B2B.com

also by Brian O'Connell

Cashing-in on the
Business-to-Business
E-Commerce Bonanza

brian o'connell

Adams Media Corporation
Holbrook, Massachusetts

Published by
Adams Media Corporation
260 Center Street, Holbrook, MA 02343. U.S.A.
www.adamsmedia.com

ISBN: 1-58062-403-0

Printed in Canada.

J I H G F E D C B A

Cataloging-in-publication data available upon
request from the publisher

This publication is designed to provide accurate and authoritative information with
regard to the subject matter covered. It is sold with the understanding that the publisher is not engaged in rendering legal, accounting, or other professional advice. If
legal advice or other expert assistance is required, the services of a competent professional person should be sought.
— From a *Declaration of Principles* jointly adopted by a Committee of the American
Bar Association and a Committee of Publishers and Associations

Many of the designations used by manufacturers and sellers to distinguish their products are lcaimed as trademarks. Where those designations appear in this book and
Adams Media was aware of a trademark claim, the designations have been printed in
initial capital letters.

This book is available at quantity discounts for bulk purchases.
For information, call 1-800-872-5627.

Visit our exciting small business Web site: www.businesstown.com

Dedication:

To my wife, Karen, and three children, Madison, Cooper, and Chip, who cheered me on while researching and writing this book, and to the many e-business entrepreneurs who walked me through life on the edge of the information world.

Acknowledgment:

Thanks to the fine people at Adams Media who supported my idea for this book, and who were there for me every step of the way. Special thanks goes to my editors, Dawn Thompson, and Paula Munier Lee.

Contents

.1 1100000101010010000   01110100010 00111101000101   11101010
0   1 0101   0000   1 100 1   1 00   0111   1   1
1   0   0   1   0 0   1   01   0   1
0 1 111 0   00   001010 10   00   1 0001   010100 010

introduction

B2B.com

"What's the catch?"

That's the response from corporate managers, small business owners, and commercial entrepreneurs of every stripe when the miracle of business-to-business electronic commerce is rolled out before their eyes. Easy access to well-stocked inventories. Ultra-fast order executions. Next-day deliveries. Price tags on goods that don't induce sticker shock. And no messy carbon invoice copies to stack on your desk.

Hey, what's not to like? These days, business-to-business e-commerce is, well, big business. And companies that take the business-to-business route aren't looking back. The irresistible, combined force of solid standards, lower costs, and decreased complexity is morphing corporate networks into intranets, making intercompany transactions more attainable. Encompassing the entire commerce cycle, from awareness to product research, comparison, selection, supplier sourcing, transactions, fulfillment, and post-sales support, business-to-business online commerce is on just about every corporation's fast track for development and implementation. Clearly, scores of businesses are warming to business-to-business e-commerce, strapping on the technology's jet engines and feeling the Gs.

With good reason. Business-to-business electronic commerce is entering a high-growth phase, increasing at a compound annual growth rate of 41 percent over the next five years, according to the

Yankee Group. Business-to-business e-commerce transaction volume in the U.S. alone is expected to grow from $138 billion to more than $541 billion in 2003.

But much of that cash may not come from simply ordering and shipping goods. Right now online commercial transactions are taking a back seat to service—the big fortunes currently being made are as likely to come from companies marketing consumer demographics online as they are from companies selling widgets or staplers. According to *www.emarketing.com*, an online business-to-business market monitoring service, roughly 40 percent of all medium-to-large-size businesses have a Web site. But only 7 percent to 10 percent of today's business-to-business Web sites are designed for direct sales.

So who are the new power brokers in the corporate e-commerce market? How are they using online business-to-business applications to turn their annual ledgers from red to black? What do their award-winning Web sites look like? And what's in store for the commercial online industry in the years to come?

That's what this book is about. We'll examine the new ideas germinating in small cubicles and on corporate drawing boards nationwide and analyze what type of fruits they will bear online in years to come. Ideas like online discount suppliers, online cybermediaries who bring businesses together, and consumer demographic seers who can tell companies who's buying their products and why and who's not buying and why not. Dozens more uses of e-business will be described in great detail.

We'll also talk to dozens of online experts, from industry seers to e-commerce business owners to see where the industry is today and where it's headed tomorrow. We'll roll out real-life case studies and anecdotes about how the online industry's leading minds achieved their greatest successes and take a peek at what they're working on now. We'll back everything up with easy-to-understand infoboxes, sidebars, and colorful industry profiles, and package it together in one lively, user friendly book.

By the time the reader has finished this book, he or she will have a greater understanding of what issues e-business faces down the road, what the technology will offer, and who's making it work best for users of all stripes.

chapter one

E-Business Pioneers Blazing a Trail in Rough and Tumble Cyberspace

Isn't it funny how the more things change, the more they stay the same? Take the global business picture. One hundred years ago, corporate managers were justifiably excited about telecommunications breakthroughs like coast-to-coast telephone calls and manufacturing advancements like the combustion engine and the automated assembly line. Toss in the imminent arrival of air travel, radio, and the typewriter and you can imagine a corporate executive's excitement about the future of business.

Flash forward one hundred years later, where equally excited business leaders have a box seat to some of the greatest advancements of the last hundred years: real-time teleconferences between parties thousands of miles away from each other; cellular phones no bigger than a stapler that carry news, names, and numbers of key business contacts, and e-mail capabilities at the flick of a button; and the advent of online commerce. Who would have imagined such wonderful business tools even 10 years ago?

Recognizing the advantages of new business tools is one thing; doing something to maximize their potential is quite another. The key to harnessing the power of these business tools, whether you ran a company in 1900 or operate one today, is adapting to new advancements and preparing for change. In commerce circles, a growing number of corporations have done just that in leveraging one of the most critical business tools of this or any other age—the Internet.

It's no secret that technology is changing our world at a phenomenal pace. Computers are radically changing every aspect of our lives, especially the way we work. The hype is now the reality, and, like it or not, your company's ability to exploit this technology will be a crucial factor to its success.

Enter e-business, the hottest trend in the red-hot Internet technology. E-business is bringing businesses, employees, suppliers, vendors, and—above all—customers together easier, faster, and at a better price tag than ever before. Above all, e-business is about using the Internet and the Web to link companies and consumers together.

Using Web technology for e-business hardly existed four years ago, but today e-business is crowded with several business models, sliced and diced into different categories by different analysts. These commerce models fight for their share of a market that, according to Forrester Research Inc., will grow from $8 billion today to $1.3 trillion in 2002.

E-Business Defined

There's a lot of confusion these days about what e-business means. Is it e-commerce, where business-to-consumer (B2C) and business-to-business (B2B) markets are drawing thousands of new customers per day? Or is e-business the business of corporate extranets and intranets, those bundled Web sites that bring companies, suppliers, vendors, and customers together at the flick of a keystroke? Or is e-business about digital marketplaces and portal partnerships, where companies can band together and sell their wares together at one venue on the Internet?

E-business means all those things and a whole lot more. Sure, e-business is about electronic commerce, intranets, and digital marketplaces, areas we'll cover in great detail inside this book. But for now, let's try to keep things simple. Simply stated, e-business is about exchanging rich information at almost zero cost using existing communications networks and standard software that runs on virtually any computer in existence anywhere in the world.

E-business processes bring greater efficiencies and improved service and add value. This results in a tangible competitive edge for companies that allows them to offer the same commodity as their competitors quicker and cheaper. These companies can grow exponentially because they are built on scalable technology platforms and run Internet linked applications, enabling them to move into new markets with relative ease. Their agility allows them to adapt to constant change and reduce costs.

What's so great about becoming an e-business? As you'll discover, that's what this book's about. But let's take a quick look at some advantages right here:

Increased Sales

The Internet is a global media. Almost anything can be sold online. You can generate quality leads, rapidly penetrate new markets (locally and globally) using your existing resources but without the costs of traditional media. Do you want to sell more to more customers?

Faster Time-to-Market

How quickly can your company respond to market changes? Using e-business you can change or update your information instantly—whenever you choose. Therefore, you can inform your customers immediately about new products, price changes, and special promotions.

Lower Costs

E-business removes the cost of traditional sales networks. It can replace expensive telephone sales operations and printed business literature that can soon become outdated, and it can provide you and your customers with a quicker, cheaper, and more convenient way to purchase.

Increased Market Share

Give your customers and, more importantly, your competitors' customers' tangible reasons to buy from you. Many companies using e-commerce as part of their e-business strategy see massive reductions in costs and pass these savings on, attracting more customers. No wonder the Internet is growing so fast.

Can your competitors provide the same products or service but in less time and for less cost? Is their business open 24 hours a day, 7 days a week? Who will take the initiative first—you or the competition?

Better Supply Chain Management

Supply chain management streamlines the distribution of real-time information, data, and goods across the entire business spectrum.

It focuses on your customers, suppliers, employees, and business partners to maximize efficiency and productivity in every area of your business network.

What a Well-Honed E-Business Site Can Give Your Organization
1. Respond instantly to market trends.
2. Release capital by removing the need to carry excess stock.
3. Schedule "just in time" deliveries.
4. Use quality information to make better business decisions.
5. Empower your work force with the tools to be more productive.

When you link your internal and external systems to your Web site they become Web enabled. This allows authorized members of your supply chain (your partners, customers, suppliers, and employees) to receive the information they need when they need it, wherever they may be.

Customer Service
Using e-business technologies and concepts in your customer service processes creates the concept of customer self-service. Customer service focuses on attracting, supporting, and retaining profitable customers. To achieve a successful customer self-service model, front-end e-business software can be integrated with Web-enabled existing back office systems, giving customers controlled and secure access to the data that they require. This way you can manage your relationship with your customers and they can manage their relationship with you. In short, you give your customers what they want when they want it.

Success Stories
How are companies embracing and benefiting from these powerful new business breakthroughs? As Thomas Edison once said, it's easier to show you than to tell you. Let's take a look at how some companies are using e-commerce to thrive in the new age of e-business.

Harley-Davidson: Born to Be Cyber-Wild
When it comes to cutting-edge companies, it's tough to beat Harley-Davidson. The $1.2 billion world-renowned designer, manufacturer, and

marketer of heavyweight motorcycles, parts, accessories, collectibles, and riding apparel is king of the road in the hearts and minds of motorcycle enthusiasts everywhere.

So it's no surprise that the company was quickly able to gain traction in the slick world of the Internet. Take a look at Eaglemark Financial Services, Harley-Davidson's majority-owned subsidiary, which provides financing for dealerships and retail customers. Eaglemark's back office functions are improving significantly with the company's recent implementation of a World Wide Web–based B2B transaction, invoice presentation, and payment software package.

With the e-payment software, Harley-Davidson dealers can access a secure Web site and tap into a wealth of invoice processing and payment data such as money owed, money received, and payment exceptions.

"With 620 Harley-Davidson dealerships to deal with, and 75 additional customers to handle, we've got our work cut out for us," says Al Ely, vice president of marketing at Eaglemark. "We used to have a manual, heavily paper-intensive office. But the automated invoicing package that Bank of America has given us on the Web has led us to that Utopian paperless workplace that everyone's talked about. Right now we're paperless and effectively communicating electronically with clients online—I wish we'd done this sooner."

As part of Eaglemark's everyday business, the company handles an annual average of $2 billion worth of floor plan financings, account openings, products, parts and accessory financing, and working capital and real estate loans. If a dealership sells a motorcycle, then that sale generates one invoice. But closing the book on the sale used to take a week at a time. "We'd present invoice statements on Thursday, process them over the weekend, and mail them out on Monday for arrival on Wednesday or Thursday," recalls Ely. "It was completely inefficient."

With the electronic payment and invoicing software in place, that process is completed in 24 hours, with real-time electronic delivery of all the invoicing data. "People can make payments anyway they want," says Ely, "but we're really encouraging them to do it electronically." That shouldn't be a problem. At a recent dealer road show in San Diego where Eaglemark demonstrated the new e-payment software, 85 out of 85 dealers signed up to use it on the spot. "That was overwhelming," says Ely.

Ely estimates that his back office staffers are 50 to 60 percent more productive with the new software. "There's been a big efficiency boost, more accuracy, and better overall customer service," he adds. "In the motorcycle business, there's a real pride of ownership with customers. So you want to talk to them as much as you can and make sure they're happy. Now, we have more time to do that.

"Better yet, our dealers have more time to sell motorcycles."

AMP Incorporated: Plugged In

AMP Incorporated is the world's largest business-to-business provider of electrical components. The company makes connectors, cables, and components used in wiring, fiber optics, printed circuits, and wireless communications. Their products are found in household appliances by Whirlpool, batteries by Duracell, medical equipment by GE, and in computers by IBM, DEC, and Sun. In a world powered by electricity and information—a world of voice, data, and video—AMP connects people to each other across the vast reaches of the globe.

Like most B2B e-commerce providers, AMP is okay with the notion that people don't realize their computers, car stereos, or console televisions are equipped with AMP's electronic wizardry. In fact, they like it that way.

But that didn't stop the company from building one of the best e-business sites in the world. The Web site, called AMP Connect, was designed to provide customized electronic commerce solutions for clients in business-to-business operations and offer consulting, development of electronic catalog database and business transactions, Web site hosting, and support and systems integration for turnkey operations. AMP called on IBM's Net.Commerce e-business system to run the site.

AMP Connect lists almost half of AMP's 200,000-plus products. The Harrisburg, Pennsylvania company, with 45,000 employees in more than 200 facilities in 50 countries, was spending about $10 million (U.S.) annually to publish and distribute its 1,400 product catalogs. AMP's e-business site not only virtually eliminated company catalog printing costs, but it provides customers with more timely product information. AMP adds products to its components lineup at an astounding rate even for Web software companies—an average of 200 new products a day.

AMP launched its electronic catalog in January 1996 to serve its customers worldwide. Today, AMP offers its customers a global product information catalog in eight languages: French, Italian, Spanish, English, German, Japanese, Mandarin Chinese, and Korean. Two-thirds of the catalog's 100,000 registered users (from over 138 countries) are engineers in industries such as computer peripherals, electronic/electrical equipment, aerospace systems, and communications equipment.

By the end of 1999, AMP's online catalog expanded to include over 100,000 parts, and business was busier than ever. Not only were catalog costs cut, customers were much happier using the site, and company revenues skyrocketed as a result.

Nautica Apparel, Inc.: Looking Good

With its implementation of an intranet/extranet solution (using Microsoft's BackOffice B2B platform), New York City–based Nautica has streamlined communications between Nautica and its business partners by giving all parties 24-hour access to design information, contracts, and sales data.

The B2B site helps Nautica bring additional licensees online and links Nautica more tightly with its licensees all over the world, streamlining communication and making time-critical design changes instantly accessible to everyone. Moreover, Nautica's e-business operation required minimal training for employees, who were already familiar with the Microsoft Windows operating system and Microsoft Windows–based desktop products.

Los Angeles County Government: Purchasing Power

The largest local government in the United States buys $650 million worth of goods and services each year from a list of 25,000 bidders—everything from hard drives to helicopters. Until recently, all of those purchases were made using paper forms. Twenty people might buy toner cartridges at one time, without knowing that a central warehouse already had hundreds in inventory. This meant the county missed out on opportunities for volume discounts and incurred unnecessary inventory costs, not to mention the delays of paper-based order fulfillment. The time delays inherent in paperwork created chaos, waiting, and huge warehousing costs. With e-commerce heating up, L.A. County got online. Using a Web-based purchasing solution, the county now lets buyers shop, order, and pay for goods over the Internet.

L.A. County immediately garnered big savings from easier comparison shopping and lower inventory costs, faster order cycles, less paperwork, and more opportunities for small businesses.

Freemarkets Online: Do I Hear $100?

At Pittsburgh-based Freemarkets Online, Inc., bringing e-businesses together online is the company's reason for being. Part auctioneer, part matchmaker, the company employs specialists called "market making engineers" who do nothing but scour the corporate landscape for the best prices for corporate clients.

Companies that were faced with the grim prospect of leafing through hundreds of print product catalogs use Freemarkets Online to winnow down the best products and the best prices for them. For example, a manufacturing company that traditionally had a list of 2,500 potential widget suppliers in the United States could spend months trying to find the best business relationship. By using an online middleman like Freemarkets Online, that company could get an "e-list" of the 20 or 30 companies best suited to buy those widgets from and then get an online comparison of the companies, their widget offerings, and their price ranges—all within one day.

Estimated savings from using an online e-business middleman can be as much as 20 percent, Freemarkets Online says. In 1998 and 1999, their market makers conducted more than 50 bidding events, and they claimed to deliver an average savings of 17 percent to manufacturers such as United Technologies, General Motors, Procter & Gamble, Westinghouse, and Whirlpool. With every deal, Freemarkets makes money from both ends, taking a fee from the buyer and a sales commission from the seller.

But the company isn't done after the vetting process is over. It continues to help the buyer choose the best supplier, often counseling rejection of the lowest bid and recommending a supplier with better delivery systems or long-term potential.

Amdahl Corporation:
Taking a Byte out of the Production Process

Amdahl Corporation, a wholly owned subsidiary of Fujitsu Limited, provides integrated computing solutions to many of the largest users of information technology in the world. Founded in 1970, Amdahl employs more than 10,000 professionals in 33 countries.

Amdahl's 350-strong sales force offers complete business solutions to organizations with a heavy investment in System/390-compatible technology that are now integrating MVS, Windows NT, and/or UNIX into their computing environment.

After trying out a client service platform to streamline its company sales efforts, Amdahl switched to an online B2B platform that enabled company sales staffers to compress the product selection process from several days involving multiple personnel to a single task as short as 30 minutes by one person. As the system guides sales representatives through building their orders, they can check their selection against an illustration on the left side of the computer. They can also print corresponding solution specifications and incorporate them into their sales proposal—increasing the probability of closing the sale. The system also screens for conflicting specifications and suggests appropriate alternatives.

While the company doesn't say how much it has saved from its new e-business venture, it has recorded its highest profits ever after the implementation of its e-business Web site.

ClaimsNet.com: Picture of Health

At first blush you wouldn't think that Claimsnet.com was a ready-made e-business success. Yet that's exactly what it is. Its specialty is the little understood and distinctly unglamorous field of moving claims from health care providers to insurers. With only 60 employees and 2,400 customers—a pittance in the health claims processing field, it's making headway in the industry thanks to its e-business Web site.

The health care industry, including doctors, pharmaceutical companies, home-care supply firms, and insurers together add up to about $1 trillion annually, or 13 percent of the U.S. gross national product. And about 25 cents of every health care dollar—or $250 billion a year—goes toward administrative costs.

Historically, the health care industry processes paperwork at a snail's pace. First the provider—whether it's a two-doctor practice, a giant HMO, a hospital, or a laboratory—must fill out and mail the forms for each insurance company used by each patient. (Multiply the number of claims by the number of patients and visits and it's easy to see how the industry racked up 4.4 billion transactions in 1998.) Then the insurer's claims processing representatives determine whether providers have sent the correct information and whether the patient is in fact eligible for treatment. If not, the form goes back to the provider, starting the whole cycle over again. The practitioner also needs to ride herd on the submissions, making sure they've been received and processed. Typically, physicians wait anywhere from several weeks to a few months for payment. But Claimsnet.com, with its ramped-up e-business site, whittles that process down to hours.

With its e-business site, Claimsnet.com has an advantage that many of its customers don't—it can process health care claims at a rate of ten cents each—about half the industry average. A dime here and there may not seem like much, but after billions of transactions, you're starting to talk about real money. These companies are at the forefront of the e-business revolution. While the e-commerce table has room for all kinds of diners, it seems that the early arrivers are going to be feasting longer and more richly than those who wait e-business out for a year or two.

chapter two

A Snapshot of Where E-Business Is Today

The blockbuster digital economy regularly surprises those who study it most closely. In 1997, for example, private analysts forecasted that the value of Internet retailing would reach $7 billion by 2000—a level surpassed by nearly 50 percent in 1998. But the industry grew so fast in 1999, forecasters tripled their previous estimates of the near-term growth expected in business-to-business electronic commerce.

Yes it's really true. There is no business like e-business.

Throughout this book we'll spend a great deal of time touching on the e-commerce aspect of e-business, particularly the business-to-business side. While we'll brush up against the B2C side as well, that's not our interest here. B2B is the subset of e-business that everybody's talking about, but there's not a whole lot of information on the topic, a situation we aim to rectify inside these pages.

Online Usage Is Skyrocketing

By any measure, the ability of consumers and businesses to reach the Internet and to engage in e-commerce is increasing rapidly. The *Industry Standard* reports that from 1998 to 1999 the number of Web users worldwide increased by 55 percent, the number of Internet hosts rose by 46 percent, the number of Web servers increased by 128 percent, and the number of new Web address registrations rose by 137 percent.

In addition, according to a recent study by International Data Corporation (IDC), revenues of U.S. Internet service providers (ISPs) will rise at a compound annual rate of 28 percent through 2003.

B2B Business is Booming

Intercompany trade of hard goods over the Internet hit $43 billion last year and could reach $1.3 trillion by 2003—an annual growth rate of 99 percent. Here's a breakdown (dollar figures in millions; percentage of industry trade):

INDUSTRY	1997	1999	2001	2003				
Aerospace & Defense	$864	$6,553	$25,633	$38,205	0.5%	3.5%	13.6%	20.3%
Computing and Electronics	$8,729	$50,379	$229,108	$395,302	1.8%	8.2%	29.2%	39.3%
Construction	$85	$1,651	$6,975	$28,610	0.0%	0.1%	0.4%	1.4%
Consumer Goods	$672	$2,946	$12,722	$51,915	0.1%	0.3%	1.1%	3.8%
Food and Agriculture	$50	$3,029	$13,019	$53,648	0.0%	0.2%	0.8%	3.0%
Heavy Industries	$12	$1,319	$4,678	$15,811	0.0%	0.2%	0.6%	1.8%
Industrial Equipment and Supplies	$88	$1,266	$4,520	$15,699	0.0%	0.1%	0.4%	1.2%
Motor Vehicles	$1,464	$9,254	$53,219	$212,925	0.2%	0.9%	4.3%	14.7%
Paper Products and Office Equipment	$561	$2,859	$14,269	$65,192	0.1%	0.3%	1.4%	5.6%
Petrochemicals	$2,087	$10,327	$48,001	$178,311	0.2%	1.0%	4.0%	13.5%
Pharmaceutical and Medical Equipment	$234	$1,431	$8,514	$44,117	0.1%	0.3%	1.7%	7.8%
Shipping, Warehousing	$505	$2,887	$15,408	$61,552	0.2%	0.9%	4.5%	17.2%
Utilities	$3,221	$15,406	$62,896	$169,545	0.7%	2.9%	10.6%	25.8%
TOTAL	$18,570	$109,308	$498,962	$1,330,831	0.2%	1.0%	4.0%	9.4%

SOURCE: FORRESTER RESEARCH

How fast is online B2B growing? Forrester Research, a Cambridge, Massachusetts–based Internet analyst, predicts that it will reach $1.3 trillion by 2003—a 99 percent annual growth rate—accounting for 9.4 percent of all U.S. B2B sales. Investment bank Goldman Sachs puts the figure at $1.5 trillion by 2004. Merrill Lynch is forecasting that 39 percent of all procurement in the computing and electronics industries will be done online by 2003—up from just 2 percent in 1997—and will be worth more than $395 billion. Similar increases are forecast for utilities, petrochemicals, motor vehicles, and shipping and warehousing.

With close to 22 percent of the world's gross domestic product consisting of materials procurement, according to the *Wall Street Journal*, the impact of a global boost in efficiency is obvious. The two main efficiencies that B2B can provide are reduced sales and transaction costs and reduced product development times. Virtual development teams can hand off projects to peers in different parts of the world, resulting in "24x7x365" productivity. That was possible before, particularly through technologies like Electronic Data Interchange (EDI), the forerunner to e-business, but the added speed of online procurement pushes the process into hyperdrive.

With e-business, new B2B business models like aggregators and auction sites are applying the trading principles of stock exchanges to every category of merchandise and in the process are transforming the supply chain into a demand chain. In short, the Internet is shifting power away from those who manufacture to those who buy.

Initially triggered as a cost-cutting move spearheaded by technology companies in the early 1990s, business-to-business e-commerce has grabbed the attention of even the most mundane of manufacturers. An industry survey says businesses sold some $138 billion of goods and services to each other through their online operations in 1999.

Nowadays, buying anything from pencils to power tools is as easy as logging on and clicking a few keystrokes. Before you know it, the overnight delivery guy is delivering your order straight to your desk. No surly telephone clerks. No messy paperwork. And no bulky product catalogs taking up space in your office.

Sounds too good to be true, right? In most cases, it's not. For the Internet savvy, buying products online is as natural as drinking a glass of water or getting out of bed in the morning. But there is a learning curve involved, albeit not a very steep one, that enables you to get the most from your e-business experience. And the first place to start is understanding what the e-business phenomenon is all about.

What Is B2B E-Commerce and How Is It Linked to E-Business?

As usual when it comes to cyberspace, the Internet means many things to many people. The same goes for e-commerce and e-business.

By most accounts, electronic commerce is a means of conducting transactions that, prior to the evolution of the Internet as a business tool in the mid-1990s, would have been completed in more traditional ways: telephone, mail, facsimile, proprietary electronic data interchange systems, or face-to-face contact. Indicators gathered from a variety of private sources show rapid growth not only in current e-commerce but in the infrastructure that will support future e-commerce development.

Most industry experts also agree that e-business is a composite of the entire commerce cycle, from awareness to product research, comparison, selection, supplier sourcing, transactions, fulfillment, and post-sales support. Companies of every size are adopting e-business for its convenience and cost-savings potential.

In a physical sense, e-businesses are brick-and-mortar businesses that are linked online. Through these online connections, computers

---

E-Business Versus E-Commerce

E-business is one of those umbrella terms that corporate honchos love to use but are never sure what it means. But one thing you should know is that e-business doesn't necessarily equal e-commerce.

"Consumer e-commerce is about branding and impulse buying—customers want convenience. Business-to-business e-commerce is about customer relationships and automation of processes—businesses want control and analysis," says Brian Valente, senior director of marketing at Just in Time Solutions, an online billing presentation software vendor in San Francisco.

Here's more on how the two differ:

Definition of E-Business

E-business describes the technology-enabled business that has certain technology and business characteristics. From a technology perspective, the intranets in these businesses are merging with the extranets, and standards and e-commerce are the cornerstone of business systems and processes. From a business perspective, the principles of e-businesses focus on seamless integration between the customer and the company, between internal and customer-facing systems, and between the company and its suppliers and partners.

Definition of E-Commerce

A subset of e-business, e-commerce is the term used to describe Internet-based electronic transactions including EDI, bill payment, order processing, fulfillment, customer interaction, etc.

can automatically ship goods and track inventories, and customers can check the progress of purchases through databases.

Many companies also use their e-business links as "intranets," or internal Internets, that are usually password protected and meant only for the eyes of company employees, vendors, and favored customers. Through intranets, managers and staffers can quickly access reports about finances, sales, projects, or personnel records. The reports are generated by networked databases that link company employees online throughout the world.

E-business sites can also mean Web pages that are simple billboards for businesses to complex sites that integrate warehouse and inventory systems that automatically order, ship, and track goods.

Procurement and Distribution

Almost all of the e-business action is in proprietary procurement and distribution sites. Distribution sites are on the push side, automating the channel through which goods and services are sold.

A good example of a "push" is Intel, which specializes in making computer microchips for personal computer makers. Like Ford Motor or Cisco Systems, Intel is blessed with a customer base that has been online for years. Since Intel's customers are accustomed to buying from Intel (the company made $1.5 billion in 1998 from online purchases), the companies "push" themselves toward Intel, an e-business vendor they know and trust.

Procurement sites, on the other hand, are on the pull side. Procurement sites "pull" customers in by allowing them to source day-to-day items such as stationery, professional services, and travel—which typically account for 30 percent of corporate spending—over the Internet, thus simplifying and expediting the purchasing process.

Many industry experts say that four types of e-businesses are emerging as dominant players these days. These include trenchant buyers, who use e-commerce to negotiate more favorable supplier discounts; vigilant sellers, who capture more of each customer's total purchases by providing convenient, buyer-centric e-commerce offerings; cybermediaries, who create a powerful position for themselves by bringing together previously unknown buyers and sellers; and Internet solution providers, who provide the enabling technologies to support these e-business efforts.

The Fab Four: The Top B2B Industry Players

These are the four cornerstones of the e-business industry:

- Trenchant buyers—who leverage B2B procurement
- Vigilant sellers—who capture more of the customer's total purchases by providing convenient, buyer-centric e-commerce offerings
- Cybermediaries—who bring together previously unknown buyers and sellers
- Internet solution providers—who provide enabling technologies

But e-business sites are a great deal more than simply meeting grounds in cyberspace where buyers and sellers gather to barter over goods. In addition to the shoppers who choose items online but pay for them offline, the Internet is an important source of research that influences offline ordering and purchasing, particularly for big ticket items such as autos. In an analysis of the impact of the Internet on 1998 customer spending, Cyber Dialogue estimates that while sales ordered and paid for online were $11 billion, sales to customers that were ordered online but paid for offline were more than $15 billion, and the value of offline orders influenced by the Internet was approximately $51 billion.

The E-Business Web Site

A true e-business site is dedicated to attracting new customers and additional revenues, all the while giving your entire organization more time to attract even more customers and revenues. On your e-business site, a new breed of integrated sales, service, and marketing applications help customers help themselves. Built specifically for the Web from the customer's perspective, e-business applications automate customer processes, driving new revenue and freeing corporate resources that can be dedicated to attracting additional customers.

Your e-business site needs to wholly satisfy customer expectations. Web-savvy customers expect sites to be highly responsive, intuitive, and immediate. They want complete control of the relationship. And, of course, they require access from any browser, any time, from any place. Customers also want a personal experience, to be closer to the company, and to be understood. This is why in a fickle Web economy—where customers are one click from a competitor's site—your e-business platform should provide a buying experience that will keep customers coming back.

On your e-business site, sales, marketing, and service processes are compressed and streamlined. A customer's life cycle becomes frictionless and exponentially efficient: Site visitors become shoppers,

shoppers turn into customers, and customers are converted to advocates. In the background, marketing intelligence is collected, providing insight for one-to-one customer relationships, enhanced product offerings, and an improved customer experience. This collection and application of shopping behavior information improves performance. The result is a self-perpetuating customer lifecycle.

To help themselves, customers need access to complete information. E-business applications combine data from back and front office systems (such as pricing, parts numbers, and descriptions) with the knowledge of seasoned employees. For example, customers can learn which products work together and which solutions are ideal. Given complete information, customers are free to service themselves—a little or a lot.

By the Numbers

While retail e-commerce and business-to-business e-commerce merge and blend in many areas (like many companies, Dell and Microsoft, for instance, have sites that accommodate both retail and commercial customers), B2B e-commerce has a built-in advantage. Compared with consumers, businesses are better equipped to go online and have more to gain from efficient electronic trading.

Even at a cost of $1 million per e-business Web site (primarily for larger firms), corporate e-commerce isn't always cheap. But a high sticker price isn't slowing its blockbuster growth.

According to the Yankee Group, B2B transaction volume will grow from $138 billion in 1999 to more than $541 billion in 2003. That's five times the level of the much more loudly trumpeted consumer online sales last year.

But it's not the money that companies are spending online that gets e-businesses excited, it's the amount of money that companies are saving by going online. A recent International Data Corp. survey projected that by 2003 online business-to-business transactions could reach $1.3 trillion annually and save companies up to $103 billion.

North America will continue to hold a significant lead in electronic commerce implementations during the next few years, but other regions are beginning to accelerate their adoption. The IDC report predicts that by 2003 North American e-commerce penetration will triple from 7 percent to 24 percent; Western Europe will grow from 3 percent to 11 percent; the Asia-Pacific region will grow from 2 percent to 9 percent; and Latin America will move from 2 percent to 7 percent.

Quick Facts:

- Roughly 40 percent of all midsized to large businesses have a Web site.
- Only 7 to 10 percent of today's business-to-business Web sites are designed for direct sales.
- By 2006, almost half of the U.S. work force will be employed by industries that are either major producers or intensive users of information technology products and services. Innovation has increased demand for high paid, "core IT workers" (computer scientists, engineers), created new IT occupations, changed skill requirements for some non-IT occupations, and raised minimum skill requirements for many other jobs. Wage gaps between workers in IT industries and all other workers continue to widen. (Source: International Data Corporation)
- Of the $50.9 billion in Internet sales of goods and services in the United States in 1998, 85 percent of them were made to businesses, according to Forrester Research Inc., a Massachusetts technology firm.
- By 2003, Forrester projects that U.S. e-commerce will leap beyond $1.4 trillion in sales—92 percent of them made to businesses.
- In a Forrester survey of 30 companies, they're spending an average $1.8 million on e-commerce.

A similar report by the Yankee Group has found that B2B e-commerce in the United States is expected to grow at a compound annual growth rate of 41 percent by 2004. In Europe, Visa International has found that B2B e-commerce will grow at a rate of about 30 times the growth of the GDP of most European countries.

Big Dogs Bark the Loudest

As far as industry usage of e-business tools goes, it's the larger companies that are driving the technology's growth right now. Forrester Research estimates that 98 percent of companies with more than 1,000 employees have Internet access, and 75 percent of them are buying and selling online. But just 45 percent of companies with 20 to 99 employees are online and 2 percent are engaging in e-commerce.

Ford Motor Co. buys $16 billion in paper, furniture, and other supplies not used in building cars. By the end of 1999, as much as $12 billion of that amount was spent over the Internet. Ford says it will save 30 percent of costs with e-business compared with paper-based invoicing.

It's the Fords and the DuPonts who are spending the $1.8 million or so on their corporate e-business platforms. For the smaller guys, prices are significantly lower.

Larger companies have larger problems. For example, that $1.8 million could mean that a company has to change from its electronic data interchange over private, non-Internet networks, a process that can be expensive and complicated. But now even small companies can process transactions over secure Internet sites for a fraction of the previous cost.

A small company setting up its own Web site for e-commerce can count on spending $20,000 or more. That amount will give a smaller company a public Web site with a section that only customers with passwords can access. That section includes catalogs with discount pricing and other features common to sales between businesses.

Words to Live by: A B2B Primer

Getting your arms around a wholesale e-business Web strategy is no easy task, but since you have to drop your oars in the water somewhere, it's a good idea to establish some goals first. Here are some good goals to start with:

Ask Yourself These Questions: Start your e-business by answering some basic questions about your site's goals: Who are you trying to serve? What are you trying to achieve? How are you going to get there? If you can answer these three questions, you can begin the infrastructure phase of putting your e-business in place with a firm grasp on what your goals are.

Buddy Up: Get business talking to IT and IT talking to customers. In too many businesses, non-technical management thinks that the information technology department is speaking a foreign language. Don't let that happen to your e-business campaign. A partnership between the IT department and the front office is the way to go. Make sure that your IT folks are included early on in the planning and development stages, and don't be afraid to share credit together. Your e-business site will be the better for it.

Hug the Middle of the Road: Customers don't want to know what you're going to build two or three years from now; they want to know what you're giving them today. So when it comes to mission critical applications, keep things simple and build them so they work right the first time. One bad experience can chase your e-business customer away forever.

Use Your Best People: You want to give your customers state-of-the-art information, but you don't want to increase your own costs by doing so. So when you're developing your e-business site, put your best thinkers and most effective implementers on the project. They can come up with ways to keep your customers and your accountant satisfied.

E-Business, Test Thyself: As you go through various stages of your Web site design, make sure you're testing your processes as you go. That can mean internal software diagnosis or bringing in beta users who can give you honest feedback on your site. And don't be afraid to ask your best customers for help. Customers like talking about doing business on a day-to-day basis: how they're paying their bills, how they're interfacing with their own customer base.

Security First: No matter what your product is, customers won't use it if they don't feel safe. So not only do you have to apply the most stringent software tools toward your e-business site, you have to prove to your customers that your site is safe as possible. Use the best security tools, and then consider a certification from an industry standards body, like the Internet Computer Security Association. They'll take a look at your site and give it their seal of approval, which will help both you and your customer sleep better at night.

Ask the Experts

For more information on e-business trends, tools, and techniques, go see a guru, specifically one of the top information technology analysts. These companies regularly issue reports and studies on Web business trends. While the studies aren't cheap—about $2,000 for a standard report—you're getting information that's hard to get anywhere else. Here's a rundown of the top Web analysts:

GARTNER GROUP *www.gartner.com*
Claim to Fame: Practically invented high-tech research industry. Tracks over 500 subspecialties.
Quote: ISP worldwide shopping spree muddies market.

INTERNATIONAL DATA CORP. *www.idc.com*
Claim to Fame: Specializes in massive surveys of end users and industries.
Quote: Don't get caught without distribution to the online nation.

META GROUP *www.metagroup.com*
Claim to Fame: Prides itself on providing clients with easy access to its analysts.
Quote: Many help-desk outsourcers 'not making the grade.'

YANKEE GROUP *www.yankeegroup.com*
Claim to Fame: Primary focus is telecom; making push in new media.
Quote: Small and medium business market missing the Internet commerce opportunity.

FORRESTER RESEARCH *www.forrester.com*
Claim to Fame: Earliest to new media. Focus: business-to-business transactions.

Quote: Eight million new-car purchases will be influenced by the Internet in 2003.

GIGA INFORMATION GROUP *www.gigaweb.com*
Claim to Fame: Concentrates on infotech implementation projects.
Quote: E-commerce will deliver huge benefits but not profits over the next 12 to 18 months.

JUPITER COMMUNICATIONS *www.jupitercommunications.com*
Claim to Fame: The go-to firm for information on consumer use of new media.
Quote: Online retailers must embrace auctions as new platform for discounts.

CYBER DIALOGUE *www.cyberdialogue.com*
Claim to Fame: Says that it's so Internet focused, even its research is conducted completely online.
Quote: Consumer demand for health information services has reached critical mass. . . . Act now.

ZONA RESEARCH *www.zonaresearch.com*
Claim to Fame: Issues popular daily e-mail bulletins on developments in tech.
Quote: Internet technology market to exceed $142 billion by 2001.

GOMEZ ADVISORS *www.gomez.com*
Claim to Fame: Rates Web sites; advises site owners on how to improve.
Quote: Internet brokers ka-gank (a technical term for snafu)!

Why E-Business?

E-businesses are springing up across the corporate landscape like azaleas in April. Why? Because the demand for their services is so high and because brick-and-mortar companies now recognize that their businesses depend on customer relationships.

Here are some reasons e-business tools are no longer considered a luxury but a necessity in corporate circles these days.

1. Keep 'Em Smiling

If your customers aren't happy, you aren't going to be in business for very long; if they get what they need, they're yours for the long haul. That's the make-or-break reality of business these days, and that's why Web-based customer service is an integral part of your business-to-business strategy.

2. Customer, Serve Thyself

Your customers aren't just the people buying your product—they're everyone you do business with, including employees, suppliers, and partners. The real advantage of customer service on the Web lies in letting all these customers serve themselves instead of navigating through recorded messages, talking to operators on the phone, or dealing with the frustration of waiting in line to talk to a representative.

3. Face-to-Face and Phone Service Is Inflexible

Most customer service counters and phone lines aren't open after business hours, which is extremely impractical for people who work during the day. Often if customers are lucky enough to get through to someone, they have to wait indefinitely. The Web is open 24/7, and service is immediate. It's almost like having your own customer service representative on hand, day or night.

Those are only some of the myriad benefits attained by adopting an e-business Web strategy. Now that you know the benefits, let's get to the more important task of building your e-business site.

chapter three

Ladies and Gentlemen: Start Your Web Engines

While interest in e-business is decidedly on the upswing, companies that engage in e-business are doing so cautiously. According to research from the Meta Group, efforts to date have focused on e-commerce (i.e., customer-facing) applications and do not reflect fundamental business model redesign or enterprise-wide thinking.

In addition, company size currently has little correlation to e-business spending. Almost one-third (28 percent) of the companies surveyed by Meta Group are larger than $1 billion (annual revenue); at the same time, only 3 percent of those companies categorize their total annual e-business investment as being greater than $20 million; and only 14 percent of companies have e-business investments over $5 million. While slightly more than 80 percent of companies reported using e-business with customers, far fewer are using e-business with their partners (43 percent), suppliers (52 percent), and internal systems (57 percent).

Shifting into Second Gear

Meta Group describes the first wave of e-business development as "brochureware," where companies merely published information on their Web sites. In the second, and most current, wave of development, the focus shifts to include the sales channel. The next wave will address supply chain issues. Because of the complex business-to-business issues that must be resolved to "e-enable" supply chains, Meta Group expects a significant new investment of dollars and resources during the next three years.

The greatest differences in the Meta Group survey were not between industries but between "e-leaders" and "e-followers." Meta Group identified fewer than 20 percent of the companies surveyed as e-leaders (based on their behaviors). E-leaders share several of the following characteristics:

- Have an e-commerce/e-business executive plus strong CEO support
- Perceive that e-business has had a significant impact on their business
- Are using e-business with customers and intra-enterprise systems
- Are spending at least $5 million
- Have multiple dedicated e-teams, and at least 2 percent of total employees are dedicated to these teams
- Are developing their core business using a new model and are building a new business

Failure Rates

The fact is that despite the rising trend of e-business, failure rates of companies attempting to capitalize on B2B commerce are alarmingly high.

According to another report by the Gartner Group, analysts there predict a bumpy ride for both traditional bricks-and-mortar organizations and the newer dot.com enterprises attempting to break into e-commerce. Gartner warns that while technologically aggressive businesses face failure from immature technology, an unready market, and poor e-business strategies, more conservative organizations that seek to avoid all risk by ignoring the Net age completely are also doomed to failure.

In fact, Gartner Group analysts suggested that despite huge awareness of the need to adopt an e-business model, many companies will tumble into e-business disillusionment by 2001 with 75 percent of projects failing to deliver on their promise.

Such failures will not be because transformation to e-commerce is wrong, but because the business model, strategies, and implementation will have failed. However, in the long term, businesses will learn from other organizations that take time to get e-business right.

How do companies get e-business right? The recipe lies in the creation and management of astute business practices combined with a company vision that will cut between the hype and the reality surrounding e-business. It will be essential for companies to strike the balance between e-business aspirations and rushing headlong into an unready market with unproven business models and technology.

Five Mistakes that Can Derail Your E-Business Express

King Midas may have had a golden touch, but that doesn't mean that every e-business has one, too. Poor planning and improper implementation can derail the most well-intentioned e-business campaign.

According to the Gartner Group, there are five key dangers to look for that, if unaddressed, may ruin your Web campaign before it even gets going:

- One of the biggest basic mistakes that organizations make when implementing an e-business strategy is to completely redesign their business in order to become an e-business. E-business is not a binary switch from traditional to e-business. The key to success is Mix Management, where the traditional business model and the e-business business model coexist and are tailored to fit the market they address. Gartner Group advises enterprises to develop an e-business road map to be implemented in stages and to look for ways to build innovation into select processes. This way, learning from step-by-step initiatives can be used to constantly evaluate the end-point goal and adjust strategy accordingly.
- Another fundamental error is for organizations to suspend good project management rules simply because "this is e-business." Gartner Group has found that most projects overestimate the potential benefits and underestimate the time needed to realize e-business benefits. Gartner Group's advice to enterprises is to carefully analyze the cost associated with each project and ensure that they employ personnel who have the requisite experience and time to devote to the effort. Only by adopting this step-by-step approach will organizations be able to truly track progress and ensure that organizational barriers are not hampering project advancement.
- The third point highlighted points to a belief in some organizations that technology can do all the heavy lifting in e-business implementation. Gartner Group points out that despite the ubiquity of the Internet, technology is only meant to serve the business need and can, at worst, be misapplied and drain critical enterprise resources. Organizations must ensure that each e-business initiative has a sound business goal at its core, with technologies being selected based on their fitness for the job intended. Those ultimately responsible for e-business strategies should be wary of letting technologies become too entrenched and should be prepared to replace installed technologies as the e-business product market matures.
- Emphasize the importance of using e-business to attract new markets and customers as part of the overall e-business strategy. Enterprises that focus solely on who their customers are today will miss the opportunity to explore what their customers could be. Business plans need to be aligned to address the threat of cyber competition and explore new sources of revenue.

(continued)

- Be alert to new competition. Gartner Group points out there will be an increase in the rise of agile and aggressive new enterprises that have no fear of doing whatever it takes to go to the top of their markets. A company that develops its e-business plan using a list of existing competitors runs a substantial risk of being blindsided. You only have to look at the mistakes that Barnes & Noble made in not recognizing the threat that Amazon.com posed to see that.

Gartner Group advises organizations to develop a comprehensive e-business survival plan that anticipates the actions of their top competitors and embraces the radical changes necessary to beat them in this new game. A dot.com subsidiary or enterprise should be considered if the enterprise is moving too slowly for the e-business plan. According to Gartner Group, "In the past, the big ones ate the little ones. In the future, the fast ones will eat the slow ones."

An E-Business Blueprint

Now that seemingly everybody is linked to everybody else, the challenge becomes managing the flow, controlling the content, ensuring the security, and facilitating the use of huge amounts of information.

A commitment to e-commerce requires an abundance of vision, perseverance, and capital—with all-out support among top management. How can you, as a responsible manager, move into the uncertainty of such new operations? The answer brings us back to teamwork and partnering, key talents in the Internet economy.

Many organizations put up a Web page and start selling products without a clear sense of what goals they are attempting to meet. These companies understand that taking large orders from strategic customers and ordering from suppliers online without human intervention to waste time or make errors is a great benefit to their bottom line, but few understand the best way to get to that point..

Of course, you can always get an e-business specialist to launch and maintain your site for you (there's much more on outsourcing in Chapter 6). However, most e-commerce development tools targeted at small and midsize businesses cost $5,000 to $100,000, while larger companies pay a lot more than that. Garden variety e-business sites generally include templates for online catalogs and databases, so it's easy to change items and prices. Dynamic database searches can serve different information when an item is out of stock or on special, and they can be hooked up to existing back-end systems for order fulfillment and a range of automatic payment options.

Companies that have a high volume of sales—especially those that deliver soft goods such as articles, reports, software, or music over the Net—require industrial-strength solutions costing anywhere from $100,000 to $1 million or more (like the $2 million or so that some Fortune 500 companies pay for their e-business site).

The good news is that as Internet-based commerce skyrockets, competition among e-commerce solutions will fuel pitched price battles much like the ones we've seen in the personal computer industry in the last 10 years. There, prices fell dramatically as companies tried to undercut each other in the name of market share. Expect the same thing to happen with e-business developers who should, as time goes on, go after your business with low-cost packages.

An E-Business Plan Outline

Moving forward with your e-business requires a strategic business plan. Begin with the following outline, created by the Sun/Netscape Alliance.

1. Summary of Net Economy Initiative
1.1. Statement of purpose—Describe the business goals and objectives.
1.2. Basic business case—Summarize the factors that are driving your e-commerce initiative; explain how your basic business case will leverage your core competencies.
2. Market Analysis
2.1. Market trends and conditions—Describe underlying dynamics of market activities and explain how the e-commerce initiative will create a new value proposition in the marketplace. Estimate the size of the market and the proportion that the e-commerce initiative will capture. Focus on market size, growth rate, and profitability.
2.2. Customer value proposition—Identify opportunities for creating and sustaining customer relationships based on one or more Customers.Com critical success factors.
2.3. Barriers to entry and customer options—What are the barriers to entry? What are the sources of sustainable competitive advantage?

What options do customers have and how readily can they switch to an alternative?
2.4. Competition—Identify competitors and summarize similarities and differences. Analyze the degree of competitive challenge.
2.5. Supplier value proposition—Identify competitive forces driving suppliers' actions and activities.
3. The Net Economy Opportunity
3.1. Customer relationship opportunities—Describe the chain of events that drives the e-commerce strategy. Emphasize how the company will maintain customer relationships and work with channel partners, distributors, and other third parties, to create competitive opportunities through network connections.
3.2. The vision for improvements—Describe the missing pieces in as much detail as possible. Identify the capabilities of the Web-based environment and the individual customer touch points. Explain how people will communicate and share information, using specific scenarios where feasible. Describe the users' experiences. Identify the features and functions of enabling repositories and communications networks.

(continued)

An E-Business Plan Outline *(continued)*

Identify commerce, content, and community features and functions.

3.3. The vision for implementation—Describe the series of steps for launching the e-commerce initiative. Begin with the plans for a pilot test at the earliest possible time. Explain what you expect to learn from the pilot, and how this information will affect the evolution of your e-commerce strategy.

4. Marketing Plans

4.1. Marketing and promotional activities—Describe the key marketing and promotional activities for creating awareness with target markets and generating traffic for the e-commerce environment.

4.2. Customer service and support activities—Describe expectations for responding to customers' inquiries, resolving problems as they arise, and reinforcing customer relationships.

5. Revenues, Costs, and Financial Justifications

5.1. A financial spreadsheet or exhibit showing your revenues and expenses related to the goals and objectives of your net economy initiative—Describe the incremental revenues expected, the potential cost savings, and the other financial opportunities that make the investment worthwhile. In addition, describe the expected improvements in customer loyalty and other important nonfinancial measurements you discovered during your assessment and analysis.

What Are Your Goals?

Knowing what price range you can accommodate is obviously important. But knowing what you want to get out of your e-business site is doubly so.

According to the experts at the Sun/Netscape Internet Alliance (SNIA), creating a value proposition for a Web-based initiative has some similarities to creating a value proposition in the more conventional brick-and-mortar world. A recent report on launching an e-business by the SNIA states that you need to begin by developing a strategic business plan to drive your e-commerce efforts.

According to the SNIA, you should start your e-business goals initiative by creating the business models that will lead to a compelling and profitable value proposition. That means examining your business performance for areas of desired or potential improvement. Do you want higher sales? More customers? Higher average sales per customer? Better profit margins?

The best way to find out what you want is to allow your business objectives to fuel your technology choices. From an understanding of your own enterprise and from watching the experience of other firms, begin by imagining how the Internet might be harnessed to stream-

An E-Business Goal's Checklist

Knowing what your customers want is the foundation for your e-business platform. To help build a better customer relationship management strategy, answer the following questions first. Your customer requirements document should answer the following eight questions:

- Who are your target customers? Remember, these are the people and organizations that you expect to use your products and services.
- What are the three or four primary things that your target customers want from you?
- Who are your critical business partners, distributors, resellers, and other third-party channels in your marketplace?

- How do these indirect channels help you to add value to your business processes and enhance your customer relationships?
- What are the communication steps, transaction events, and information flows that are part of these third-party business processes?
- What information do you send directly to your customers?
- What information do you send to your customers through third parties?
- How are you able to capture and recall information about your customers' needs and expectations as they interact with your products and services?

(Source: Seybold Group)

line your business processes. Try to quantify your goals and test them for reasonableness.

Starting Points

Start from the premise that the Internet enables you to instantaneously communicate and interactively share information with the various parties in your value chain: your customers, suppliers, business partners, remote offices, distributors, resellers, and other intermediaries who add value to the activities of your firm. Using the information power of the Internet, you can create, improve, and maintain relationships with all the various parties you depend on for success. As you identify the ways you reach and interact with the people in each group, notice that multiple people are often involved in a single process, ranging from the individuals who specify design requirements to purchasing agents, and from those who approve orders to those who actually use the product.

The overriding principle is to focus first on your end customers—the individual people, business enterprises, and other organizations that actually use the goods and services that you provide. You need to identify your target customers and build on your knowledge of what these customers are doing with your products and solutions.

Identify how your customers are incorporating the results of your goods and services into their own environments and discover what they are actually trying to accomplish. Describe how to make it easy for your customers to do business with you by simplifying your business processes and ensuring that customers have access to the information they need—just when and where they need it. Be sure to identify the value propositions that affect your company's relationships with your customers and how you can contribute to their ongoing satisfaction.

To help you start this process, build a catalog of your customer-facing business processes. This will help you identify how you currently communicate with customers and suggest opportunities to enhance customer interaction with Web-based solutions.

Then, identify your current cost factors in sales, marketing, and customer service. Ask the following questions.

- How much do you spend to actually close individual sales?
- How are you spending your marketing budget? What are your returns from the marketing expenditures?
- What are your costs for customer service and support?
- How many sales leads are in your pipeline?
- What is your prospect-to-customer conversion ratio?
- What proportion of customers contribute the majority of profits?
- What is the rate of customer defection to your competition?
- How many complaints do you receive per month?
- What is the turnaround time for responding to customer inquires?
- How many inventory turns per year do you make?

The answers to such questions help you identify problem areas and help set financial benchmarks for your e-business operation.

After reviewing your own internal processes, compare them to successful competitors. If your business is juice bars, compare your internal processes against the industry leaders. Much of this information is available on the Internet, and much more is available at industry conferences and seminars where your competitors speak. Also, check and see if any magazine articles or books are available so you can glean more information.

Keys to E-Business Success

According to a hands-on survey of business Web sites by Forrester Research, there are a handful of things that can go wrong on your e-business sites that will drive customers away for good. These are at the top of the list:

- The quality of a site's search function (only 12 percent list items in a usable order).

- Whether a site delivers satisfying content (only a little over 50 percent of the sites Forrester looked at provide a meaningful payoff).
- Whether a site actually works (4 out of 10 sites have serious breaks in them).

Identifying Improvement Opportunities

Many new ideas will flow from the assessments. As you target the opportunities for improvement be sure to identify the benefits—both more measurable monetary and less measurable relationship-oriented benefits. For example, how much are you likely to save in sales and support costs by allowing your customers to search for catalog information on their own?

Certainly you will economize on the printing and distribution of hard copy documents. But what about the ability to directly remove items from sale as soon as they have gone out of stock—and thereby avoid the support calls and customer frustrations? Alternatively, how are you likely to increase customer satisfaction by being able to correctly track customer demand and accurately ramping up production schedules in anticipation of future sales? Your customers expect you to have the goods on hand and available for timely delivery. Otherwise, even if the price is right, they will look elsewhere.

Identifying Your Goals and Objectives

Once you have completed your assessments, developed your new business model, and estimated the business benefits of various opportunities for improvement, you are in a position to prioritize various approaches and solutions in terms of their importance and timing. It is often advisable to identify the goals and objectives of an overall project and then plan to implement it in terms of a series of discrete and tactically executable phases.

Once your business objectives are in focus, use your research to highlight the approaches and strategic actions to move you toward reaching your objectives.

Be Innovative

You need to assess your business processes in a thorough fashion. As you consider your end-to-end business processes, you will invariably identify opportunities for innovative Web-based business initiatives.

Depending upon the outcome of your assessment, the characteristics of your firm, the nature of your distribution channels, and the underlying dynamics of your marketplace, you will develop your own set of strategic approaches on how to manage and control your business operations.

Emphasize the agility of your Web-based business. A Web-based business model shrinks the cycle times for routine business operations and thus reduces many non-value-adding operational costs. Companies doing business on the Web develop a very rapid information metabolism. They can respond quickly and cost-effectively to changes in their marketplace—and accommodate the speed of operating in the cyber economy.

When customers place their orders interactively over the Web, the information can be automatically captured electronically and does not have to be re-entered into your order processing or accounting systems.

And when the engineering group updates the specifications of a product or when a marketing manager changes the pricing and packaging of an item, the revised information can be automatically distributed to the sales force and customers—without the delays and costs for printing new brochures, updating printed catalogs and price lists, and sending paper documents to the field.

Tracking Customers

It's also important for your e-business site to track customer activities in near realtime. A Web-based business can track customer activities in near realtime—including, if desired, the consequences of every mouse click or every interaction. As a result, a business can develop detailed profiles of their customers—what content they are looking for, what kinds of questions they are asking, what types of products and services they are buying. A firm can anticipate future market demand by tracking what its customers are saying and doing within its e-commerce environment.

This also enables a business to easily test both new products and innovative marketing programs with little initial investment—and get results from customers within a short period of time. Marketing and promotional activities that in a conventional environment take months to plan and implement can be completed within days or weeks, saving time and money and increasing the productivity of an agile organization.

Personalized Services

Your e-business site should also offer personalized service at an affordable price. Do that by focusing on the specific needs of targeted groups of customers. As individuals search for information and seek to buy goods and services, an enterprise can capture this information and then respond to the requests based on what it knows about the customer. As the firm learns more about its individual customers, and as people explain their interests and preferences, the Web-based firm can appropriately tailor its offers and suggestions.

Saving Time, Earning Trust

Your e-business site should also enable customers to save time and increase satisfaction, which in turn leads to greater loyalty. Once you invest in the network connections and the underlying infrastructure of the Web, you need to create the customer-facing scenarios that describe how your customers will do business with you. Be as specific as possible, and, where relevant, incorporate the contributions of distributors and other channel partners. Much of the information that people need to do their jobs is available online and quickly accessed interactively—provided of course that they know where to begin looking for it in the first place. As a result, customers no longer have to waste time on the telephone seeking answers to routine questions—and waiting in calling queues for minutes on end. This reserves person-to-person telephone calls for the hard problems, those not easily answered through online queries.

Estimating Costs

As the final step in creating a strategic business plan, you need to determine the costs of your e-commerce opportunities, taking into account both current expenditures and likely expenditures for later improvements. This is obviously a difficult kind of estimate as there are no hard and fast rules for modeling situations and automatically calculating the results. Respond to this challenge by proceeding incrementally, basing your estimates on the best assessment you have for near-term initiatives and giving best estimates for the later work, together with a promise to refine it as you gather experience.

Some of the specific design and development factors in your costing estimates include:

- Hosting and network communications services
- Platform, infrastructure, and software applications
- System administration
- Content management, including designing the look and feel of the environment
- Integration with existing legacy environments

In addition, consider related expenses such as marketing, sales, and promotions. It helps to relate these costs to the ways you will identify your unique capabilities in the marketplace, differentiate your firm's solution from your competitors, and build market momentum behind your particular vision with online and offline advertising, link-exchange partnerships, and community Web site sponsorships.

E-Procurement a Profit Center?

A recent study by Grainger Consulting Services, a division of W. W. Grainger, Inc., confirms that e-commerce procurement is a significant benefit to both buyer and seller. The study shows that buyers who made investments to acquire and implement e-procurement methods averaged a return on their investment of between 265 and 400 percent, while sellers showed gains of 10 to 15 percent. Sellers did, however, receive the additional average benefit of a 300 percent increase in sales.

What Does Your Customer Want?

We'll talk a lot more about customer service in Chapter 8, but including your customers' needs in your business plan is imperative. Begin by focusing on what your target customers will need from your online environment. Describe how customers will use the electronic connections—the kinds of inquiries they will make, the types of information they will be looking for, and the ways in which they will incorporate your interactive resources into their work activities.

Then plan for the continuing evolution of customer needs and expectations. In many cases your customers will begin interacting with your Web site by doing simple things at first, such as quickly checking an order status rather than calling you on your toll free number. Over time, as they become accustomed to the interactive medium, they will expect new (and higher) levels of service. Savvy customers will want one-click access to product data sheets, for example, and the capability to troubleshoot and order replacement parts online.

Define your customer requirements by reviewing your existing market segments and listing the capabilities, characteristics, and demographics of your primary groups of customers. For instance, a company selling office products needs to use different marketing strategies to appeal to office managers in large enterprises, administrative assistants in small firms, and individuals working in home-based businesses. Each of these types of customer represents different segments of your market, and buyers in each segment have different needs and buying preferences. By tailoring its messages to different buyers, a company can more effectively execute its marketing plan across a wide range of potential customers.

Check and verify that your market segmentation strategies actually work, that the groupings that make sense in a conventional, offline world are still applicable in the interactive environment of the Net economy. Examine not only current market profiles, but also customer trends.

Also attempt to describe the key characteristics of your target customers. Depending on the objectives of your underlying business strategy, you might focus on people and groups who are:

- The most profitable
- The easiest to acquire
- The most influential

Be explicit about who these people actually are. Identify their attitudes, aspirations, and actions, and don't forget to describe what it is about their business tasks that makes them potential customers for your products or services. Describe the barriers they face to getting their jobs done. Categorize the kinds of information that each of them needs in order to do business with you.

Who's Calling the Shots?

While your customer determines how successful your Web efforts will be, your company leaders will determine if and when your Web efforts even get off the ground. A successful e-business campaign needs a high-level executive sponsor, somebody who can advocate forcefully for your customers' interests and concerns throughout the multiple levels of your company's operations. This person needs to be a hands-on leader who can create the business vision, spearhead the implementation efforts, secure financial resources as necessary, and motivate the key groups within the firm to align their activities toward the new initiatives. Your sponsor may be the CEO, a divisional executive vice president, or a vice president for interactive marketing.

Additionally, the executive sponsor must be able to work with senior managers to build consensus and commitment behind a shared vision of fostering customer connections. Together, the sponsor and the senior managers will be faced with directing and managing the linkages among all the various independent parties who are involved in your end-to-end business processes.

Even when your visionary leader is coming from high up in the corporation, that person cannot succeed without the support of line managers and the cooperation of front-line personnel. Not only do front-line operations people understand fully what the customers' issues are, they have the power to make your initiative work or to sabotage the whole thing. You and your sponsor need to secure the commitment from the various functional groups within your organization—including marketing, sales, product development, customer service and support, and operations—by showing how a customer-facing interactive environment will help to solve each group's most significant customer relationship issues and concerns.

Building Your E-Business Team

To gain the maximum benefit from your e-business campaign, it's important to have your entire company, as well as your company leaders, sign on to the project. That's not as hard as it appears, but it does take some diplomacy, some internal coordination, and some old-fashioned team management.

It is not necessary to have a huge staff on your e-business project; many organizations have only a handful of people. What is important is to make sure that each of the roles is covered, even if it means that some individuals will be playing multiple roles.

There is a lot more to a successful Web site than a Webmaster who manages its day-to-day operations. You will need a focused team that is dedicated to the evolution of your entire e-commerce environment—ranging from tactical business decisions to routine management. This team will form the hub for various kinds of distributed activity that will take place throughout your organization as new documents are written, new products are designed and marketed, orders are taken in new ways, and customers are served.

The core team should comprise people working in three distinct roles: marketing/sales, content, and technology. Please note that we are talking about distinct roles here, not necessarily new full-time positions.

Many of the roles (described later) are undertaken by people who already have jobs in the relevant areas. Most core teams are small—often comprising no more than six to eight people—and frequently individual staff members fulfill multiple roles.

E-Commerce Director: While the title itself depends upon the culture of the organization, an e-commerce environment needs to be led by a seasoned marketing professional who has senior management-level status (such as vice president) within the company. The e-commerce director is responsible for the business direction and operational management of the e-commerce initiative. The scope of this person's activities begins with product marketing responsibilities and includes strong linkages into the product development, product marketing, manufacturing, and logistics operations of the firm. This person also needs to direct the customer service, advertising, and interactive marketing activities on the site.

Web Channel Manager: The Web channel manager has the key role of turning the e-commerce vision into a set of practical and readily implemented operational activities. This person is someone with a strong marketing background who is also technically savvy—or at least not technophobic. He or she needs to have a strong ability to build consensus, and, thus, to do internal marketing. This person has to get buy-in from the different line organizations within the firm that need to proactively provide content and support to the e-commerce environment.

Customer Profile Manager: The customer profile manager is a marketing professional who takes responsibility for managing and evolving the information about individual customers. He or she ensures that customers are only asked to supply information in exchange for a relevant and valued service or product, that customers are never asked more than once for the same information, that the information is kept up-to-date, and that individual customers can review their own information. This same person may manage the development of targeted offers and promotions based on customers' profiles.

Customer Traffic Analyst: The customer traffic analyst tracks the reports of customers' activities on the site. He or she analyzes the Web site traffic logs to identify dead ends that customers may be encountering, what products and services they are looking at, where they are coming from, and what they are actually doing on the site. This person interprets the information and disseminates it quickly to all of the other people in the organization who need to see it.

Customer Service Manager: As a seasoned customer service professional, the customer service manager is responsible for overseeing all of the customer service functions on the Web site. These functions include resolving the barriers to customer interactions (using the information provided by the customer traffic analyst), developing processes for responding to customers' e-mail inquiries, and ensuring that all outbound communications (such as e-mail messages) arrive satisfactorily. This person is ultimately responsible for the quality of customer service delivered through the Web site.

Content Manager: In a publishing operation the manager for content is called the editor-in-chief. In your core group this person decides what type of information should appear on the site and is responsible for managing both editorial and content review processes. This person also monitors the organization of content on the site, makes sure that stale content is removed, and tracks broken links. This person supervises the editorial workflow processes and procedures to ensure that all copy has been reviewed and approved by the appropriate parties before it is posted.

Graphic Design Manager: This person is responsible for the quality and consistency of the overall appearance of the site. Often working in conjunction with an outside design firm, this person defines and then evolves the guidelines for the overall look and feel of the site. He or she works with external departments and divisions to ensure design consistency. This person is also responsible for creating and managing the series of templates that are used by people throughout the firm when publishing content for the Web.

Webmaster: The Webmaster is the person who is responsible for the Web site's presence on the Web, even if the operations and hosting is outsourced to an Internet service provider. He or she ensures that the Web site is performing as expected and that all of the related applications are running properly. The Webmaster manages the customer tracking and logging applications and provides the data to the marketing group. This person is also responsible for implementing security policies, monitoring and resolving performance issues, and detecting operational problems that will inevitably occur. In terms of continued management, the Webmaster decides when and how to upgrade the site with new software releases and applications and participates in the planning for expanded operations.

There are many other technical tasks that fall into the Webmaster's lap, so it is also important to identify what he or she should not be doing. The person in this role should not have to manage the content distributed on the site, answer customers' e-mails, write copy, or develop the customer-facing marketing strategies.

Programmers: The programmers are the people who develop and continually refine your Web applications. The programmers will probably include a combination of internal and external developers. Regardless of where they come from, it is very important that the programmers assigned to your Web development team understand your existing operational systems and can integrate your Web environment with various external business systems.

Nuts and Bolts: Building the Perfect E-Business Beast

What is the best way to acquire the products and services needed by your e-commerce project? Your choices here involve a set of key decisions. Successfully achieving your project within your cost/time targets depends on getting the most appropriate hardware, infrastructure, and software, and also skilled implementation assistance.

There are many factors to consider in your analysis, such as your available internal information technology capabilities and the different features of software offered by vendors of varying reputations.

Developing your site should be an iterative process, with prototypes being continually evaluated. Prepare detailed task plans that define each of the activities, with a timeline for prototype, review, and revision.

Integration should not wait until the site is complete. Integration with internal systems such as inventory, accounting, and customer relationship management needs to be built in from the beginning. Otherwise, as schedules get tight (as they invariably do), there is the tendency to leave this integration for Phase II, a strategy that in the short run will make more work for your internal staff and in the long run could cost a lot more in both investment and dissatisfied customers. Integration with payment and certification services is generally straightforward but should not be left to the last minute.

Populating the site and the databases with content is perhaps the step that is most overlooked and causes the most delays. Frequently, this cannot begin until the site is almost completed, as developers generally do not provide the needed data entry tools until they have solved all of the other "difficult" problems.

A critical strategy is not to wait until the last two weeks of the project but to begin the process even during the design phase. At that point you can begin to inventory and catalog existing content sources, such as:

- HTML pages used on your internal site
- Databases and other electronic repositories
- Hard copy catalogs and other paper-based information collections
- The results of ad hoc activities
- Information obtained from your suppliers/partners (ideally, electronically and continually updated)

You can also begin to assign content creation tasks and start thinking about ongoing content management responsibilities.

Launching the Working Environment

Finally, you have finished developing your e-commerce environment—at least for the first iteration of your plans. It works. It meets

Helpful Hints

Obviously, there's no shortage of work when it comes to building the perfect e-business site. Here are some things you can do to make the process go a bit easier on you and your staff:

1. Question Everything. Ask for views on which products, customer groups, and processes are ripe for seizing the customer-first opportunity. This helps ensure that plans are the best they can be—and begins to develop buy-in down the line. Get help from marketing visionaries and operations people who know how information flows. Highlight potential conflicts and opportunities. Notice what others in the industry are doing.

2. Set Goals. Make a short list of measurable items—and be realistic about the timeline. Expect a number of discrete chunks of accomplishment before the grand vision is realized. Work in teams, with help from experienced planners to define assumptions, business events and rules, and critical success factors.

3. Who's Minding the Mint? Nothing can replace a supportive visionary executive. Get a sponsor on board as soon as possible to help articulate the e-commerce vision and develop a mental model that everyone can support. High-profile funding legitimizes the project and engenders enthusiasm for change.

4. All Aboard! Listening and responding never stop, so hold stakeholder workshops to vet the vision, air concerns, set clear priorities, and discuss models for customer-focused operation. Use workshop experts and set up regular progress reports. As buy-in proceeds, bring customers and partners into workshops.

5. There's No "I" in Team. Start with a strong project leader and recruit representatives from many departments including sales, marketing, operations, and IT. Build on their perspectives and identify issues for early treatment. Here's where enlisting experts and veterans gives critical leverage to avoid costly pitfalls and speed the process.

6. Plan Accordingly—and Everything Will Go According to Plan. Include a business assessment and schedule covering long-term justification from profit increases, productivity, and cost savings. These gains are likely to be foreshadowed by early signs of nondollar progress such as reduced complaints and increased online usage by customers, prospects, and partners.

your requirements. It meets your customers' needs. It is finally time to launch the working environment.

There are two steps to deployment.

- First, install, test (particularly the integration), and tune the application on the production server or servers. This may be done internally or may involve shipping the server(s) to the hosting outsourcer.

Questions Before Your Site Goes Live

- As you launch your e-commerce environment, how will you begin to build traffic to the site?
- How will you continually test and assess the performance of the site? Are your customers able to find the information they need within a reasonable period of time?
- Do you have the business processes in place to accommodate your customers' requests from the Web?

- Have you defined your quality of service targets? How quickly do you expect to respond to online requests? What are your measures of success?
- What is your feedback system for monitoring customers' experiences and Web site performance, and for then implementing changes?

(Source: Netscape/Sun Alliance)

- Second, migrate any users and any remaining content from the staging server to the production environment. Again, test the results of this migration to see if the security system works. During this time you may be running two systems in parallel if you already had a first-generation system.

Once you have launched your e-commerce solution on the Web, you can begin to exploit the capabilities of the new environment. Now that your business can change and respond on Internet time, recognize that you need to continually adapt and enhance your environment lest it become out-of-date. There are two areas that require continual attention and continual improvement: the interactive content that you compile and publish, and the design of the site itself.

Maintaining the content on your e-commerce site is fundamentally an editorial and publishing process. Staff members or independent writers need to author the product descriptions, data sheets, news articles, analyses, and other kinds of content that will appear on your site. Other people are involved in the review and approval of these pieces. You will find that your e-commerce organization is repeating this editorial and publishing process on an ongoing basis with a frequency determined by its business goals and objectives.

As your site is primarily intended to sell products and services, then each content owner must maintain the current content as well as the lists of resellers, branch offices, product catalogs, data sheets, online help guides, and other electronic resources.

Once your site is up and running, maintaining the content is no longer a strategic task undertaken by an ad hoc business team. Maintaining the site needs to be viewed as an ordinary part of running a business and incorporated into the operational responsibilities of individual line organizations. Maintaining the site should be funded and managed just like any other kind of core operational activity.

What Tools Do I Use?

Choosing what software and Web services you'll use on your e-business site doesn't have to be a zero sum game. In other words, feel free to use what you need to make the system run smoothly and securely, ostensibly within the confines of your budget.

Here are some guidelines to follow.

First, the software must run natively on your platform of choice. You can have more future flexibility if the software also runs on multiple common platforms. The software must be easily integrated with other solution subsystems, such as legacy order-processing systems, product databases, customer databases, and customer-support systems.

Choose software that is able to handle your business's anticipated transaction volumes for the next few years of forecasted activity, with a substantial margin for upside growth. Avoid trading increased transaction volume for restrictions on other aspects of scale, such as file-size handling or directory membership length.

Modularity and extensibility can be critical determinants in creating the solution you envision now and new capabilities that will occur to you in the future. A tightly bound all-in-one approach lacking either of these can be extremely frustrating as your needs evolve. Dealing with such limitations can be extremely expensive.

Above all, don't select any software that doesn't provide robust security provisions. Your buyers and partners must have confidence in conducting transactions. This includes simple support for encryption protection, secure communication of user IDs and passwords, authentication, support for digital certificates, and delegated user administration for partners.

The next level is being sure that the software has appropriate functionality for its intended purpose. The software must provide as much of the needed functionality as possible, leaving only minor gaps to be filled in by custom development or separate programs. Prebuilt software modules may be the best choice to support online purchase transaction processing, billing and payment, content publishing and delivery, directory support for multiple applications, security services, integration/conversion support, and workflow. Be sure that you can obtain a good set of application program interfaces and tools for the software you select to help your technical staff create functional extensions and satisfy ongoing business. And look for conformance with open standards.

While in-depth features and functionality encourage creative implementation for users, it is also important to examine the way the features are expressed to the user. For example, a parametric search feature in a product catalog can be valuable to your customers, but they'll never use it twice unless it's easy, intuitive, and rewarding.

Installation and Maintenance

System administration that is easy and flexible will pay dividends in terms of the time and training it saves. It also strongly affects the morale of the administrator. The software must have good provisions for many ongoing system administration tasks that will arise such as editing users, privileges, products, customers, promotions, prices, and banners. Check to see whether and how much of this can be done remotely through Web browsers by nontechnical people.

The software must have relatively easy support for setup and configuration tasks, with logical procedures, clear terminology, helpful defaults, informative status indicators, and flexibility. Be sure the software makes it easy to back through transaction records and untangle broken orders. Audit capabilities help diagnose security problems, especially with payments. Look for built-in reporting functionality and activity analysis aids.

Quality and Cost

Evaluate the quality of the software as to the number and severity of bugs in the current release and the vendor's approach to dealing with bugs. Look for software that will provide a good balance in the level of experience and skill required for installing, operating, integrating, and extending the software because that affects the cost and availability of developers.

Finally, consider the software in terms of several cost considerations such as initial cost, recurring maintenance fees, and the cost of developer support in the future.

Choosing a Vendor

When choosing a Web tools vendor, software attributes are extremely important, but they are only part of the evaluation. A complete analysis and evaluation examines the qualities and capabilities of the software vendor as a supplier. When looking at sourcing alternatives for software and services, here are a number of criteria to examine:

- How long the vendor has been developing and deploying the kind of software you need? Robust e-commerce has not been on the market very long. It is relatively easy to determine how many years have gone into developing and refining a vendor's knowledge of customer requirements and getting feedback on their approaches. The more knowledgeable they are, the better their software, and the greater help they can be.

- How often have new releases been issued? This includes both dot-release upgrades as well as full-integer releases that take the software to a new level. Although the pace of prior releases may not necessarily continue in the future, it is an indicator of relative smoothness and efficiency of the vendor's product planning and development processes. Although on the one hand you may be disinclined to revamp your entire operation to absorb new releases, on the other hand you want to have the benefit of timely improvements rather than waiting a long time for problems to be corrected.

- Can they add capabilities to your Web site? You're best served by a vendor with vision and the proven ability to execute on their vision. Every vendor faces tradeoff choices for use of their scarce development resources. They must make hard choices about which aspects of their products they improve and what new capabilities to introduce. As you listen to their plans for new software enhancements and forward products, consider how well these directions map to your own e-commerce strategy.

- Will they be there for you? No matter how well the vendor's software meets your feature and performance requirements, you will inevitably require technical support, especially in the early stages of installation and startup. As you consider different vendors, get a reading on their relative strengths in the area of technical support. The key factors include response time and quality of information. Consider also the quality and completeness of technical documentation.

Should You Use an Intermediary?

The e-business marketplace is being transformed by the emergence of e-market makers that facilitate online transactions. According to Dataquest Inc., analysts estimate e-market makers generated approximately $12 billion in 1998, and this excludes e-marketplaces focused on financial products (mortgages, bonds, securities, and so on), where volumes exceeded $100 billion.

Dataquest defines e-market makers as business-to-business reintermediaries. They enter supply chains in vertical industries and horizontal business functions, introducing new efficiencies and new ways of selling and purchasing products and services. An e-market maker is an organization that develops a business-to-business Internet protocol (IP), network-based, e-marketplace of buyers and sellers within a particular industry, geographic region, or affinity group.

E-market makers will revolutionize trading relationships and business-to-business e-commerce, diverting a significant percentage of transactions from extranets, electronic data interchange (EDI), and Web storefronts while creating opportunity for a new breed of e-commerce transactions. They will also change the way organizations purchase and sell strategic and nonstrategic products, the way they purchase and deploy software, and the way they evaluate professional services companies, financial institutions, and Internet service providers.

Dataquest segments e-market makers into four categories:

Content and Community Portals. These portals provide value-added content, such as specification sheets and part descriptions for design engineers, buyer's guides for small companies, and hosted software. They may also provide bulletin board functionality for sellers and buyers to post information about products and services for sale. These portals earn revenue by posting advertisements or collecting subscription fees. They may also charge sellers a finder's fee for sales leads.

Channel Enablers. E-marketers sell commerce software and hosting solutions to help the channel participate in e-commerce. They are common in industries in which suppliers have ceded so much supply chain power to channels of distributors, brokers, and agents that suppliers may now be hesitant to initiate direct sales.

Efficient Commerce Networks. These organizations manage a trading network that generally maintains existing supply chain relationships and pricing models but attacks industry inefficiencies.

Efficient commerce networks often aggregate suppliers' catalogs; they may compete with brick-and-mortar distributors.

Dynamic Marketplaces. These marketplaces employ a commerce model whereby product pricing is negotiated within the marketplace through auctions, request for proposal/request for quote processes, or bid-ask matching exchanges. These dynamic marketplaces can represent seller advocates, buyer advocates, or be neutral online exchanges. The neutral online exchanges manage purchases and sales among multiple buyers and sellers. These exchanges work best for commodity and near-commodity products for which descriptive information facilitates reasonable price/quality comparisons.

Initially the e-market makers will drive adoption of catalog software, search engine software, and buy-side software. Over time, Dataquest analysts say, the e-market makers will either compete with software providers or will provide a channel. E-commerce software vendors that do not have a strategy for partnering with and in the long term potentially competing with e-market makers need to develop a strategy. Developing an e-market maker strategy is critical for buy-side software vendors as enterprise procurement evolves to the extended enterprise and trading communities.

Good to Go

While the points addressed here are some of the most important issues to consider before you plan your e-business site, they're not the only ones. In Chapter 4 of the book we'll address in detail how e-business will affect your organization, from your sales department to your back office. Then we'll address deeper concerns on key areas like outsourcing, whether portal partnerships are a good idea, marketing your e-business site, and reaching customers overseas.

We'll also take a closer look at some of the more successful e-business sites operating today. So what are we waiting for?

chapter four

Gauging E-Business's Impact on Your Organization

s any philosopher worth his sandals will tell you, every cause has an effect. With e-business, the big picture tells you that the effect will be a positive one on your outfit: easier access to customers, profitable new distribution channels, and a rosier bottom line.

But what cost, if any, will implementing your e-business platform have on your company? What changes need to be made before you get going? And what adjustments do you need to make as an organization as your e-business operation, which will touch every corner of your business along the way, unfurls itself across the corporate landscape?

The impact your e-business initiative has on your company is an enormous one. Your employees will view your entire company differently after its implementation, as (obviously) your customers will, too.

The Impact of E-Business on Your Business

So how does e-business impact your business? In myriad ways. Remember, e-commerce is all about providing the opportunity for businesses to communicate, coordinate, and transact with anyone, any time, anywhere. Traditionally, communication and coordination have been expensive, leading to the concentration of activities in firms and relatively inflexible production.

Customers had limited choice in products. Goods were distributed through complex distribution channels that were slow, relatively uncoordinated, and inefficient. Service levels were often erratic and often reflected what was best for the manufacturer or the distribution channel rather than the customer. All this has changed in the world of e-business and e-commerce.

E-commerce provides the tools to create much more efficient, speedy, and responsive supply chains. Instead of manufacturers pushing product down the supply chain, customers pull the product through it. This results in enormous savings, particularly of inventories and wastage within the supply chain. Procter & Gamble saved billions of dollars through redesigning its supply chains. When the supply chain becomes much more flexible and responsive, the customer receives higher-value, better-quality products and services.

E-commerce allows for just about any business process to be run more efficiently, particularly those that span a number of organizations. Rich information about all aspects of the process is available anywhere, any time, allowing processes to be far better managed. Processes can be streamlined, hand-offs and errors minimized, performance can be tracked, and appropriate information made easily available to support any stage of the process.

E-commerce also allows you to link yourself directly to the customer. That means dramatically reduced costs and improved ability to add value by sensing and responding to customer needs! For companies selling physical products such as cars, computers, bicycles, and so on, e-commerce means being able to have direct communication with the consumer for specifying, ordering, paying, and tracking the product from manufacture to final delivery. However, remember that the consumer is not satisfied until she receives a physical product— getting physical distribution right is critical.

Of course, if you produce information products like software applications or Web content, the actual product can be delivered directly to the customer's computer via the Internet. Many businesses are only just beginning to come to terms with the possibilities and threats inherent in the raw power of the Internet and the Web to deliver their information directly to the consumer. You must be prepared to start experimenting with direct distribution of information products, because you can be sure that if you are in a viable business someone else will be doing the same.

Although the greatest potential of e-commerce is in linking organizations and individuals together, using e-commerce within organizations can also provide very significant benefits. Even in areas such as buying supplies, large companies have saved millions of dollars by developing Web-based purchasing sites.

Maximizing Your E-Business Efforts

According to Judith S. Hurwitz, president and CEO of Hurwitz Group, Inc., a Framingham, Massachusetts research and consulting firm focused on electronic business applications and services, companies must do three things to ensure that their e-business campaign is a coporate-wide success.

- Clean house. Implementing E2K requires opening your computing infrastructure to customers, employees, and partners, meaning that your customers may spot problems before you do. To minimize risk, identify areas where your company may run into trouble.
- Create a "hypertier" applications architecture. Without an applications architecture underlying your E2K infrastructure, you won't be able to compete with startups that have no legacy and no expenses. To start, conduct an audit of the structure of your current applications and underlying architecture. Match this against a hypertier architecture that's based on a fluid design and that lets you react in realtime to changing market and customer requirements.
- Strike a balance between effectiveness and efficiency. Traditional companies specialize in becoming efficient. They cut costs out of processes and send invoices on time. In stable markets, efficiency is paramount.

Hurwitz also advocates an e-business initiative that has the right mix of decision-makers, expert analysts, and dependable implementers in place. Here's what the core of that line-up should include:

- A chief e-business officer who looks to the future and helps the company prepare for success.
- Executive producers who lead from technology and business standpoints.
- Web strategists who can extend the Web structure to meet the business's strategic objectives.

The Sales Department:
All Office Politics Isn't Necessarily Local

Another potential land mine for organizations looking to set up e-business sites is the time-honored corporate tradition of "turf," particularly the kind of turf where some company staffers feel threatened by the potential encroachment on their turf by the e-business site.

Offering Web e-commerce directly to customers can be disruptive to the sales channel because if distributors and dealers become threatened with a direct-to-consumer approach from their vendors, they may stop selling that company's products. Few vendors can transform their distribution methods overnight. So, while selling directly to customers

seems like an important future direction, alienating existing distribution channels can result in disaster.

There are many examples of companies that have successfully
navigated these new waters and created innovative sales and distribution strategies in response to the Web. Companies that have experienced the smoothest transitions, such as Dell and Cisco, are ones that
didn't require radical changes in their traditional business processes
because they were already selling directly to customers. As a result,
shifting the direct customer relationships to the Web wasn't as risky
as it has been for companies totally dependent on distribution.

Some companies that have been more reliant on multitier distribution have worked to make the Web a win/win for themselves and
the channel. For example, PC Order's business is designed to maintain positive and profitable relationships between manufacturers of
technology products—including Quantum and Hewlett-Packard—
and their channels by facilitating the online referrals of customers to
dealers. The service lets manufacturers offer a customer-friendly
referral service while helping the dealer consummate the sale. Time
will tell if these creative approaches to resolving channel conflict will
be successful. The true test will be in where and how consumers
choose to buy.

Yet struggling with traditional sales channels is more the norm
than the exception. One vice president at a major auto manufacturer
tells the tale of successfully lobbying the top brass for $250,000 for a
Web-based order entry system. Standing in his way was the company's venerable sales staff, many of whom tried to deep-six the Web
sales initiative believing it to be a threat to their jobs. Some sales
staffers bad-mouthed the site to customers, telling them that the site
was less than secure and potentially glitch-prone.

Only another successful lobbying effort on the part of the vice
president prevented the system from collapsing under the weight of
the sales department's negative energy. Immediately, orders came
from the top to institute automatic sales commissions for each Web-
based transaction. Dinner meetings were held with top company executives and sales managers where the CEO and other senior executives
took turns reminding the salespeople that the Web was their friend,
allowing them to focus on bigger and better relationships with customers and spend more time wooing new ones. In addition, each sales
staffer was given a CD-ROM kit detailing how to best sell the site to

customers, along with brochures and information packets detailing the site's benefits for use by their customers.

The pitch worked, as the sales staff began to see the Web site not just as a tool for marketing, or for sales or any other division, but as a great tool for customers.

Another good idea to build a sense of interdepartmental community for the site—and to ward off any negative corporate political power plays that could mitigate a site's effectiveness—is to include everybody in on the planning of the site, from the ground floor up.

The same auto manufacturer, realizing how close it came to squandering the site's potential by not explaining its benefits to staffers, embarked on a new campaign where one member of each corporate department—sales, back office, marketing, manufacturing, etc.—was included in the design and implementation process. That way, each corner—and each cornerstone—of the company was heard from throughout the process, fostering the type of goodwill that isn't available by adopting an exclusionary e-business site development process.

The Back Office: Accounting for New Procurement Procedures

A new B2B site not only will give your company a new look, it will give customers a new way to look at you, too. Even though the concept of electronic procurement, most notably through electronic data interchange (EDI), has been with us since the early 1990s, buying goods online is still a new experience in the eyes of your customer.

That's why it's important that the financial and accounting officers in your company understand how electronic procurement works. Simply stated, electronic procurement is the most commonly used component of e-business. It connects buyers and suppliers to electronic catalogs of nonproduction purchases such as MRO (maintenance, repair, and operational) goods and services and eliminates rogue purchasing by unauthorized buyers in your organization.

Most industry studies confirm widespread cost reductions in electronic procurement. The National Association of Purchasing Managers estimates that the traditional paper handling of procurement processes ranges from $50 to $200 per transaction, whereas the automation of these same procurement practices has been documented to cost between $0.42 and $0.93 per transaction.

Start from the Top

Rome wasn't built in a day, and neither were the 1927 Yankees. But both had a head start—great leadership from the top.

According to Arthur Anderson's e-business practices team, building the perfect e-business is a campaign that starts from the top down. Here's their list of "must do's" when putting your e-business team together:

1. E-business initiatives are typically brainstormed by a few stakeholders who form alliances and gain support within an organization. When an initiative's operation grows complex, there's increasing justification for a formal project management structure to ensure proper execution and accountability.

2. A challenge facing many organizations today is the staffing of Internet-based initiatives. While many skill sets can be transformed from traditional roles, hiring experienced e-business personnel is recommended to avoid the pitfalls of developing an e-business strategy and rollout plan.

3. Any e-business initiative affecting a business process or communications should have two important participants—a senior executive on the steering committee and a project leader who understands the profound effect that the Internet will have on the company's future.

4. A popular e-business team-building structure model includes a steering committee, a project leader, and a supporting management team. The steering committee offers high-level direction to the project leader who then coordinates specific tasks with the supporting management team. Each group's level of involvement depends on the nature of the project and the overall impact of the initiative. This traditional model works well when organizing an e-business initiative. The level of involvement by each participant should be directed by the steering committee.

Here's how the electronic procurement process works. Customers enter the Web site through a home page or Web portal and can immediately choose from a menu of potential goods. The purchase itself is captured by e-procurement software for routing and approvals. This way, control of the purchase and prenegotiated price breaks stay in the e-procurement system. When users have filled a virtual shopping cart with the items they want to buy, the entire process of order routing, approval, and delivery is automated through the software, with status messages delivered at each stage of the procure-to-pay process.

The Web's ubiquitous "shopping cart" experience is viewed favorably by e-shoppers, primarily because it gives them a high comfort level and bolsters their service levels because they control buying the supplies and services they need. Electronic procurement also reduces administrative tasks associated with the buying process such as routing purchase orders and obtaining manual sign-off to buy commonly used office supplies.

Customers who use your site to buy goods and services can expect to save a great deal of money in their new electronic procurement efforts. These cost savings are due to an estimated 45 percent reduction in the cost of goods realized by eliminating most of the manual processes to purchase a good. A cost reduction of 25 percent for automating purchasing and payment has saved its commercial line of business billions of dollars annually.

Quantifying dollars saved from the e-business supplier's side is an inexact science, but some studies show that giving customers an electronic procurement option benefits you, the supplier, in many ways. For example, since e-businesses do not have to rekey invoices or get purchase orders out faster, they can spend more time capturing data about suppliers and customers and learn how partners are responding to products. Consequently, with this qualitative electronic information, the e-business can begin the process of driving down the cost of the goods itself.

The Marketing Department: To Market, To Market

The dynamic nature of the Web creates an opportunity to transform the communication between the company and the visitor from a one-way communication into an ongoing dialog. This lets companies learn more about their prospects and customers so information can be tailored to their interests.

But as e-business may have been in existence for several years now, it's only in the past year or so that company marketing executives are giving e-business a good chunk of their time and attention. While initially it was seen as an issue for the IT department, it is now widely recognized that e-business must be considered as an integral part of the marketing mix. That's why, in addition to the traditional supply chain and channel distribution challenges associated with launching a business-to-business Web site, a business-to-consumer site involves additional planning that requires the skills of a senior marketing executive.

Web-based marketing relies on many traditional skills that should be transferred from the existing marketing team. Maintaining appropriate relationships with customers through Web-based marketing and interaction is critical to the success of an e-business site.

Initial planning and opportunity assessment of a retail site should involve the steering committee and (at least) the vice president of marketing. Marketers understand the importance of the customer experience and are best able to direct methods of communication, content, and market segmentation. As the project progresses into the design and development phases, the project team involves supporting management and staff.

Customer Service: New Call Center Options in the New E-Conomy

The continuing evolution of e-business brings eye-opening news every day. Traditionally, collecting information about customers has been expensive, and merging this information into customer profiles has been even more difficult. But with an e-business site, you can now track your customers online to find out what they look for in a product, what they buy, and how they feel about your product and your online shopping experience.

Products are also being linked into the Internet. Manufacturers can now interact directly with the product. Previously, products were sold to the customer and there would be no communication with the manufacturer unless something went wrong. Now, if the product is connected to the Internet, its performance can be monitored. If problems occur, it may be possible to fix them directly, or the consumer may be able to fix them herself if she is provided with appropriate information. Many service calls may become a thing of the past.

E-businesses also allow customers to take an active part in defining their own needs and crafting a product or service to satisfy those needs. Rather than deciding in advance what products or services will satisfy the customer, use your knowledge and skill to assist the customer in designing her own product or service.

Then there's the issue of customer trust. How do you get your customers to trust e-commerce? To gain that trust—and keep it—e-businesses must have well developed customer service policies, and these must be communicated clearly and unequivocally to the customer. E-businesses must provide customers with accurate descriptions of products and services and their prices. Customers must be given the price of a product or service, not just part of the price. Delivery costs, handling charges, customs, and brokerage fees should be transparent to the consumer. If you are supplying customers in another country, you should indicate the cost to the consumer in their own currency.

Privacy is an increasingly important issue for the customer. What practices do you have in place to keep customer information (particularly payment information) secure? Under what circumstances will customer information be divulged and to whom? Although selling customer information to a third party may result in short-term revenue, it may result in losing customers in the long term.

Customer Service Skill Sets in the Age of E-Commerce

Arthur M. Rosenberg, president of Unified Communications Consortium, advocates some obvious staffing requirements to make sure that an e-mail or Web mail customer drive call center culture has the required "human" element to succeed. In the book he co-authored with Paul Anderson, he points out that if a customer call center rep can't type or is unfamiliar with old-fashioned communications skills, even the most advanced Web-based call center won't get off the ground. Here are his requirements for what customer call center reps must know and what skills they must possess to ensure that your e-business customers are well taken care of:

- E-mail message management. Sending, retrieving, addressing, routing/forwarding, replying, archiving, data attachment handling, etc.
- Written language skills. Reading and screening Web caller text content, grammatically correct writing, selective use of technical terminology, properly employing customer-sensitive verbiage, etc. Multilingual language skills and being able to understand poor English text will be important considerations for global e-business.
- Typing proficiency. Fast and error-free typing to minimize the time to create a text message response. Accurate name spelling and data entry will be extremely critical. This includes accuracy in procedural keyboard entries for e-mail messaging and data file management.
- PC usage literacy.
- Internet/Web site navigation skills.
- Web caller applications procedures and information.
- Understanding Web caller perspective, mindset, and physiology. Text message processing is still going to be more time consuming than voice, even with the use of skilled personnel. And because such personnel will be more expensive to recruit and retain, their time has to be used much more selectively on an exception basis. The real solution is to be much more organized and automated for e-mail response processing.

Considering the differences in skill requirements involved, Rosenberg says, real-time voice connections and message processing for Web callers may be most effectively handled initially by separate staffing resources in a call center environment.

In addition, typical call center management responsibilities will apply to staffing for Web mail processing. These include recruiting, training, work force scheduling, and performance monitoring. Management must also specify the rules that will be applied to message routing and disposition, based upon content analysis and elapsed-time priorities.

External Partnerships: Bringing in Fresh Blood

Sometimes the best partnerships you can make aren't always inside your company, they're outside. In the new world of e-commerce, communication needs come from all sides. A manufacturer needs to know that a contract supplier monitors inventory and replenishes it automatically. A customer needs to know how to specify exact configurations for an order and schedule delivery—without waiting to connect to a person in the call center.

Take the concept of "complementors." A complementor is a firm with information that can give you a competitive edge if you establish the right relationship. For example, Century 21 is a complementor to AT&T by giving it house-sale information for phone service sales leads.

Business-to-business e-commerce exploits the fact that almost every business is connected to the Internet in some way. To take advantage of this universal connectivity, enterprises are upgrading and extending their internal systems to allow exchange of essential business process information such as parts, prices, orders, inventories, production schedules, payments, preferences, and shipments.

Corporations are also taking advantage of well-designed, personal electronic interactions that bind customers through data-rich services. Formerly private databases now invite customers to review order status, inventory availability, account history, shipping status, FAQs, and custom catalogs. Satisfaction comes from information, entertainment, and need fulfillment.

This multidimensional model of cross-communication replaces the old linear model with expanded enterprise relationships. Today, for example, Home Depot's order department can collaborate with Nextel to automatically notify contractors via Nextel cell phones that building material orders are ready for pickup. This illustrates the concept of "complementors." The relationship expands both businesses.

The IT Department: Managing Chaos

Nobody wants to start from scratch, especially if you've already made a big investment in information technology. The Web's real business value lies in increasing your efficiency and effectiveness by leveraging business applications built on platforms you already have.

It's not that easy. Connecting the systems you have to the Web requires knowledge of some complex and often disparate technologies. But it's equally important to understand the issues surrounding your particular industry, because to do e-business you need more than just technology—you need people who understand how technology interrelates with your business.

That's where your IT department enters the picture. Even though there is no universal solution to e-business implementations, there is one constant and that's your IT staff. Whether you migrate to new platforms and technologies or simply Web-enable the systems you already have, you're going to need the full resources and support of your IT staff.

Here's what they'll face:

1. Round-the-clock workloads requiring new architectures and active management.
2. Resources—everything from floor space to processing capacity to staff skills—may be maxed out due to an ambitious e-business effort.
3. Your IT infrastructure will also place a huge demand on traditional IT platforms. Web servers, application servers, content servers, firewalls, load balancers, and storage systems will be more important than ever, as will be their management and maintenance. Also, because e-business applications depend on the seamless interaction of all these pieces, data center technicians are also under increasing pressure to manage end-to-end services, not just devices.
4. Another immediate impact that your company's IT staff will feel on the threshold of an e-business campaign is a drain in resources. As you'll see in Chapter 5, the lion's share of the e-business budget doesn't go to technology tools, it goes to the people who know how to work those tools. Most companies now have at least two or more IT staffers dedicated to the e-business effort. And the larger the company, the more employees you'll need.
5. Working with customers. Many companies are extending their e-business solutions by creating Web extensions to their ERP systems. To successfully integrate other best-of-breed applications or legacy systems, your IT team must build and maintain your e-business applications as close to your partners as possible to

IT Haters and Other Strangers

When it comes to calling the shots on an e-business campaign—or at least having a say on what kinds of bullets to use—you'd think the IT department would have more of a say. But they don't. According to a recent study by London-based Commslogic, only 15 percent of IT departments lead e-commerce projects. Surprisingly, the survey indicates that it is the sales and marketing departments that are overwhelmingly driving and retaining ownership of e-commerce strategies. Other highlights of the e-commerce study include:

- Despite the fact that the technology of e-commerce is new to IT departments and IT is not generally the instigator of e-commerce projects, 60 percent of respondents reported that their projects are being managed in-house; 30 percent have outsourced, and of those indicating that they intend to outsource, the majority will give the projects to existing suppliers rather than seeking specialist help.
- Integrating e-commerce into existing systems varies quite widely: 33 percent of respondents reported that their e-commerce system was integrated into the supply chain; 29 percent of businesses had re-engineered their existing systems to accommodate e-commerce; while 33 percent had taken the opposite approach by making e-commerce fit their established processes.
- Over 70 percent of organizations place a high importance on Microsoft's NT operating environment in their e-commerce solutions; 23 percent indicated a preference for UNIX-based platforms.
- More than half the e-commerce solutions surveyed have required platform upgrades since their inception, indicating either under-specification of the initial systems or growth from early tactical or pilot projects.
- Forty percent believe that business-to-business transactions will be where they achieve major e-business gains; 27 percent opted for e-shopping as the most important area, with a prediction that cost savings of 18 percent could be achieved.

extend applications and enable collaboration. Four key e-business areas in which your IT team can collaborate on business processes with external customers, suppliers, and partners are online sales, order management, supply chain management, and customer service. Let's examine them one at a time.

Online Sales—Enabling online business-to-business and business-to-consumer sales, including creating new retail channels and empowering existing distribution channels and salespeople to sell complex, configure-to-order products

Order Management—Enhancing the speed and accuracy of order processing and fulfillment and providing a superior purchasing experience for customers and business partners

Supply Chain Management—Facilitating the information flow throughout the supply chain, from raw materials suppliers to retailers, for better and more efficient inventory and production management, and faster response to customer demand

Customer Service—Providing customers and partners with easy access to accurate, in-depth information directly over the Internet or through a customer service organization

Down the road, your IT staff can expect some formidable barriers to the continuing success of your e-business operation. For instance, some e-businesses will start instituting policies that give preferred customers superior access to e-commerce sites. Implementing policies across company networks may not take off as quickly because of the complexity of setting up and managing these policies.

In addition, the market for mobile wireless devices that let workers access e-mail and connect to the Web will take off. As palmtops, cell phones, and hybrid platforms grow in sophistication, more companies are figuring out how to use them to increase efficiency.

11 11000001010010000   01110100010 00111101000101   11101010
   0   1 0101   0000   1 100 1   1 00   0111 1   1
   1 0   0   1   0 0   1   01   0   1
   0 1 111 0   00   001010 10   00   1 0001   010100 010

chapter five

Managing the Finances of Your E-Business Venture

Thomas Edison had it wrong. Success isn't 99 percent perspiration and one percent inspiration; it's actually equal parts inspiration, perspiration, and trepidation.

Why add trepidation to Edison's time-honored mix? Because when you're sailing in the uncharted waters of e-commerce, it's only natural to feel a bit anxious about what could leap out of the water and bite you next.

Take your business, for example. After all, businesses are all about costs and revenues. Regarding the former, there are at least two types of business costs: production costs and coordination costs. Being able to exchange information easily and cheaply can help you reduce production costs, though new technologies often have a much greater impact.

The big impact of e-commerce is on coordination costs. Making sure the right activities are completed in the right order at the right time is what coordination is all about. Improving coordination within firms can yield significant savings. Often the most dramatic reductions in coordination costs occur when we improve coordination between firms.

Another way of reducing costs is to transfer them. Get your customers to place their own orders, configure their own systems, and track their orders. Not only does this drastically reduce your costs, but it also improves the quality of service to the customer.

What about using e-commerce to increase revenues? By knowing more about the consumer and being able to provide her with richer information potentially increases the value of the product or service to the consumer. Even more significantly, linking the consumer into an extended network may add even greater value. Allowing consumers to share information about a product or service provides increased value at very little or even no cost to you. It may also allow you to identify ways of improving the product, thus increasing its value further. Increased value equals the potential of increased revenues.

E-commerce also helps you find out the value each individual places on your product or service. Consider airline seats. An airline can now dynamically adjust prices via its Web site. Those customers who are particularly risk averse may be prepared to pay a significantly higher price to be sure of getting exactly the seat they desire on the flight of their choice. Customers who are prepared to take the risk that they will not have their precise needs met may be prepared to wait with the expectation of paying a lower price. Airline seats can also be auctioned off to make sure that each flight has as few empty seats as possible.

Money Matters—Business First

E-business technology is powerful, sexy, and exciting. You don't think so? Try telling the person sitting next to you at your next dinner party that you've built an e-business platform and then try to get a word in edgewise for the next hour or so.

It's already a given that e-business will have some application in most organizations now or in the very near future. Many who have been there on the front lines of e-commerce say that when it comes to funding and allocating your e-business budget, it's best to adopt a strategy of "business first, technology second." That means identifying your macro goals first (How will I use e-business to maximize my business?), and then identifying your micro goals later (What tools should I use and how should I use them?).

Remember, one reason the stakes are high on your e-business venture is because your investment is so high. Web site development costs have grown into a $10 billion industry, while revenues generated online will reach $226 billion in 2000, according to ActivMedia Research.

In fact, ActivMedia's "Real Numbers Behind 'Net Profits'" study of electronic commerce found the average budgeted investment for e-commerce Web site development in 1999 across all Web sites

Banker Beware

Financial service companies are pumping bigger budgets into e-commerce without focus and strategic direction, warns Ernst & Young. The big five accountant and consultant says technology can help add customer value to retain and attract customers when similar-type products leave little room for differentiation. The survey predicts 14 percent of companies' technology spent will be on e-commerce by 2002.

(excluding ISPs) was about $37,000. Media and portal sites committed the most to e-commerce site development, averaging $78,000. Business-to-consumer sites selling exclusively online averaged $68,000, and typical retail and business-to-business sites committed in the mid-$20,000 range. In addition, Web sites anticipating profitability in two to five years had far higher development budgets than sites that were already profitable or expecting profitability soon ($59,000 to $26,000).

Having grown 25 percent from 1998 to 1999, Web budgets (including Internet, intranet, and extranet) rose by more than 35 percent from 1999 to 2000, with Web site budgets of medium-sized businesses increasing the fastest (more than 150 percent). Small and large business Web budgets are anticipated to grow about 30 percent, according to the Bear Stearns survey.

As usual, putting good talent to work will take up most of your e-business budget. A survey by the investment firm Bear Stearns that examined the spending patterns of Webmasters found that personnel costs continue to consume the largest portion of Web site budgets. The top three budget costs reported in the Bear Stearns survey are personnel, hosting fees, and servers.

In absolute dollar terms, all budget line items identified in the survey climb year over year. The barriers at the top of a Web specialist's list? Lack of funding, lack of qualified personnel, and lack of support from corporate management, Bear Stearns says.

Going on the Offensive

Another key element that budget analysts don't talk about much—but should—is the health of the global and domestic economies. Let's face it, things are rolling now. But if the U.S. financial picture fades as it has with regularity in the past, the first thing that companies do is to rein in expenditures. That could well mean a limit on capital spending, which will cause a lot of e-businesses to take it in the shorts.

This is the type of thing that drives CEOs crazy. They get paid to worry about the big picture, and there's always room in the frame for a dark economic cloud or two.

Since selling your e-business budget to the executive suite is a prime consideration for any corporate Web guru, it's a good idea to go aggressive rather than have your CEO cast aspersions on your ambitious budget and begin whacking away. Here are some tips to use for your boardroom chat with the chief:

- Emphasize how dominant B2B e-commerce is to the overall e-commerce picture. According to Forrester Research, the B2B market is projected to represent over 90 percent of the dollar value of Web transactions going forward, amounting to trillions of dollars. CEOs like it when you can use the words "revenue" and "trillions" in the same sentence.
- Bone up on all the e-business research you can (like this book, for example). The more you know about how e-business can advance your company's long-term interests, the more your CEO will want to hear about e-business.
- Break out a spreadsheet and figure out just how much your company can save in order entry via the Web, as opposed to human order-takers. Sure, your e-business is a profit center, but it's a budget saver, too.
- Emphasize the departmental benefits of an e-business. Spell out how customer service will be able to handle more customers easier online than over the phone. Stress the benefits of a sales staff that can spend more time developing real, long-term relationships with clients. Mention how marketing's printing budget is going to go way, way down as a result of your Web site. Offer a new supply chain vision that links directly to your Web site.

Above all, lay off the bits and bytes talk as much as possible. Use a business-focused sales pitch, emphasizing how everyone wins with your e-business operation and how it will create value, and you're more likely to get the budget you want.

The Human Element

In the case of an e-business site, not only is money an issue, but human resources as well. Most costs associated with building and maintaining an e-business site are labor related. In addition to programmers, a successful e-commerce team will need graphic designers, content creators, and business analysts. Many companies wind up having to do a lot of application development in-house, tweaking off-the-shelf systems and integrating them with back-end systems. Forrester Research says that a CIO can expect to spend about 40 percent of his or her company's e-commerce budget on content management, data cleansing, and legacy-system and supply chain integration.

That's a lot to put on the plate of just your CFO or your IT department. So why not spread the responsibility for your e-business budget around the company? That's what some companies are doing.

At Hallmark, the IT budget committee meets monthly and reviews any initiative that requires more than 10 days' implementation time or an investment greater than $10,000. At PG&E Corp., the holding company of utility Pacific Gas & Electric, an e-business committee meets regularly to focus on staying on top of a rapid-fire IT project schedule. PG&E's technology council includes CIOs and senior business managers from each of its subsidiaries. More often than not, these hybrid committees act as project gatekeepers that apply criteria based on business value as they prioritize e-business initiatives. Some of the questions they ask include: Does the project affect infrastructure? What is its return on investment? Does it affect the customer, or is it an internal project?

At one paper manufacturing company, the e-business budgeting committee was able to learn from a competitor's mistake. The competitor, putting into play a budget tactic that e-business professionals frown upon but that is used with regularity, "shorted" its e-business budget up front. Shorting means testing the e-business waters by building a template-type site with a few items for purchase. The rationale here is that you can save mega bucks by building a test site and sitting back and watching what interest the site attracts. The trouble was, the competitor found that a barebones site with few products won't attract anybody, and their efforts to save money did more harm than good.

Tracking E-Business ROI

Of all the key elements of your e-business spending plan, make sure to leave room for a solid return on investment (ROI) analysis plan.

A sense of urgency is forcing many companies to push ahead with projects without considering ROI. CEOs are less concerned about a dollar return than with enhancing the company's competitive edge, creating a marketing channel, or improving customer satisfaction. Less strategic initiatives are still subject to stringent ROI calculations, and some companies are beginning to develop new metrics to help them assess the value of all of their e-business projects.

According to a survey conducted recently by Primary Knowledge, at many e-businesses nobody really knows if their online commerce investments really pay off. Primary Knowledge queried more than 25 leading-edge Internet marketers for the survey, including barnesandnoble.com, NetGrocer, MotherNature.com, e-centives, and Webstakes.

The key finding: While many e-business executives deem ROI initiatives "mission-critical," these same businesses are still only in the planning stages for doing anything about it. Surprisingly, the survey found that the most common stumbling block is not lack of funding or management cooperation but simply insufficient expertise in developing advanced measurement tools.

"This dearth of tools and services is forcing e-marketers to rely on 'homegrown' solutions, which hinder them from converting the flood of available Internet data into meaningful business insights," says Primary Knowledge founder and CEO Peter Adams. He adds, "E-businesses today are moving at the speed of light and are selling in an increasingly price-competitive, low-loyalty marketplace. They are not coming close to the level of business success they could be enjoying if they maximized the yield of their online customer relationships." The survey respondents, comprising senior executives from a broad range of key e-business segments, were nearly unanimous in their opinion that what is needed is a one-stop solution that essentially stores, slices, dices, and breaks down all their marketing and customer-related data according to their respective needs.

But traditional ROI analysis tools are somewhat dull in the era of cutting-edge technologies like e-commerce, which prove hard to quantify. According to a recent survey by Gartner Group Inc., of Stamford, Connecticut, of 100 IT professionals, fewer than 5 percent perform any post-project analysis to determine benefits, direct or otherwise.

The gap is far more conspicuous with e-business ventures. Companies under fire to get e-commerce systems up and running are much more inclined to forgo rigorous cost justification, especially when traditional ROI methods seem stretched by the uncertainties of the dot.com culture.

That's because Web-based projects are as likely to open new markets or improve key metrics, such as customer affinity or supply chain efficiency, as they are to cut the cost of business as usual. In addition, post-project ROI analyses can take too long, a serious flaw in a world increasingly based on quick-turn e-commerce projects. Consequently, e-businesses are beginning to come up with new ways of judging IT investments. Appropriately enough, many of these techniques—such as real options—have their origins in the world of financial investing where the ability to adjust to rapidly changing markets is a must. Adopting these techniques will require IT managers to embrace risk. But, experts say, the payoff for IT could be big: the ability to communicate and collaborate more effectively with business units.

One trend in ROI analysis that is really gaining steam these days is a budgeting technique known as "real options." Here's how it works. Real options takes into account not just immediate benefits, such as cost savings, but also the future benefits of an investment. Using real options, a corporate budget analyst is able to show management how the investment in their e-business would not only improve short-term productivity but also make it easier for the company to deploy critical new applications, such as Web-based collaboration tools. Other companies treat ROI analysis as a stock market spreadsheet, with IT budgeting and overview a continuous cycle, reviewing capital appropriations with a senior executive committee every other month. Other top-level managers review those recommendations as often as every other week.

Of course, it's easier to measure the ROI of an e-business application that cuts back-office processing costs than one that improves customer satisfaction. As companies struggle to come up with new metrics that measure the ROI of e-business projects, they must also take into account another key aspect of nearly all e-business initiatives: they're cross-functional. The investments companies make in e-business stretch out across the entire organization, from marketing to customer service, from the back office to the sales department.

Tracking the Top E-Business/ROI Factors

What do corporate budget analysts look for when they crack open their e-business ledgers? According to a study by *Information Week*, they check out customer service first, then tend to budget issues. Here's the top five factors they look for:

1. Improving customer or client satisfaction (cited by 87 percent of IT and business executives)
2. Lowering the cost of promoting products and services (70 percent)
3. Increasing direct access to customers (68 percent)
4. Lowering operational costs (85 percent)
5. Adding new customers (72 percent)

One national parcel delivery company had some success with its e-business/ROI effort by emphasizing that cross-functionality in its ongoing budget analysis. Says the company chief financial officer, "E-commerce cuts across the entire organization, and if we just continue to focus on the person who runs the shipping dock, that's not going to cut it. We have to look at accounts receivable, order entry, customer service—the whole value proposition. We need new metrics because no company makes a huge investment without monitoring the return at some point."

That's a tactic that many companies looking to quantify their e-businesses will have to take if they want to get a new snapshot of their Web enterprises.

Recovering from E-Failures

It's not a "budget" issue as much as it's an IT issue, but the risks involved in not making your e-business disasterproof can cost you plenty of money in the long run. Take eBay.com. In the summer of 1999, this online auction site suffered an outage disaster that shut the company down for 22 hours, a lifetime in the e-business game. Customers were apoplectic, and investors sent the company's stock down more than 25 percent in the two business days after the problems began, slashing nearly $6 billion off its market value.

It's the curse of e-commerce. Even the best-prepared sites are vulnerable to outages; hardware and software change constantly and must be updated, leading to a potential witches' brew of conflicting systems. And the most successful sites are even more vulnerable to trouble, because more traffic means more stress on the system.

Even worse, businesses may face lawsuits or regulatory scrutiny if customers sustain financial losses as a result of system failure. This happened in the securities market after the stock market crash of October 1997. Online brokerages lost millions of dollars in lawsuit settlements, commission refunds, and trade executions. Merrill Lynch, for example, paid close to $10 million to investors. Customer complaints also prompted the Securities and Exchange Commission and the National Association of Securities Dealers to investigate online brokerage firms. Ultimately, brokerage firms took it upon themselves to correct deficiencies in their systems.

Risk and concern of failure are not limited to online brokerage firms. Dell Computer, for example, has successfully embraced the Web as an extension of its sales channel. During the third quarter of 1998, Dell's Web site exceeded $10 million in daily sales. One hour of system downtime during that period could have cost Dell $416,000 in revenue.

So remember, inaccessible support forums, malfunctioning search capabilities, or limited hours of operation negate the financial benefits of an e-business platform. Customers who can't access Web-based support forums may well revert to contacting a company through traditional support channels such as toll-free telephone support lines.

Here are some steps, from the *Wall Street Journal Interactive*, to take that will allow your e-business to stay up and running—and out of harm's way.

- Take the long-term view—Try to maintain a cushion of 40 to 50 percent more data capacity than you need; tomorrow can come early in the Web game.
- Be negative—Crashes are more likely to hit those who haven't prepared for them. Have backup systems in place before disaster hits and investors, analysts, and reporters descend.
- Be a nurturer—Having proper backups and redundant systems allows for what Microsoft's Tim Sinclair calls "well-baby care"— preventive maintenance such as taking servers offline to keep your site crash-resistant.

- Get good help—A well-run Web site needs people available round-the-clock, in constant communication, whose goal is to make sure things keep running smoothly.
- Losers weepers—Downtime is bad, but losing data is worse; it undermines the sometimes still-shaky trust people have in electronic commerce.
- Be up front—Let users know what's happening—and in plain English, not tech-speak. Sure, people will be mad if your site is down. But they'll be madder if they don't know what's going on.
- Keep the memory of an elephant—Now that you're back up, what went wrong? Was it an unavoidable Web gremlin, or was there something you could have done to prevent the outage?

Web Spending: An Industry Breakdown

Share of IT Budget for Implementing E-Business per Industry	
Construction & Engineering	11%
Banking & Financial Services	9%
Media & Entertainment	9%
Information Technology	8%
Retail & Distribution	8%
Electronics	7%
Food & Beverage Processing	7%
Health Care	7%
Manufacturing	7%
Metals & Natural Resources	7%
Pharmaceuticals & Medical Equip.	7%
Professional Services	7%
Chemicals	6%
Telecommunications	6%
Transportation	6%
Consumer Goods	5%
Insurance	5%
Utilities	5%
Energy	4%
Hospitality & Travel	4%
Overall Average	7%

Web Support

Portion of Companies Providing Customer Service on the Web per Industry

Information Technology	100%
Pharmaceuticals & Medical Equip.	92%
Insurance	88%
Transportation	84%
Electronics	83%
Telecommunications	83%
Media & Entertainment	79%
Retail & Distribution	78%
Utilities	76%
Metals & Natural Resources	75%
Banking & Financial Services	74%
Manufacturing	74%
Energy	71%
Health Care	70%
Chemicals	69%
Consumer Goods	63%
Professional Services	58%
Hospitality & Travel	56%
Construction & Engineering	50%
Food & Beverage Processing	47%
Overall Average	74%

E-Business Sales

Share of Total Sales from E-Business per Industry

Pharmaceuticals & Medical Equip.	54%
Food & Beverage Processing	33%
Electronics	27%
Metals & Natural Resources	27%
Banking & Financial Services	26%
Health Care	25%
Manufacturing	25%
Consumer Goods	24%
Telecommunications	22%
Information Technology	21%
Chemicals	20%
Energy	19%
Retail & Distribution	19%
Transportation	19%
Hospitality & Travel	16%
Media & Entertainment	13%
Professional Services	13%
Construction & Engineering	8%
Utilities	6%
Insurance	5%
Overall Average	21%

Web Service Sales

Portion of Companies Selling Services on the Web to the Following Industries

Telecommunications	92%
Information Technology	80%
Transportation	80%
Banking & Financial Services	76%
Utilities	55%
Electronics	50%
Health Care	50%
Media & Entertainment	50%
Professional Services	50%
Chemicals	46%
Retail & Distribution	45%
Construction & Engineering	42%
Energy	36%
Pharmaceuticals & Medical Equip.	33%
Consumer Goods	32%
Food & Beverage Processing	26%
Hospitality & Travel	25%
Insurance	25%
Manufacturing	25%
Metals & Natural Resources	15%
Overall Average	47%

Customer Links

Customers Included in Electronic Supply Chain per Industry

Pharmaceuticals & Medical Equip.	41%
Information Technology	34%
Banking & Financial Services	33%
Metals & Natural Resources	33%
Electronics	32%
Food & Beverage Processing	30%
Consumer Goods	29%
Manufacturing	28%
Retail & Distribution	25%
Telecommunications	23%
Transportation	23%
Health Care	22%
Energy	20%
Chemicals	19%
Media & Entertainment	19%
Hospitality & Travel	16%
Insurance	15%
Professional Services	14%
Construction & Engineering	10%
Utilities	7%
Overall Average	24%

Supplier Links

Suppliers Included in Electronic Supply Chain per Industry

Industry	Percentage
Retail & Distribution	46%
Hospitality & Travel	45%
Health Care	38%
Manufacturing	35%
Information Technology	33%
Telecommunications	32%
Utilities	30%
Metals & Natural Resources	28%
Food & Beverage Processing	24%
Chemicals	23%
Consumer Goods	22%
Electronics	22%
Energy	22%
Transportation	22%
Banking & Financial Services	21%
Media & Entertainment	21%
Pharmaceuticals & Medical Equip.	21%
Insurance	18%
Professional Services	16%
Construction & Engineering	10%
Overall Average	29%

Source: *Information Week*

chapter six

The Outsourcing Dilemma

F or some companies, especially those with deeper pockets,
building an e-business Web site is a simple proposition—just
hire someone else to do it. If you buy into the notion that time
is as big a commodity as money and your time is better spent
building your company products while a Web specialist takes care of
the design, implementation, and maintenance of your site, that's
fine. But if you go that route, you should know what you're getting
yourself into. If you don't go the outsourcing route—and decide to
build your own e-business site—there are issues to consider in that
scenario as well.

Either way, it's a big decision. E-business initiatives require such
a broad range of services—from design to development to integration,
marketing, and hosting—that it's not always easy to find someone
who can handle the whole ball of wax. One e-business IT executive
recalls having to assemble and coordinate seven professional services
companies—from Internet-only designers and system integrators to
marketers and ad agencies—to get his site rolled out.

Keeping each of those e-business services providers focused on its
piece of the project and in sync with other providers—and reining
them in when they tried to expand the scope of their efforts—turned
into a full-time job for the IT manager. Key employees had to meet with
the e-business services providers every few days to assess progress,
monitor schedules, and assign responsibilities. But in the end, the
manager saved tens of thousands of dollars by not using his own staff
and by leasing instead of buying the vendor's e-business package.

Like the IT manager, many companies are discovering that finding the right e-business services provider and getting the most out of them presents unique challenges and requires new skills. Finding one with the right experience and expertise to handle all aspects of an e-business launch can be tough.

But it's not impossible, and the savings can be significant. So let's take a look at both sides of the e-business outsourcing issue.

The Outsourcing Picture

There's little question that outsourcing is a big trend in the e-business world. In a recent survey of 50 U.S. companies, Forrester Research Inc. recently found that the median budget for e-business outsourcing is $750,000 today and will double to $1.5 million by 2001. About half of IT managers expect to spend more than $1 million on outside services suppliers by then, with 28 percent planning to invest more than $5 million.

The goal for IT managers looking to outsource their e-business operations, either partially or totally, is to keep it simple. A good first step is to do your homework and conduct some solid due diligence on a handful of e-business services providers. Get to know their skills and capabilities, talk to their customers, and take a look at the site work they've done. When you hit the actual selection process, begin with a request for proposal (RFP) to the vendors you like and then ask for an onsite presentation.

As you review your vendor proposals, keep everyone at your company informed and on board. The last thing you want when hiring a Web outsourcer is to have individual departments bickering over who owns the outsourcing vendor this week. That may lead to an e-business

A Seller's Market?

The Internet is quickly becoming a crucial factor in many small companies' growth strategies. According to an e-merchant study released earlier this year by Internet market research firm Keenan Vision, the number of e-merchants will number 400,000 in 2003.

That's a lot of dot.coms, and the e-business vendor industry has noticed. With so many companies looking for outsourcing help, the price of a good e-business vendor package keeps going up.

Fast Fact: A Burgeoning Market

Forrester Research predicts that the market for Web server hosting services will grow to more than $10.5 billion, and complex Internet hosting will grow to $8 billion by 2002.

site that isn't integrated, causing gaps in the system that can hurt you when you're up and running. To alleviate that scenario, choose a vendor that works well with its team and yours, so everyone works well together throughout the enterprise.

It's also imperative that you understand your audience. The technical and architectural decisions you make regarding a business-to-business site should differ considerably from the choices you'd make if you were planning a business-to-consumer site. A business-to-business site can largely overlook the need to support credit card payments because transactions flow through the company's traditional billing systems. A retailer, on the other hand, would make credit card processing a prime consideration.

If you're starting from scratch, most e-business server vendors make going online a snap. Some offer a variety of templates for basic e-commerce functions. For example, IBM's Net.Commerce Start software comes with three prototype storefronts, bundled database services, various payment collection services, and links to legacy accounting systems.

But if you're creating an e-commerce architecture that taps into existing business systems, you'll have to hire outside developers or, at the least, be prepared to spend a lot of quality time with your e-commerce server vendor.

The Business Case for Outsourcing

The business case for outsourcing standard e-business services is a convincing one. At the top of most IT managers' lists is the elimination of the "worry" factor. While nobody guarantees a good night's sleep in the software applications world, there's a lot an e-business vendor can do to ensure you'll sleep like a baby when you hit the pillow each night. By outsourcing your e-business enterprise, for example, you don't have to worry if your site receives more visitors than anticipated or if some of the equipment fails. In addition, an e-vendor will take

Farm It Out

According to Creative Networks, Inc., these services are cited as the ones companies are most likely to outsource in the near future:

- Web hosting
- E-commerce
- Intranet administration
- Intranet application development

care of the all-important back-end of your Web system, an area where most companies don't have a lot of experience. Your provider will handle a laundry list of items that are critical to your e-business's success, like capturing orders, processing electronic coupons, calculating taxes, and getting purchasing authorization. On top of that, they will make sure you are up 24 hours a day, 365 days a year.

Some companies will take things a step or two further, with features like fraud screens, charging for tariffs on international orders, and placing your e-mail address or your 800-number on every transaction so your customers can reach you with questions.

Key Factors in Outsourcing

- Cost, control, and expertise/staffing are still the primary factors that influence whether companies manage service internally or outsource.
- Cost savings and avoidance are the primary decision factors that influence companies to outsource. A third factor is emerging that will far outweigh these benefits: reducing cycle times.
- The most common reason companies keep services in-house is control. In addition, they cite cost. Security and integration among various applications and services are also important.

When Outsourcing Is a Good Idea

Do any of the business issues listed here apply to your organization? If so, it may be a good idea to consider outsourcing your e-business enterprise.

- Can't afford to buy
- Fast growth

- Small to medium-size company with annual revenues of less than $1 billion
- Don't need extensive software customization
- High IS turnover
- Skills shortage

Table 6-1
Average First-Year Costs Including Development and Operations
(for a company of 500 employees)

	Web Services	Communication	E-Commerce
Service	$353,508	$297,131	$501,225
Internally Provided	$278,815	$90,483	$84,811
Savings	$74,693	$206,648	$416,414

- The first-year savings are significant in all three areas examined. The first-year savings for a company of 500 people are shown in Table 6-1.

The biggest savings are from reduced development costs (the initial costs associated with creating the application such as application development, design, and planning). Operational costs were significantly lower for communications but slightly higher for Web, and significantly higher for e-commerce.

In many cases, hiring an e-vendor is case of addition by subtraction—it keeps you from making a big budgeting or systems integration mistake. Most companies don't know how much they spend on internal labor costs to upgrade and maintain particular applications, especially newer, more complicated applications like those found in Web circles. CIOs often grossly underestimate internal costs—sometimes by as much as 50 percent—because costs are spread in many different areas. For example, CIOs may neglect to include a portion of data center costs when figuring the price tag for implementing and maintaining applications.

But even as cost savings and avoidance are the primary decision factors for whether companies outsource, a third factor is emerging that will far outweigh these benefits: reducing cycle times. Some

Table 6-2
How Services Are Managed

	% E-Business Sites Managed Internally	% Services Outsourced	Both
Web Services	81%	6%	13%
Communication	78%	14%	8%
E-Commerce	53%	21%	26%

Source: Creative Networks

companies view this as a strong motivator to outsource. It is this area that will provide the greatest benefit over time because it results in more rapid ROI, faster time to market, and greater value to the company. Reducing development and deployment time has several effects on cost, ROI, and value, specifically:

- Reducing time to benefit results in realizing more rapid ROI.
- Freeing up development and deployment resources allows those resources to be applied to other systems and increases opportunities.
- Accelerating deployment reduces the time when the system is operating at less than steady state, which reduces the "cost of chaos" associated with operating redundant systems, increased downtime, lower user productivity, and higher support costs.

Not surprisingly, cost was sighted most often as the compelling impetus to outsource.

Improved system responsiveness and security are not seen as reasons to outsource, even though they are important reasons that companies manage services in-house.

Even with all these advantages, there's still a lot of handholding needed for traditionally minded, Web-shy companies. "There's a big fear of what going online really means to companies," says Anish Dhanda, president of NetNumina Solutions Inc. (www.netnumina.com), a Web application development firm. "One home appraisal company that we helped get online with an e-commerce package wasn't sure if they wanted an e-commerce or e-business site. They didn't understand the distinction. They also weren't sure whether or not they should leverage their own existing systems or not. There's no shortage of anxiety out there."

To help assuage customers' Web fears, NetNumina includes a blueprint and a 10-day discovery phase when it starts out on an outsourcing project. "That's the relationship part," Dhanda says. "Both parties should know where they're going and how they're going to get there—together." Dhanda says that the most legitimate concern on the part of clients is the possibility of getting stuck with a Web vendor they don't like. "That's why we take things so slowly at first—being tied to a vendor they don't care for is a huge concern to companies with limited budgets." Even with the 10-day period, Dhanda says that all of his company's clients are up and running at full capacity within 60 to 90 days.

What Can an E-Vendor Do for Your Small Business?

Comprehensive and complicated software—and thereby potentially the most expensive—presents the best argument for renting over the Web. That's why e-businesses are prime outsourcing candidates.

Farming out your e-business site can be a quick way to acquire top-of-the-line enterprise applications with a modest upfront cost. That's true especially for small and medium-size businesses that often don't have the resources to buy, implement, and maintain their own software.

According to Carolyn Brackett, vice president of First Data Merchant Services Corporation, building an electronic storefront may seem particularly daunting to small businesses and retailers as the maze of e-commerce products and services available makes it easy for a merchant to get lost. Many small companies find building and hosting a Web site on their own to be cost-prohibitive, and generating traffic to their sites can also prove to be a difficult undertaking.

But, Brackett says, an outsourcer can help your small business in unique—and very beneficial—ways. Here are Brackett's five areas where a small business can benefit from an outsourcing relationship:

1. Domain Name Registration. Getting your Web site name isn't as easy as one might think. First you choose it and hope nobody else has first. Then, you have to register it with InterNIC or one of the newer agencies that register and maintain a database of domain names. Fortunately, your Internet service provider or your e-commerce service vendor(s) will often perform this task for you.

2. Web Store Design. With many Web building services and software products available to assist businesses in designing a Web site, there's plenty of help out there. Your e-business vendor will help you decide what products/services you want to sell, what you want the look and feel of your logo and your site to be, what type of navigation tools you want to use, what forms of payment you

wish to use to transact business, and how you are going to calculate tax and shipping charges.

Once you've made these decisions, your e-business vendor will help develop your product catalog. You'll need to provide necessary information on each product (i.e., description, color, size, and price). This catalog is expandable, so that you may add to it as your business and product offering grows.

3. Server Hosting. Another major decision that businesses joining the electronic marketplace must face is whether to buy a server and host their Web site in-house or to outsource the entire operation to a service provider. For many smaller businesses, outsourcing is the most viable and cost-effective option. Establishing your own operation is complicated and can take several months to set up, whereas using a hosting service can take less than an hour to set up. It will also speed the time it takes customers to download pages on your Web site, improving the customers' experience on your site.

4. Payment Solutions. In order to become truly e-commerce enabled, you must have the following: payment software, a merchant account, payment processing services, and a gateway to connect all these elements of the payment process. You also will need cash register software to help easily calculate sales tax as well as shipping charges, and you may want to include a shopping cart function as well.

In order to start transacting business and accepting payments, you must first open an account with a merchant bank. Again, your e-business vendor can help you with this task.

5. Traffic Coverage. No matter how great your Web site is, no one will come to it if they don't know you are there. This is where driving traffic and transactions become an essential element of your e-commerce plan.

The first step in building traffic is registering your site with search engines. Again, there are vendors that will do this for you. Your e-business vendor will also help you choose where and how you place your site. Many Web specialists say a virtual shopping mall, like a Web portal, is the way to go. And they can help you get there.

In addition, one old rule that still holds true in the virtual economy is "location, location, location." Much like putting

Big Benefits?

E-businesses can realize these big benefits from outsourcing. Unlike death, taxes, and the Yankees in the World Series, there are no certainties in life. That goes for e-businesses, too. But if you outsource your e-business enterprise, the chances of your organization reaping the following benefits should rise:

Cost savings. Because you don't have to buy and maintain hardware and software and operate the system 21 shifts a week, they'll have more functionality and better reliability for 90 percent less cost.

Rapid time-to-market. Because there is nothing to install or learn, you can turn a marketing site into a selling site in literally less than an hour.

Reduced risk. You won't have to store customer information on their site, and because you rely on experts who serve hundreds of merchants, you won't have to worry about your technology choice becoming obsolete, your site not working properly, and your developer getting a better offer or your success exceeding the scale of their installation.

Source: Internet Commerce Services Corporation.

your store in a real shopping mall, having your storefront in a business-to-business shopping portal or industry-related site not only gives higher visibility but helps draw in "window-shoppers."

The Business Case to Keep Things In-House

Choosing whether to outsource is like a tale of two businesses. Are you starting from scratch or are you adding your e-business site to existing legacy systems?

The difference is significant. Many e-business specialists say that starting from scratch is actually an advantage, price-wise. You simply choose a Web package, plug it in, and off you go. But if you're adding to existing systems that have been in place for years, maybe you don't want an outside company fooling around with your IT systems. In that case, keeping your e-business in-house, with your trusted IT team in charge, may be a better option.

Another issue that's causing companies to shy away from farming their e-business operations out is the availability of good help. Many managers evaluating outside providers of e-business services are finding that the selection process is often a two-way street. Services providers are in a position to pick and choose the companies for whom they'll work.

Outsourcing Motivators

When asked what would motivate
respondents to outsource specific
services, the services with the highest
number of respondents in the Creative
Networks survey said what they would
not outsource at all are:

- calendaring and scheduling
- voice mail
- wireless messaging
- directory
- content development

That's because, as we've noted many times so far in this book,
e-business services is a booming market, with analysts and vendors
saying that demand far outstrips supply. That gulf could worsen as
more companies come out of budget freezes from Y2K in 2000 and
increase their spending on e-business. Forrester Research Inc. predicts that the U.S. market for e-business services will grow from $10.6
billion in 2000 to $64.8 billion in 2003. All this means that top-notch
e-business consultants often have the luxury of being picky about the
clients they choose.

Some have backlogs of eight to nine months before they can start
work for a new client. As a result, some have decided that they will
only take new business from clients that plan to spend at least $1 mil-
lion per year. Global 2500 companies and dot.com startups with venture capital funding often make the cut, but midsize companies with
$250 million or less in revenue and 1,000 or fewer employees can be
left behind.

That said, the most common reason companies keep services in-
house is an old-fashioned one—control. Few IT managers want to give
up control of their shops, particularly in an unknown area like e-business.
Other reasons cited in the Creative Networks study for not outsourcing an e-business are lack of expertise of the outsourcers, security, and worries over integration among various applications and
services.

Cost Issues

What can you expect to pay for your e-business outsourcing help? It
varies, with some of the larger vendors, like IBM and HP, charging up
to $1 million for large-scale packages (they offer much cheaper versions
for smaller companies), and some other companies offering to build

your site for as little as $3,000. Of course, in many cases, that's just for design. One of the little known secrets of the e-business vendor game is that fees can pile up like leaves in your yard in late autumn.

Beyond design, there are fees for almost everything imaginable: server setup, number of servers, type of OS, Web server and commerce platform, custom programming, application setup, application licensing, back-end integration, domain name, digital certificate support, chat service support, monthly maintenance, secure server and encryption fees, varying disk allocation allowances with corresponding fees, for megabytes of data transferred, for statistics reporting, for online cost calculation setup, tax calculation, shipping calculation, fulfillment services, fax orders, transactions (CyberCash, merchant bank, and CSP), mailing list management, Real Audio and Video, e-mail, banner advertising, and for specific numbers of catalog entries. As the old saying goes, a fee here and a fee there, and pretty soon you're talking about real money.

The best advice in dealing with fees is to either opt for a uniform pricing package or have your lawyer write a contract stating in advance what fees for the Web features listed here will cost you. That way there won't be any surprises.

But that's the bad news. The good news is that most companies do save money from their outsourcing ventures. According to the Creative Networks study, the first-year savings realized by companies who engaged an outsourcing development vendor (including planning, design, initial deployment, application development, pilot, etc.) plus administration and management (operations) are significant.

In the study of 500 e-businesses that outsourced, the biggest savings are from reduced development costs. Operational costs were sig-

Cost Reducers

Over time the greatest impact outsourcing has on reducing costs is:	The greatest impact outsourcing has on realizing rapid ROI and increasing value is:
• Accelerating time to steady state	
• Minimizing downtime	• Stable infrastructure
• Increasing service levels	• Reducing cycle times and time to benefit
	• Freeing up internal resources that can be applied to business-critical and high-value applications

nificantly lower for communications (as shown in detail in the next section), but slightly higher for Web and significantly higher for e-commerce.

Web vendors are quick to defend their pricing platforms, emphasizing that the return on investment far outweighs costs. "We've seen $12,000 investments turn into $300,000 returns," says David Dunn, president of VC3, Inc., an Internet solutions integrator. "Costs are always going to be a big deal, but not only are you making a smart financial move you're also ridding yourself of some real headaches in managing these tasks as well."

The cost for developing Web services, communications, and e-commerce far outweigh the costs for outsourcing development in these areas, particularly for e-commerce services (including storefront, transaction systems, bill payment, customer interaction processes, etc.). Development costs include design, planning, application development, and initial implementation costs.

Communications have the best cost savings for annual operations (administration and management). Even with a marginal loss for outsourcing the operations of Web services, the savings in development costs plus the ROI benefits of outsourcing Web services (described earlier) make outsourcing Web services a good proposition. Since the operating costs are high when outsourced, the decision is more complex on the e-commerce side. In this case, companies look closely at the opportunity costs, the benefits beyond cost savings, amortizing hardware and software costs over time (3 to 5 years, generally), and the additional staffing required to operate the environment.

So What Do You Do?

The business case for outsourcing standard e-business services is a tempting one: Companies that outsource are, by and large, realizing cost savings and more rapid ROI on their investments. However, the market is emerging slowly, and it is critical that you pick and choose those services that will provide the best return for your business and to manage the outsourcers to get the best results.

Cost savings and avoidance can be achieved through outsourcing and demonstrated with a solid business case. But, in some cases, it's just as compelling not to outsource standard services. This is best expressed in the value achieved by shorter cycle times, shorter time to benefit, and redeployment of resources to high-value business applications.

If you want to go the outsourcing route, the best way to plan which services your company should consider is to:

1. Compare the service levels outsourcers can deliver with those actually delivered internally. Quantify the cost of downtime and the value of uptime to determine your ROI.

2. Focus first on standard infrastructure services and specific business applications that are highly standardized, such as messaging, Web hosting, and e-commerce.

3. Allocate appropriate staff to manage the outsourcer and to supplement parts of the service that make sense. For example, many companies outsource remote e-mail while managing the rest of the users internally.

Other, less tangible considerations that companies quantify when making the decision of whether to outsource include:

- The reduction in risk brought about by shifting the burden of implementing new technology to the outsourcer
- Reduction in upgrade and update costs
- The ability to quickly take advantage of new technology without the high transition or "rip and replace" costs

Who You Gonna Call?

Companies come and companies go, but the following list includes some of the top e-business outsourcing vendors in the world.

Corio Inc. (*www.corio.com/*)
Forrester Research Inc. (*www.forrester.com/*)
Great Plains Software Inc. (*www.greatplains.com/*)
IBM Global Services (*www.ibm.com/services/*)
J.D. Edwards & Co. (*www.jdedwards.com/*)
Oracle Corp. (*www.oracle.com/*)

PeopleSoft Inc. (*www.peoplesoft.com/*)
Sunburst Hospitality Corp. (*www.sunbursthospitality.com/*)
USinternetworking Inc. (*www.usinternetworking.com/*)
DocuCorp (*www.docucorp.com/*)
NoWonder Online tech support services (*www.nowonder.com/*)
NuoMedia (*www.nuomedia.com/*)
Telecomputing (*www.telecomputing.net*)
Centerbeam (*www.centerbeam.com/*)
MiconPC (*www.micronpc.com/subscription.html*)

Finally, some services are more strategic than others, which influences the outsource decision. Utility services such as network services and even e-mail and Web hosting today are more easily outsourced. Other applications—such as some e-commerce applications—will be a utility in some companies but a competitive advantage in others.

For example, one company may consider rapid customer response a competitive advantage and invest millions of dollars in developing and operating highly integrated systems. Another may consider customer response an administrative system that can be very cost-effectively outsourced.

In the end, the business case needs to analyze costs, risks, ROI, and the associated benefits, which are highly specific and take into consideration all the areas mentioned here. The bottom line is that there is a strong, highly skilled emerging channel for outsourcing that will allow companies to effectively share the risk of technology innovation, reduce operational costs, and focus their investments on those systems that bring competitive advantage and the highest value to the company.

chapter seven

Any Portal in a Storm?

o portal or not to portal? That's the question a lot of online
e-business planners are asking themselves these days.

The term "portal" lends itself to a sci-fi, *X-Files*–type definition
where a portal might be a two-way interdimensional door opening
into several realities. In the online business world, a portal may open
doors all right, but you aren't going to greet Elvis or ET on the other
side. Instead, you hope to find customers with their checkbooks open
waiting to buy your product.

Where Customers Meet

Businesses are trying to create enterprise Internet portals, or at least
align themselves with a brand-name portal that can lead them to more
customers. Portals are the place where businesses can connect to their
customers, their investors, and their suppliers, and it is often the first
page you see when you connect to the Net. Portals, in short, are the
most fought-over territories in the Net gold rush.

Why? Because of those two paramount business commodities—
access and information. Portals can give employees, business partners, and customers a central access point to critical data, including
Web sites, internal reports, news feeds, even enterprise applications
such as enterprise resource planning and customer relationship management software.

Portals generally rely on a host of underlying technologies,
including databases, transactional systems, online analytical processing

software, query and reporting tools, data mining, search engines, Web browsers, and push/publish delivery mechanisms. Indeed, because portals tie in to so many technologies, implementing one can be tricky. A portal that provides access to legacy reports highlighting a company's financial health, links to competitors' Web sites, weekly reports from a business intelligence system, and customized news feeds requires weaving together numerous systems.

Internet portals were once pitched as places for nonexperts to find things on the Internet. They're still that, as well as search engines and directories. But they're quickly evolving into full-service hubs of electronic commerce, mail, online communities, and customized news. The four biggest Internet portals—Yahoo, Excite, Lycos, and Infoseek—compete for "eyeballs" with cable TV, magazines, and newspapers; they attracted more than 200 million page views per day in the second half of last year, according to the U.S. Securities and Exchange Commission. They've even started calling themselves "networks."

Portal Advancements

On the e-business side, we're beginning to see better integrated electronic commerce, more multimedia (especially audio) clips, and the ability to personalize portals to access specific information. We're also witnessing a trend where general interest portals will start to be eclipsed by niche portals for areas like finance, manufacturing, and medicine—all big venues for business-to-business e-commerce. Meanwhile, customized intranet portals are also beginning to replace brand-name portals in corporations. Recently, it has become popular for large and medium-size companies to build portals to their intranets, which have been spinning out of control for years.

Essentially the benefit of the portal approach is that it can offer multiple windows to different data sources in a single interface. That could be an internal application or database data or external Internet data. The idea being that someone could be working on an order entry application, for example, in one window and have details of stock availability in another window. Multiple tasks can therefore be carried out without the user having to continually change applications. The real value with e-business portals is they create tighter, more streamlined value chains so e-businesses can personalize what their customer sees and what their partners see, creating a market space through the portal.

Hot B2B Portals

B2B portal sites are popping up in every industry. Here are some of the more successful ones:

Institutional markets: Epylon.com
Electronic components industry: Questlink.com

Natural gas and energy: Altrade.com
Circuit boards: Fastparts.com
Marine products: marex.com
Farm products: Farms.com
Maintenance, repair, and operating products: findmro.com

That's an important ingredient for cyber success for e-businesses, as the market for e-business Web portals is huge. According to Merrill Lynch, sales of online portal products will reach $15 billion by 2002. And in a recent Delphi survey of 300 IT and business managers from Fortune 500 companies, more than half were introducing a corporate portal. Another quarter will follow suit by the end of 2001.

"[Enterprise portal] technology is being applied very rapidly into the whole B2B market," said Steve Dille, vice president of marketing at Viador, a developer of e-business portal solutions. "Companies are using it as a way to get their B2B business models up and running faster and at less cost than they could by building it themselves."

Why Portals for E-Business?

Many e-businesses, frustrated over customer service glitches and looking to consolidate their buying audience, are taking a harder look at Internet portals. Portals also have value throughout the e-business enterprise, where corporate intranets merge with e-business sites to give buyers, sellers, suppliers, and staffers a place to meet to hash out problems, drum up more business, and create more transaction opportunities.

Consequently, B2B e-commerce portals and Net market makers are now investing millions of dollars in exciting new "e-frastructure" software applications to connect multiple buyers and sellers across emerging or fragmented markets on the internet. These transactional applications include auction solutions, e-procurement and marketplace technologies, and exchange systems for horizontal and vertical e-markets.

But the common thread to e-business portals is the ability to manage information about customers up and down the customer care cycle. A typical application of a customer information portal might be a salesperson who, on the eve of closing a deal, finds his customer complaining about a slow service call on another product. With access to his company's e-business portal, the salesperson can directly access data about the poor experience rather than having to place a phone call or wait for a paper report.

Portals specifically target the problem of the "divided enterprise," where enterprise applications are in place but data from the applications isn't effectively shared among departments

Managing Your E-Business Portal

Companies that use portals as anchors for their e-business efforts emphasize getting the right people together. That means employees, customers, executives, suppliers, distributors, partners, and investors. Your portal strategy's objective should be to establish and enhance relationships with these stakeholders in a way that fosters a sense of community. Your customers must become more intimate, suppliers must become part of an integrated marketplace, employees must benefit through operational efficiencies, and executives must achieve decision-making improvements.

Providing content, applications, and processes to your stakeholders through the enterprise portal creates a valued experience that becomes habit forming. Business customers like familiarity and comfort—if you can win them over with good customer service through a portal-based strategy, they'll be more likely to stick with you. And since your portal can provide the brass ring of the Internet shopping experience—one-stop shopping—then you may have a leg up on your competition.

Tools for Trade—What Business Benefits Can You Get from a Web Portal?

1. Productivity and collaborative applications—e-mail, knowledge management, joint product design, discussion forums, spreadsheets, document and text management, distance learning applications, browsers, and file-system managers.

2. Transactional applications—ERP, CRM, supply chain, and legacy applications.

3. Commerce applications—sales transactions, order fulfillment, and customer service.

4. Analytical applications—access to internal and external transactional and operational data that enables decision support.

Implementing an e-portal strategy involves business initiatives such as using direct mail and cobranding to attract traffic, and creating a compelling experience for visitors. Technical initiatives of security and scalability must also be implemented to avoid the downtime problems major brokerage sites and the eBay auction house have experienced. The strategy should also use customer feedback and access problems to effect continuous improvements.

The benefits of a successful e-portal strategy are compelling in terms of product differentiation, cost savings, time-to-market benefits, strategic advantage, and shareholder returns. Organizations that have used e-business portal strategies have also benefited from significant "early mover" advantages.

What companies should avoid doing is stuffing their portal site with noncritical content, thus distracting from your sales efforts. When it comes down to brass tacks, customers really don't need raw data, an abundance of sales pitches, boring cyber-brochures, and other ancillary materials. Just show them how they can easily browse your product and service categories and make purchases.

What's the necessary nontransaction stuff that stays on your portal site? Usually anything with information that will lead a customer to buy from you and stay there as a repeat customer. Besides giving customers and resellers 24-hour access to product and release information, some portals include things like news flashes, frequently asked questions, technical bulletins and tips, and marketing literature. Users should also be able to provide feedback to your technical staff via the portal. By providing customers with a self-service portal where they can find answers to common questions, customer service reps are freed to focus on customers' high-level technical issues.

Corporate Portals

On the intranet side, your portal can be an easily accessed gathering place for your employees as well. For example, a product line manager could be checking manufacturing data, supply chain data, and sales data from multiple internal applications in a single interface, while also having links to information on competitors available via the Internet. Internal data from human resources could also be held in the same screen, giving them a quick link to the right people within their own organization.

Enterprise information portals (EIPs) are gaining acceptance as a way to open up an enterprise's internal and external knowledge stores. An EIP, a browser-based system, provides ubiquitous access to vital business information contained in reports, Web sites, databases, business intelligence tools, and documents in the same manner that Internet content portals such as Yahoo! provide a gateway to the wealth of content on the Web. An EIP lets users access and filter personalized topical information from a single window to make better business decisions.

For example, easy access to current sales performance results, combined with marketing program plans, could be used to reallocate resources into the most productive areas to optimize revenue. Access to travel expense information could be used to negotiate better rates in areas with high travel. Without a cost-effective, simple delivery mechanism, this information is often unavailable to the employees who can really use it to effect change.

Corporate portals can be tailored to meet the needs of a wide range of workers, from secretaries to chief executives. Salespeople, for instance, can personalize their portals to include the latest news and developments about their customers and competitors. A CEO could choose to see up-to-the minute business data, such as that week's sales-per-region figures. This data could be garnered externally from the Web or internally from the company's database and business software applications.

And of course, corporate portals allow employees to do their jobs better, according to industry experts. For instance, some portals sport templates that show new employees how to write a proposal, conduct an interview with clients, or create a PowerPoint presentation.

If you really want to create a transactional portal where you can buy and sell goods and services with partners or suppliers, or even sell your own wares to the public, then you will probably need an application server or Web-to-host connectivity system and portal-specific development tools. If you're just looking to create a more collaborative or user-friendly intranet interface, you may well require some of these tools, but at the same time you may also get all you need from going to the likes of Lotus or AOL/Netscape.

Corporate America is starting to see the light. According to a recent Gartner Group report, approximately 80 percent of companies on the leading edge of technology usage have or soon will implement a corporate portal. More than half of the Fortune 300 companies are working on—or already have—a corporate portal. And by 2003, a majority of all businesses will manage a portal. Major companies such as Charles Schwab & Co., Wells Fargo, Boeing, and even the U.S. Postal Service have embraced corporate portal technology.

E-Portal Additions

Your e-business portal should have a heavy dose of corporate benefits for your employees, too. Companies are organizing their internal Web sites as destinations where employees can look up information, get work done, and exchange ideas. Here are some ideas that might work for you:

- A directory hierarchy that structures all content on the intranet. This part of an intranet is sometimes called a "Mini-Yahoo." Much can be learned from the design of directory services like Yahoo and LookSmart since they expend more usability efforts than any intranet project, but it is ultimately necessary to construct the actual topic hierarchy locally since it has to reflect the specific content and concerns of the intranet. The methods we used to structure Sun's first intranet portal in 1994 still work perfectly.
- A search field connecting to a search engine that indexes all pages on the intranet. In contrast to generic Internet searches, an intranet search engine should reflect available knowledge about the relative importance of various areas of the intranet; for example, it could denote official pages with a special icon.
- Current news about the company and employee interests. Typically, the intranet home page can replace traditional employee newsletters and the flood of e-mail announcements and memos that reduce productivity in many companies. Coupling the news listings with an archive and a good search engine ensures that employees can retrieve information as needed and frees them from having to store and manage local copies (something that is very expensive considering the poor information management capabilities of current e-mail software).
- Employee essentials, such as templates for writing a proposal or creating a PowerPoint presentation.

- Self-service features so that employees can sign up for or change their 401(k) on the portal. They can also fill out expense reports, order office supplies, and report a change of address online.
- An office locator where you can click on a particular office and see a picture of the person who sits in that office, as well as his or her resume, phone and e-mail info, projects in progress, and personal information such as favorite foods.
- Morale boosters such as employees celebrating birthdays that week or links to restaurant reviews submitted by coworkers.

Bigtime Players

On the business-to-business side, a host of companies are jockeying for portal supremacy. One of the biggest Internet portals is MarketSite.net, operated by Commerce One. MarketSite.net supports real-time automated buying and selling through the use of extensible markup language, or XML, that allows businesses using different systems and technologies to trade with each other. What XML does that electronic data interchange cannot do is create a common vocabulary that businesses using different systems all can use. XML provides virtual name tags in the data stream. If everyone agrees on what the name tags mean, they can exchange information.

In 1999, Commerce One announced the addition of 50 new suppliers to MarketSite, including Boise Cascade Office Products, Office Depot, Fisher Scientific, Silicon Graphics, and Lucent Technologies, thus becoming one of the first e-business portals to create a single global source for e-business needs.

Another up-and-comer in B2B is VerticalNet, based in Horsham, Pennsylvania. The company creates vertical trade communities that focus on specific industrial sectors. According to Blair LaCorte, head of strategy for VerticalNet, the company has 53 communities in eight industrial categories. Each community has three components: editorial, content-specific product information, and tools that enable auctions and trades.

LaCorte said "storefronts" on the site cost around $7,500 per year. Companies can market goods through their storefronts to targeted customers and can monitor the onsite traffic, a valuable market research tool, said LaCorte. For around $15,000 companies can set up e-commerce centers where they can post catalogs and job listings and sell excess inventories through auction.

Close to 3,000 companies have purchased storefronts or e-commerce centers on VerticalNet, said LaCorte. Last year the company processed $400 million in trade leads, 15 percent of which were finalized as sales within a month, with an average worth of around $25,000. Another 25 percent of the leads became completed sales within three to six months. LaCorte said 50 percent of buyers purchased product from parties with whom they had never done business, underscoring the Internet's ability to bring buyers and sellers together.

Right now, though, most companies build their portals from scratch. But a host of other vendors with names like Plumtree, Glyphica, Viador, and Epicentric are popping up to provide the technology in a single, off-the-shelf package. They sell software to create the sites as well as do a lot of the integration work to link together disparate applications and data. Analysts estimate that there are about 15 to 20 such vendors in existence in early 2000, with many more sure to follow.

Consortium Power

Another trend in the e-business portal sector is consortiums (i.e., like-minded groups of companies that band together and share the same portal space). In early 2000, an agreement was announced between EDS CoNext, a new subsidiary of EDS, and Ariba Inc. to facilitate consortia-based buying across 12 net markets, which the two parties called "leveraged sourcing networks."

The consortium put in place technology that reduces transaction costs, improves efficiencies of companies working together, and creates markets that work faster. At the time, statements from both companies summed up the consortium as "bringing the concept of management network to bear—to manage the deployment of technology to create unique B2B solutions instead of huge open portals." Beefing up the consortium was a group of A-list companies like Prudential Insurance, Bethlehem Steel, Clorox Co., Entergy Services Inc., Fort James Corp., Kellogg Co., Tyco Healthcare Group, EDS, and four other Fortune 100 companies.

The Evolution of "Vortals"

Any doubts that B2B portals had arrived were erased in November 1999 when both Ford Motor Co. and General Motors Corp. announced that their vast supply chain operations would be put online. Ford and GM have in one stroke created B2B ventures that render business-to-consumer stars like eBay and Amazon.com puny by comparison.

Some Web observers are calling these vertical portals that Ford and GM have launched "vortals," which may become the source of incredible opportunity as vertical markets are developed around these new technologies. "The activity being built and the communities evolving around these vortals are not to be trivialized," emphasizes Tom Koulopoulos, president of the Boston-based Delphi Group. "GM estimates $500 billion will flow through its vortal in just a few years' time."

That is just scratching the surface of market potential. "Imagine marketplaces virtually devoid of transactions, where myriad vortals coordinate, orchestrate, and execute the many pieces of the value chain inherent in any business process," says Koulopoulos. "General Motors' and Ford's core identity may still be manufacturing in five years time, but their greater value and core competency will most likely be in building vortals."

"Vortals expand the community of providers, suppliers, and buyers in a value chain by an order of magnitude and create high interchangeability between these participants," explains Koulopoulos. "Most importantly, they apply the recent overabundance of capital to the innovative process in all industries at a velocity that can keep pace with increasing expectations for higher returns. In many ways vortals are the economic model that will justify and support the inflating Internet economy."

Challenges to the consortium option include the same challenges that threaten most consortiums—differences of opinion among the members. The obviously different needs of companies that engage in e-business portal ventures will make it difficult to satisfy everyone. At the end of the day each participant will have to make an evaluation. Are they doing better on these deals than we could on our own?

For example, supplier changes will have to be made in some cases, and there are explicit and inexplicit costs associated with those types of changes. And there are also economies of scale created by a product in high demand for one company and only slight demand for another that could cause rifts as well.

The E-Market Ten Commandments

For your e-business portal to be the transactional engine you envision, people have to see it and start talking about it first. Advertising and marketing people have had a name for that process for years—buzz.

To generate buzz about your e-business portal by emphasizing the community aspect of your site, follow these steps from Buzzcompany.com, a leading Internet portal developer.

1. Enable E-Market Communications via E-Boards—An e-market on the Internet is not simply the sum total of various transactional applications but is in fact the rich fabric on all ongoing communications between potential buyers and sellers. E-boards (commerce-centric message boards) foster continuous e-discussions about products, services, and vendors and help build a base of "e-members" enrolled in an e-community of shared interests. They are a powerful means to enable this fabric of "e-market communications" and provide real substance and texture to your B2B Web site. No serious B2B contender should be without them.

2. Detect Market Opportunity and Gain Market Focus via Ratings— Concentrating fragmented physical markets and building efficient e-markets is all about focus. Drilling deeply into vertical markets, or extending broadly across horizontal markets, are ongoing processes of market opportunity detection.

   E-community technology allows you to refine your focus and detect emerging market opportunity by leveraging the power of e-members to participate in rating products, services, vendors, even the messages and opinions of other influential e-members. B2C Web sites like BizRate.com have demonstrated the power of member ratings to drive business opportunity to highly rated products, services, and vendors.

   It's important that your B2B e-boards are ratings-enabled. The information you glean from these e-member ratings will help you in staking your claim to undeveloped e-market real estate, thereby differentiating you from your competition.

3. Design-In E-Member Permissions and E-Community Incentives—An efficient e-market deploys technology to take both time and cost out of the e-business process. Providing your e-member buyers with a way to grant their permission to be solicited by your e-member sellers can accelerate "time-to-transaction" and enable private member communications leading to special pricing and cost savings on both sides.

   This solicitation can occur via private messaging on the e-boards, via e-mail, or via the integration of industry standard

chat or instant messaging technology. The key is to have a permissions engine built into your e-community platform that
allows buyers to escalate their level of permission based on their
market need and/or increasing trust with particular vendors in
your B2B marketplace.

The permissions engine is made even more powerful when
tied to an incentives model, where buzzpoints can be utilized to
encourage market efficiencies and repeat buying. These incentives are specifically tied to permission-to-solicit granted by buyers
to sellers.

4. Use E-Discussions Context to Target Advertising and
   Sponsorship—Advertising and sponsorship revenues are
   becoming a regular part of B2B business models. The e-discussion
   topics on your B2B e-boards provide you with a way to more effectively target your banner advertising and sponsorship opportunities and deliver above-average ad impressions to your sellers.
   That's called "contextual targeting."

   For example, a search for the words "paper suppliers" within a
   given e-discussion could result in a list of e-member comments
   on various paper suppliers, with a banner advertisement placed
   by the sponsoring advertiser for that particular e-discussion.

   Since e-discussions frequently use common terminology (e.g.,
   "best price") you can offer key word sponsorships to your sellers,
   and whenever those terms are used in posting a message to an
   e-board the sponsor's advertisement will appear.

5. Embed E-Community Buzz in Content Applications—First-
   generation virtual community technologies tended to be deployed
   as standalone discussion silos and were not creatively integrated
   into the overall application set of the particular Web site. For
   forward-thinking B2B Net market makers, the challenge is to
   embed e-community buzz throughout the entire fabric of your
   business model. For example, you may publish content on trends
   relevant to your particular e-market ("Online Procurement of
   Industrial Supplies"), and within that story provide embedded
   discussions related to that topic.

   These embedded discussions will drive a positive member feedback loop that serves to either reinforce or challenge the published
   content in the story. In either case it makes the content section of

your B2B portal increasingly stickier and allows your editorial organization to begin mining e-member feedback in new ways.

6. Improve Member-to-Customer Conversion Ratios via Transactive Buzz—Analysts report that many B2C e-commerce Web sites suffer from low visitor-to-customer conversion ratios. In other words, perhaps only 2 percent of Web site visitors ever buy anything from their online store. In efficient B2B e-market membership models, this does not have to happen.

   Why not implement "commerce connectors" between your e-boards and your auction, exchange, procurement, or marketplace transaction systems? Some call that building transactive buzz (i.e., a rich architecture where e-members can move from an e-discussion directly into a transaction), thus improving member-to-customer conversion ratios. This is particularly powerful if your business model is based on generating transaction fees or referrals.

7. Foster E-Member Self-Publishing of Storefronts, RFQs, and Classifieds—A dynamic B2B e-community empowers its seller members to promote their products and services and empowers its buyer members to solicit competitive bids for the products and services they need. In B2B e-markets, sellers want storefronts (sponsored home pages listing their products and services) and buyers need easy RFP (request for proposal) capabilities. And both buyers and sellers need to place regular classified advertising to match seller offers with buyer needs.

   In other words, e-member self-publishing becomes an important value-added service offered by Net market makers to enhance the fabric of their chosen e-market. These services can become additional sources of revenue for Net market makers or can be offered on a free or sponsored basis to serve your specific business model needs.

8. Deliver "MyCommunity" Personalization Capabilities—E-community is not static community. Good e-community technology lets both buyers and sellers personalize their view of frequently accessed e-boards to concentrate on the comments of e-members relevant to them, or to browse product, vendor, and service discussions that may directly lead to transactions.

   In other words, some customers only want to access "MyCommunity," not your community. This type of personalization, popular in the B2C space, also applies to B2B marketplaces seeking to concentrate a critical mass of buyers. Put another way, many e-markets basically consist of lots of different "markets-of-one," whether that market-of-one is an individual consumer or corporate procurement organization with its own processes and procedures.

9. Offer Peer-to-Peer E-Services and E-Support Applications— E-boards, e-member self-publishing, embedded and transactive buzz, new revenue models based on ad and keyword sponsorship targeting—that's a lot for any e-community platform. But it's not the end of the story.

   B2B portals and Net market makers need to offer member-friendly e-services and e-support applications that allow for self-service and new peer-to-peer collaborative service relationships. Connecting multiple buyers and sellers in an emerging e-market demands new ways of ensuring customer help and satisfaction.

10. Leverage XML-Enabled E-Discussion Syndication to Build Intercommunity Networks—No e-market is an island in the Internet economy. E-discussions taking place in one e-community may be equally valuable in another. In a world of fast developing alliances and ever changing business models, it's important that a well constructed B2B e-community have the capability to import e-boards' content from partner Web sites or export its own e-discussions to other partner, vendor, or customer Web sites.

chapter eight

What Do Your Customers Want?

With all the changes we've seen with technology and the Internet, is it any surprise that customers have changed, too? Hardly. With the advancement of the Internet, companies are seeing a different kind of customer—a customer who is more IT savvy, knowledgeable, demanding, knows his or her rights, and has high expectations.

If anything, customers are getting pickier in cyberspace. The e-business customer who arrives looking for a new and improved banking experience online knows his or her way around the Web. These people have been to eBay and Ameritrade; they've bought some shares or tickets at an airline site, maybe even bought a car or researched a home. So they enter the door with expectations. They come with a sense of entitlement because they have taken the steps necessary to get there.

They are, for these reasons, different from earlier customers. They don't wait in line, and they won't spend the time helping you iron out your organizational inconsistencies. They don't go from department to department to solve a problem, and they sure don't wait for answers to arrive by snail mail.

Instead, they send e-mail requests for information in the wee hours of the morning. They ask a variety of questions, from the commonplace to the extremely complex, filling customer service inboxes daily. And while they don't expect an immediate reply to such inquiries, they definitely expect to have an answer to their inquiry some time the next day. After two or three days without a response, they often give up and move on to another company with better customer service.

In short, today's e-business customer wants every Web encounter to be as fast and easy as their best experience to date because every breakthrough experience gives them a better understanding of the possibilities.

The Bottom Line

There's real business value in Web-based customer service, regardless of what kind of business you do. Consider the following:

- A computer screen can convey much more information than a telephone receiver. Web-based service improves service by getting customers more information in less time than it would take if they were using the phone.
- Businesses can save a bundle—running a customer service switchboard or face-to-face service counter can be expensive and still leave customers frustrated and unsatisfied.
- Companies that offer toll-free numbers as the only means of customer service will get much more phone traffic than those that also offer a URL.
- Small businesses can now offer customer service, even if they don't have an end-to-end e-commerce site. Simple and inexpensive solutions—like e-mail correspondence or FAQ pages—can go a long way.
- Having a customer service Web site can free you and your employees from busywork so you can focus on real work—like making sales calls.

Service Barriers

It is estimated that 80 percent of the total calls made to a typical customer service center ask one or more of these four questions: "Do you have...? How much is it? Is it in stock? Where is my order?"

The trouble is, companies that engage in online commerce aren't answering these questions as quickly—or as accurately—as they should. As many e-businesses struggle to close the gap between what the Internet promises and what they can deliver, the initial focus has been on technology. Not surprising given that technology is often perceived as the first step in the e-business evolution.

Some experts point to the rapid growth of the Internet as the reason customer service efforts are struggling. With so many people to deal with so fast, many e-businesses have found customer response to be literally overwhelming. Businesses are finding themselves buried in e-mail and Web-based queries, and traditional FAQs can't handle the task. The result is these companies must either hire and train more people or let customer service lag. Both options are expensive in terms of overhead costs and loss of business.

Unfortunately, the e-business customer service center may get worse before it gets better. Current data indicates that e-businesses are facing an uphill fight when it comes to providing good customer service. A recent study by Jupiter Communications showed that 42 percent of companies tested didn't respond to a relevant e-mail inquiry, took more than five days to respond, or didn't list an e-mail contact at all.

When a company can't deliver what it promised, when it promised, and at the price it promised, it's an open invitation to trouble, and a troubled customer is willing to click to the next-best competitor. The old adage used to be that a disappointed customer will tell 10 others. Now, if you disappoint one, they can tell 10,000. If you doubt that, spend some time on one of the hundreds of Web sites dedicated to trashing companies.

Considering the People Factor

There's a big difference in the vendor/customer relationship in the Web world. Customers become more autonomous and have less direct contact with the company when the Web becomes the way they experience a company. In this nonpersonal mode of interaction, developing trust is more critical than ever before. How well the site delivers a positive and productive experience is the stuff of which trust is built.

But in a hard-wired world, it's easy to forget that the recipient on the other end of your e-mail message is a human being. One of the downsides of the information revolution is that the human aspect of business relationships has suffered. After all, the computer that lets you shake a customer's hand hasn't been invented yet.

But companies that forget the human factor are the ones that will suffer most in the new cyber-economy. Keeping the individual in mind, instead of the invoice number, isn't difficult. Companies can take several steps to ensure that it treats its flesh-and-blood customers like flesh-and-blood customers:

1. Strive for good leadership, all the way up to the CEO's office. In the past, almost by definition, e-business leaders came from the technology area. Some would argue that technologists are best suited to take the lead in e-business development. Others say they tend to be too close to the engineering to see the broader context of the total business. The fact is, e-business leadership is not a matter of position, it is perspective. Good leaders can be former heads of information, law, marketing, even CEOs—as long as they have the right mix of skills. Looking back over the past few years, the first successful e-business leaders were entrepreneurs, visionaries, even dreamers—people unable and unwilling to take no for an answer.

2. Work on integrating personnel into the system. It is critical that an organization not force-feed an e-business with people ill-equipped to handle its demands. Any company moving to the Web must accept the fact that it will face some critical choices: upgrade, certify, or requalify people's skills; relocate them to another part of the organization; or, where appropriate, help them find opportunities in line with their desires. Fortunately, comfort with technology is not the hurdle it once was. Chances are good that most people will have some online experience.

3. Create the needed channels of information. E-businesses must approach customer service decisions the same way they do technological ones—with a clear plan leading to a clear set of objectives. Customers can't be viewed as a consideration to be addressed after the technologies are in place. Whether or not customers are to be tightly integrated into the system, the decisions must come early in the process. And if customers are to be part of the system, their selection and development must be viewed as an investment every bit as important to the e-business as the technologies that support it.

4. Build trust. Linking business functions such as fulfillment and support into your customer's Web shopping experience not only builds a trusting relationship with customers, but it can help your company reduce operational expenses (e.g., support phone calls) related to costs. Companies such as Cisco Systems and Ford Motor have saved millions of dollars by transforming their support operations to the Web.

It's no coincidence that all of these factors rely on e-businesses bringing good people into the customer service mix, be it a senior executive or a call center representative. To gain leverage in a new age of customer service, where money never actually changes hands, where customers never see a salesperson, and where people with problems to be solved are as important as ever (may be more so), companies have to be able to depend on real people to solve real customers' needs.

The Three Phases of E-Service

We mentioned at the beginning of the chapter how slow many e-businesses have been in implementing quality online customer service operations. For some companies, it's just part of the progression to e-commerce—get the technology going first, then worry about the people part. For others it's lack of planning. In both scenarios, e-businesses are finding after the fact that even the most sophisticated and powerful systems have fallen short of their initial promise because they haven't laid the groundwork with the human part of the online equation. Often they fail to ask and answer key questions. For example: What is their strategy to communicate to the organization that e-business is a fundamental shift in how the business works? How will they staff an e-business effort with people who may be uncomfortable in a radically different environment? Have these organizations certified and requalified the skills and mind-sets of people who will make the overall system perform for customers? What technological tools will they need to meet the new expectations of a new kind of customer?

Companies inevitably come face to face with these questions as they evolve through three stages of e-business development. The first is experimentation, in which there is an awareness of the technologies but little business focus. There also tends to be little cohesive planning behind the spending, which is not tied to specific returns on investment.

The second stage is infrastructure, which a company begins to develop to achieve operational efficiencies. This effort points to savings—instead of return on investment—as justification for a project because people are baffled as to how they quantify the benefits. Still, they move much closer to business reality.

In the third stage, transformation, e-business is elevated to a strategic imperative. There is a pervasive brand strategy in place, and the organization begins to see some major business opportunities. The return on investment is clearly articulated and well integrated within the fabric of the business. It is impossible to move from stage two to three without factoring in people. The reason is simple: The technology infrastructure might be fine, but the service to customers will fall considerably short because people aren't equipped to provide it.

Forward-thinking companies are finding ways to address this problem, realizing that every opportunity to touch a customer is an opportunity to strengthen the brand and grow the business. New e-mail technologies allow companies to sort through customer service inquiries quickly and efficiently, directing requests to the appropriate department or person and in some cases even automatically responding to questions.

What's Happening in IT?

The successful e-businesses understand early on that they have to develop a customer-centric model for the enterprise customer that includes a unified view of consumers and services. That model links the Internet, Web, and e-commerce applications with back-office systems and presents information in ways the customer wants. In addition, the rapid rate of change combined with competitive pressures means businesses must repeatedly create added value for customers. The challenge for IT organizations is to continue to assimilate commercial packages and legacy systems while managing the escalating costs of implementing and maintaining integration among them.

As usual, profits and competition drive the process. World-class customer service operations are becoming increasingly popular as more products and services become commoditized and companies find that customer service is one of the only means to differentiate themselves from their competitors. However, while traditional customer service has been done through snail mail, telephone, and fax, more customers—the more fickle and demanding customers—are using e-mail.

Integrating Web-based customer service into your overall customer service strategy begins the moment you realize you need to include it in your strategy. Some issues to consider include:

- *Giving the customer options.* Today's technology offers many ways to solicit and collect customer feedback. The most common methods are hot-linked e-mail addresses and simple HTML forms. Hot-linked e-mail opens a new browser, allowing the customer to send a message and not lose his or her original location on the site, and HTML forms include a single text box, in which the customer can type his or her message, pull-down menus, or various choices with check-boxes. Any method can give the customer a simple way to communicate via the Internet.

- *Perfecting your e-mail operation.* While some companies have devoted entire customer service teams exclusively to addressing e-mail inquiries, other companies incorporate e-mail response services with existing telephone customer service representative responsibilities. Either route you take, you should strongly consider administering a written exam to those people responsible for sending e-mail replies. This will ensure that you are sending intelligent and grammatically correct messages to your customers. Both methods have advantages and disadvantages that depend on your specific business and customer service model. What you have to keep at the top of your mind is that you need an adequate staff to accommodate all the inquiries your company receives, whatever method they arrive.

- *Redistributing customer information.* Once a message comes into your company, how will you deliver it to the appropriate people? Can one person or a team of people do the job, or is it more efficient to automate the process with an automated e-mail response system? If you find your customer service reps becoming frequently backlogged, you should consider an automated system or designate an individual or a small group of people to deliver the message. Studies show customers still prefer speaking to someone—anyone—rather than a machine.

- *Is outsourcing an option?* Many companies, especially those involved in seasonal sales fluctuations, find that they can more efficiently outsource e-mail customer service. Tracking and monitoring your customer service needs should help you with this decision. Working with an outside vendor eliminates many of the headaches associated with periodic upsizing and downsizing staff and can better accommodate unexpected spikes.

- *Keeping tabs on customers.* The very nature of e-mail communication allows you to easily automate a benchmarking and tracking system. In fact, many automated e-mail response systems include tracking components. To track and use the information effectively, determine your requirements up front in your design: How soon do you want to respond, how do you want to prioritize inquiries, and how much time should each request take?

Which tools and techniques? Again, technology provides many options for providing information, but you must decide which ones are appropriate for your operation. Consider, for example:

1. Making sure that answers coming from different people are correct and consistent by frequently updating your staff with current information. A great way to do this is posting a frequently asked question (FAQ) page on your Web site and giving your customer service people access to it for referencing and updating. Another benefit is that FAQs have the tendency to head off customer inquiries completely.

2. Capturing e-mail addresses for future marketing purposes. Always ask your customers if they want to hear from you on upcoming promotions, and if they do, you can add them to your database.

3. Following up some e-mail responses with a telephone call. This is a great way to ensure that your customers are satisfied with your customer service.

4. Tracking and monitoring the questions/complaints and using this information to help you determine what areas of your site need to be updated. Since customers also have a tendency to complain when items are out of stock, this can be a helpful tool when it comes to managing your inventory.

Sign Here.com

Nobody, with the exception of corporate lawyers, are thrilled about haggling over business contracts. The Internet isn't much help in straightening out the red tape on sales and service contracts, but it is speeding up the process in one key area—the signature.

These days, e-commerce is changing the manner in which contracts are executed and is rapidly making ink a thing of the past. It's high time, too, as customers are no longer identified by a face but with an e-mail address.

Contracting on the Internet, while enabling a business to reach customers it may once only have dreamed of, has the corresponding problem of allowing the identity of the person on the other side of the deal to be concealed. The key element of basic contract formation that is relied upon so automatically, being able to verify the identity of the parties to the transaction and that they have agreed to the contract by executing it, is difficult in electronic deal making.

That's the beauty of the digital signature. A digital signature is actually nothing like a traditional written signature. Rather, it is an encryption technology that verifies the integrity of the document and authenticity of the sender.

While there are several different digital signature technologies, most commercial digital signature products use public key cryptography. Public key cryptography operates by means of matching cryptographic keys that are associated with the user and the recipient of the message. Only the intended recipient of the message can decrypt it, and by doing so, the identity of the sender is confirmed.

Automated Responses

The most efficient way to address e-mail inquiries is to incorporate an automated response system. Such a program can automatically categorize, prioritize, respond or route, and track messages, greatly simplifying the process and ensuring a timely and accurate response.

Keep in mind that an auto-response system should first and foremost generate a confirmation to the customer, informing them that their message was received. Many systems stamp the message with a tracking number and send a confirmation immediately upon receipt of the inquiry. Your customer will feel better knowing that his or her message has been received and that an answer is on its way.

The system then needs to categorize the message. By "reading" through the text, the auto-response system can look for frequently asked questions and keywords that will identify the type of response required. Based on how the message is categorized, it can then prioritize the message and route it to the appropriate place.

Auto-response systems can follow one of three general paths:

- *Automated.* If the question is clear and easily interpreted—such as driving directions, addresses, and operating hours—the system can respond automatically from a library of responses or with an appropriate Web link. Note that in the first stages of such an operation it is critical that an experienced customer service representative reviews the inquiries and responses to ensure the responses are appropriate.
- *Automatic routing.* Using the identified keywords, this system can route the message to a customer service representative for a personalized answer. This step is particularly useful if your customer service system is designed to route messages to the most appropriate CSR rather than simply the next one available. The CSR can then respond, sending the message back through the auto-response system to gather and include the appropriate tracking information.
- *Manual routing.* Even the smartest computer can't compete with a live CSR, especially when it comes to complicated customer inquiries. The auto-response system must have a human backup who can review complex questions and manually route them to the right CSR.

Automated e-mail customer service programs are nearly a requirement for doing business in today's Internet world. Providing customers with fast, valuable, and consistent information in response to e-mail inquiries allows you to meet and exceed customer expectations. By strategically reviewing your customer service and Web programs—and by integrating the two into a comprehensive system—you can ensure that every point of customer contact is a positive one that grows your customer base and your bottom line.

A Blueprint for Success

While marketing, sales, and product delivery increasingly become integrated with each other on the Web, customer support often remains the function of a single departmental Web site within a bigger organization. This presents a special challenge for a company looking to build what Laurie Windham, President and CEO of

Cognitiative, Inc., an e-strategy consulting firm, and author of the book, *Dead Ahead: The Web Dilemma and the New Rules of Business*, calls a "Whole Experience" Web environment. "Being easy to do business with—providing access to support, service, news, and information, and creating a sense of community among your customers—are actions critical to building customer loyalty in the online arena," writes Windham in her book.

Windham says that many companies are realizing significant returns on their online customer service initiatives. For example, 70 percent of Cisco's requests for technical assistance are now handled electronically—letting the firm cut costs and retarget that money elsewhere. Web real estate destination Homeshark.com is on its way to reducing the costs of serving its customers by 50 percent. And Autodesk, the world's largest design solutions software company, launched an aggressive technical assistance effort via the Web that has provided a 1,600 percent return on investment for the company.

Unfortunately, too many companies offer second-rate customer service via the Web, as exemplified by not answering online questions in a timely fashion (or at all), not providing telephone numbers when a phone call is required to resolve a problem, and not providing enough in-depth product and pricing information to truly facilitate a purchase transaction. Online features that may benefit the company, such as static FAQs, personalization technology that only uses the data for marketing purposes, and "e-mail us" buttons that don't seem to be connected to a living person don't benefit the customers. For too many online customers, self-service can often mean no service.

Innovative companies have built "Whole Experience" Web sites that not only pull visitors through the consumption cycle but help facilitate the exchange of information, enable electronic commerce, and provide an environment for social interaction. "Many of these sites go even further," says Windham, "allowing personalization and customization—moving from generic experiences to customized experiences that meet the needs of the individual."

A "Whole Experience" Web site anticipates user needs based on data that's collected on them as they interact with the site. Over time, these unique preferences let a Web site greet each user by name, serve personalized marketing messages, stimulate aftermarket sales, and deliver a more satisfying personal experience.

Four Steps to Better Customer Service Online

- Improve customer satisfaction by meeting their needs on the first point of contact—with a knowledgeable staff.
- Boost efficiency through the creation of a contact center that fuses the call center with the Web.

- Increase sales by creating a new avenue for collaborative up- and cross-selling.
- Create a competitive advantage by providing a superior continuum of services to customers.

With targeted messaging, many companies have discovered their online customers are more likely to buy into techniques (e.g., personalization) if their experience helps improve business processes, such as making it easy to find products they're interested in based on their previous purchase behavior, or determining special negotiated pricing for their corporate accounts.

E-Business Service—the Good and the Bad

Aspects of a good e-business customer experience:

- Clear, concise wording: Customers don't want to read long paragraphs of text on e-commerce sites. Get to the point.
- Quick page download: Under 10 seconds on a 28.8 modem, as tested through a public ISP like AOL or Mindspring—not the internal corporate network.
- Appropriate page width: Most customers view the Web at 800 x 600 resolution, and some still are at 640 x 480. Choose a resolution and fit your pages inside that width. (Vertical scrolling is OK.)
- Simple page design: Where appropriate, use simple page design focused on moving customers toward completion of their goal. Don't clutter the page with dozens of features and links that most customers don't want.
- Few, and small, supporting graphics: Decorative graphics can help create an aesthetic feel to the site that supports the brand image. But use these sparingly. If customers have to spend valuable time downloading lots of unnecessary graphics, your brand image suffers.
- Large graphics only when good for the customer: Large graphics should be provided only when relevant to the customer's goal. For example, if customers click to zoom in on a product picture, the

large graphic is appropriate. But never include large graphics just to make your site look good.

- Jargon-free language: Use wording that customers understand. For example, on a travel site, don't refer to the "equipment"—call it the "plane." On retail sites, give clear product names, not abbreviations.
- A good search: Include a prominent search function, but only if it gives accurate and concise search results.
- Easy navigation: The site structure should be based on what the customer wants, not how the company is organized. For example, a site selling books and music should make it easy to buy both products in the same buying process. The company may be organized into two different divisions (in two different buildings) for books and music, but to the customer, they're just two kinds of products on the same site.

Aspects of a bad customer experience:

- Error messages: For example, typing in the credit card expiration date as "10/02" generates an error on some sites, which want the date as "10-02." Instead, the site should interpret both dates as right and not tell the customers they did something wrong.
- Long instructional text: Customers don't want to read how to use the site; they just want to use the site. Give the value; don't talk about it.
- Excessive technology: Don't require unnecessary plug-ins or include irrelevant Java applets.
- Fatal errors: Don't delete the customer's order. Don't allow servers to give a database error in the middle of the buying process.
- Distracting screen elements: Don't include text tickers or irrelevant animated graphics. You want your customers to move through the buying process, not be mesmerized or distracted or stopped by it.
- Irrelevant or flashy features: Don't design your e-commerce site just to make your company look good. Instead, serve the customer with simple, clear design.
- Typographical errors: Misspellings, grammatical errors, and other textual errors not only make your site harder to understand, they also make your company look unprofessional.
- Excessive or inaccurate search results: If your search function makes customers wade through thousands of results, it would be better if you didn't offer search at all.

Calling on Your Call Center

These days, the bulk of online user requests go straight to the company's call center for action. According to Arthur M. Rosenberg, president of the Unified Messaging Consortium, the world is moving swiftly into two-way digital messaging, which includes both personal e-mail and enterprise "Web mail." Industry research indicates only 30 percent of Fortune 500 companies respond to questions directed to the Web site's Webmaster—and that means a large number of customers aren't getting the answers they want. Consequently, they may go elsewhere to get the answers they want.

One way to bulk up your e-business customer service efforts is to bulk up on call center staffing and technologies. Rosenberg's study of 258 companies with call centers that support e-mail shows that those companies receive approximately 300,000 e-mail messages per year. Fifty-five percent of those messages go straight to call centers. These businesses expect to receive approximately 2 million messages per year by the year 2000. The current average response time for handling e-mail (the response being in the form of e-mail or fax) was 17 hours; the average cost of handling e-mail was $17.85 per message; and 54 percent of the cost is directly related to labor cost.

As a result, customer service centers will soon begin to move away from balky telephone-driven response systems to e-mail and Web messaging systems.

The Medium Is the Message

Messaging is a call center communication access option that Web callers can exploit to either request an informational message response or schedule a telephone callback. Because Web callers have their own e-mail mailboxes, two-way messaging exchange is now a more viable alternative to live telephone connections. Not only is there public access to the Web caller's personal mailbox, but multimedia informational attachments that might normally be mailed or faxed can also be immediately e-mailed or faxed in response.

Rosenberg says that there are many practical reasons why Web callers will choose to send a message instead of establishing a real-time voice connection with call center staff, including the following:

- They can't or don't want to wait for someone to assist them.
- They will use the context of Web page information for the basis of their message inquiry or transaction.

- They need the convenience of 24/7 messaging access.
- They don't necessarily need to "discuss" anything about the information they want or the transaction requested.
- They may want to send information and data attachments first, before any interactive discussion takes place.
- They want a well-documented audit trail of the two-way messaging interchange.
- They want to eliminate the time, errors, and effort involved with transcribing detailed information during a live conversation.
- They don't have a required second telephone line for an immediate live callback while still connected to the Web.
- They want to direct their communication to a very specific group or individual that may not be readily accessible in realtime.
- It's just more convenient and cheaper than a live connection.

As customer service centers rely more on Web-based communications to interact with clients, company executives must make sure that call center personnel understand the most effective way to communicate with customers via e-mail or Web mail. Apart from standard FAQ pages and having staffers manually type a complete e-mail response to customers, there's a lot more that company managers can do to take advantage of Web-based customer call center exchanges. These solutions can include:

- Automated acknowledgment of message receipt ("mailbots"). These do not do anything with a Web caller's message but send a canned response to every message received.
- Automated text content scanning and analysis, with fully automated e-mail (or fax) responses. These responses can still be personalized based on message content and customer database information.
- Automated text content scanning, with automated skills-based assignment to an appropriate, available WSR.
- Automated routing to an available WSR, with manual message content review and response generation.
- Use of standard response message templates, with "cut and paste" information from a dynamic knowledge database.
- Manual transfer of difficult Web-mail messages via e-mail to more expert staff, complete with the necessary context information.
- Return telephone calls (callback) rather than an e-mail response, based on complexity, need for discussion, and urgency of situation.

Some Good Reasons for Beefing Up Your Customer Service

Your customers can be a fickle lot. Sure, they'll stay with you as long as they're satisfied with your service, but they'll do so with one eye on your competitor's products, prices, and programs. Here are some numbers indicating how hard it is to keep customers—and what it can cost you when you don't keep them:

- Fifteen to 40 percent of customers who say they are satisfied defect from a company each year.
- It costs five to seven times more to find new customers than to retain the customers you already have.
- Ninety-eight percent of dissatisfied customers never complain—they just switch to other competitors.
- In a recent survey, two-thirds of the customers polled said they believed their suppliers either seriously or somewhat misunderstood their needs.

The number one reason (68 percent) that companies lose customers is that customers turned away because of an attitude or indifference on the part of a company employee.

The good news is:

- Totally satisfied customers are six times more likely to repurchase a company's products over a span of one to two years than merely satisfied customers.
- A 5 percent reduction in customer defection can result in profit increases from 30 percent to 85 percent.
- If companies increase their customer retention by 2 percent, it is the equivalent of cutting their operating expenses by 10 percent.

- "Instant Messaging" or "chat" connections can be activated if the Web caller is logged on to the Internet.
- Where customized responses are always necessary, new "cross-media" messaging techniques can be applied. It is faster and easier to create a "voice e-mail" response (sent as a .WAV attachment), which avoids the problems of spelling and typographical errors and increases personalization of the response.

chapter nine

Have E-Business, Will Travel

For years now we've been hearing about the promise of a global marketplace. But it took the Internet to make it a reality.

Riding on the wave of e-commerce—a market recently estimated at $400 billion by the year 2002—e-business gurus have this vision for the world: A billion people connected with a million e-businesses and more than a trillion intelligent devices across the globe.

"Electronic Commerce is opening untold opportunities for small businesses in this country and anywhere around the world to expand their businesses to a global marketplace in both the business-to-business (B2B) and business-to-consumer (B2C) areas," says Harris N. Miller, president of the Information Technology Association of America. "The E-Commerce growth numbers are almost incomprehensible. E-Commerce is here and will provide small, medium, and large businesses with access to global markets."

That access is provided by technology and the Internet—or what Frances Cairricross of *The Economist* calls "the death of distance." With the death of distance, the traditional relationship between a seller and buyer in the pre-Internet world, even with supersonic airplanes, telephones, and faxes, was substantially circumscribed by the physical distance between the two, especially when it came to exchanging information. Not only was it relatively difficult to share needed information easily around the world except for among larger businesses and organizations, it was also very costly in terms of time, human resources, and out-of-pocket charges. Even larger organizations were limited in their selections, as they could not afford to be in

Hands Across the Water

One way to achieve global e-business harmony is through partnerships. Take the one between Chevron Corp. and Ariba, Inc. that resulted in creation of the Petrocosm Marketplace, the first global independent Internet marketplace to be owned by buyers and suppliers across the energy industry.

Petrocosm Marketplace is an open Internet marketplace and exchange that offers browser-based access with Internet-hosted procurement to enable companies of all sizes to buy and sell products and services that span the oil and gas industry supply chain: drilling, electrical, pipes, valves, and fittings and professional, engineering, and construction services. Based on independent market research, Petrocosm estimates that Net market electronic trading benefits such as aggregated purchasing, lower transaction costs, and seamless access to larger global markets could drive $11 billion in oil and gas industry savings and efficiencies.

Here's how it works. Petrocosm Marketplace uses Ariba's B2B e-commerce platform to enable oil and gas industry suppliers to rapidly develop and manage a high-quality, integrated catalog. Petrocosm Corp. is an entrepreneurial, venture-backed company in which Ariba, Chevron, and Crosspoint Venture Partners each have invested to hold minority stakes. The majority of equity ownership in Petrocosm is expected to be held by energy industry participants of all sizes.

With Petrocosm, not only has a new independent company been created, but the players have taken the concept of neutrality further by creating an equity structure that encourages industry ownership and broad participation from both buyers and suppliers. Not only is there an equity play for participants, but they can also benefit from the efficiencies created by such exchanges. For buyers, savings potential is estimated to between 5 percent and 30 percent.

The marketplace includes rationalized, energy industry-specific catalogs with millions of items together with services for supplier enablement, hosted and enterprise e-procurement for goods and services, auctions, reverse auctions, bid/ask exchanges, strategic sourcing, spot buying, customer-specific pricing, electronic payments, logistics, integration to ERP systems, and online community forums.

touch with a multiplicity of suppliers or customers. The Internet has virtually eliminated those cost factors.

Predictions abound for the global growth of e-commerce. E-commerce sales in Latin America by 2003 will reach $8 billion; in Europe sales will reach $430 billion by 2003; and global e-commerce sales will reach $3.2 trillion by 2003.

Boundary Barriers

Even though the Internet makes geographic distance, language, and cultural barriers almost irrelevant, the rest of the world has a lot of catching up to do before matching the breadth and scope of e-business in the United States. Cultural, technological, political, language, and currency-related issues top the list of barriers to e-businesses overseas emulating the success e-businesses are finding in the United States.

The basic configuration of an e-commerce system outside the United States may not differ that much from a U.S. installation, with the use of internationally known suppliers of Web servers, Unix or NT platforms, and router hookups. But once you leave the four walls of a company installation, the similarity diminishes.

Challenges that follow an overseas e-business implementation include managing different marketing strategies in different markets, securing adequate resources, and managing channel conflicts. Then there's the problems of managing content, technical obstacles, and legal barriers. "In some ways, global e-commerce doesn't exist," says Martha Bennett, VP of research for Giga Information Group. "The moment you have to deliver physical goods, you're up against every piece of legislation that exists in the real world."

Another problem is that international telecommunications can be unreliable. In most countries outside the United States, Internet access is more expensive, access speeds are slower, and many people are still using older versions of popular browsers and paying for every minute they're online. Even business-to-business leased-line charges cost an average of 10 times as much as they cost in the United States. To preserve customers' patience, many experts recommend that companies code tightly in HTML and create text-only versions of their Web sites early on, giving visitors a choice as the site starts loading.

An additional problem for global e-businesses is fulfillment. Not many countries can match the delivery channel infrastructures of the United States and Europe. According to QM Soft of San Diego, when people purchase over the Internet in the United States, 15 percent of the addresses are undeliverable based on customer information entry. In the United States and Canada, companies have very good postal databases; Australia and Japan are next in line, tied with Europe. Beyond that, it falls apart.

A lack of telecommunications infrastructure is another barrier to global e-business. Entire cities exist worldwide that don't have a telecommunications infrastructure at all, much less the ability to get on the Internet. In regions of the world farther removed from the standards of globalization, the future of e-commerce is developing more slowly. A number of third world countries, such as Pakistan, or regions, such as Africa, are showing very little interest in e-commerce because they don't have the telecommunications infrastructure to drive demand. In addition, many foreign countries, like those in Africa or Eastern Europe, simply don't have the capital to give e-commerce a go.

Global Policy Directives

According to the Information Technology Association of America, businesses want some fundamental principles to shape the policies that govern global electronic commerce. Here are some suggestions from the ITAA:

1. The development of electronic commerce should be led primarily by the private sector in response to market forces.

2. Participation in electronic commerce should be pursued through an open and fair competitive market.

3. Government intervention, when required, should promote a stable legal environment, allow a fair allocation of scarce resources, and protect public interest. Such intervention should be no more than is essential and should be clear, transparent, objective, nondiscriminatory, proportional, flexible, and technologically neutral.

4. Mechanisms for private sector input and involvement in policy making should be promoted and widely used in all countries.

5. Electronic commerce is global by nature. Government policies that affect it should be internationally coordinated and compatible and should facilitate interoperability within an international, voluntary, and consensus-based environment for standards setting.

6. Transactions conducted using electronic commerce should receive neutral tax treatment in comparison to transactions using nonelectronic means. Taxation of electronic commerce should be consistent with established, internationally accented practices and administered in the least burdensome manner.

7. Regulation of the underlying telecommunications infrastructure, when necessary, should enable actors to compete, globally, in an open and fair market. As competition develops, regulation should be phased out and there should be a greater reliance on competition law.

8. The protection of users, in particular with regard to privacy, confidentiality, anonymity, and content control, should be pursued through policies driven by choice, individual empowerment, industry-led solutions. It will be in accordance with applicable laws.

9. Business should make available to consumers and, where appropriate, business users the means to exercise choice with respect to privacy, confidentiality, content control and, under appropriate circumstances, anonymity.

10. A high level of trust in the Global Information Infrastructure–Global Information Society (Gff-GIS) should be pursued by mutual agreement, education, further technological innovations to enhance security and reliability, adoption of adequate dispute resolution mechanisms, and private sector self-regulation.

Cultural Challenges

Then there's the traditional cultural and language barriers for cross-border e-businesses to overcome. It has been noted that international customers are three times more likely to buy a product if it is available and communicated to them in their own language. Furthermore, an e-commerce Web site has to provide international users with the same quick access to information as domestic users, or you will quickly lose their attention.

Some say the main challenge of Web site globalization can be described as an inherent communication gap between Web developers and translators. On the one hand, Web developers are experts on how a site is structured and operates, but they probably do not understand foreign text, how it should be formatted, and what site designs best suit a particular audience. On the other hand, translators understand how a foreign language site should look and feel, but they are not technically savvy enough to transform the vision for a culturally hip Web site into a functional reality.

Early efforts to bridge the language gap have met with marginal success. Many companies bite the bullet and hire developers and translators to go through the painstaking process of manually extracting content for translation from HTML, scripts, templates, and programs.

Once these extracted elements of the site are translated, they need to be embedded back into a site's underlying code. Making translated elements actually function in a Web environment is extremely difficult. It often requires rewriting the original code, which can be exceptionally complicated, especially in cases where the target language is Asian and the foreign language text is in double-byte characters. The extracting-reprogramming-embedding process basically amounts to a reinvention of the wheel.

Alternatively, other companies pursue an equally time-consuming method, commonly known as the "parallel sites" approach, to Web site globalization. Simply put, these companies do (and spend) whatever it takes to build from scratch and separately maintain multiple foreign language versions of their English language Web site. While expensive, this method accommodates the need to tailor some amount of Web site content for a specific audience. What is compromised, however, is the ability to centrally manage and update those elements of the Web site that should be consistently represented in all languages. If a company's Web site normally experiences frequent content and functional updates, managing these changes across multiple sites can spiral into an impossible task.

Until recently, no single technology has existed to help companies efficiently build, deploy, and manage multilingual Web sites. But now, Web site globalization technology solutions are being developed and used to more elegantly combine Web development and translation expertise.

One such solution, from a company called Idiom Technologies, takes a "World Server" approach to globalizing e-commerce sites and interactive Web portal applications. The idea behind World Server is to nonintrusively integrate with an existing Web site infrastructure while facilitating and streamlining the globalization process. Consequently, companies can maintain up-to-date multiple foreign language sites, while actually continuing to manage only a single original language Web site.

E-business Web pages can also be converted to different languages via a process known as "localization." Localization is the linguistic adaptation of a product for specific geographic markets. In addition to the linguistic and cultural challenges that this conversion presents, localizers have to deal with many technical challenges.

And as new Web technologies emerge, more options are becoming available to content developers and Webmasters. Different file formats, databases, forms, and software scripts such as CGI and Java are all intermixed into creating current Web pages. Furthermore, to reduce rework, many of today's Web sites are based on dynamic HTML, as opposed to static HTML, where information drawn from databases is displayed on demand. Pages are built on the fly on users' browsers, automatically customized to best meet their needs.

Some global e-businesses are also adopting a "mirroring" approach, where the Web site is emulated on international servers available to local users. One way to do this is to create servers in all the countries the e-commerce solution is provided for. However, this process can be costly in hardware and maintenance expenditures. Another way is to outsource this requirement to third parties that are servicing companies in this area. Companies such as Adero and PSINet are providing a solution to their customers by having servers worldwide available to mirror their sites. For a fee, they host, manage, and maintain the sites as necessary.

Regardless of the approach, however, there are two critical objectives to consider when thinking about Web site globalization. First, you want to centralize Web site development and management wherever possible. Redundant resources are certainly not cost-effective, and they are also not efficient. Second, you want to retain as much flexibility as possible in dealing with textual and graphical content, as well as with "context." When it comes to colors, design, layout, and functionality, you may not know exactly how you will need to redesign or revamp your site next week, next month, or next year, but you do know that you will.

Location, Location, Location

Growth barriers aside, some international venues are striving to keep pace with the rapid acceleration of the U.S. e-business market. In fact, Northern Europe, parts of Asia, and some countries of Latin America are all expected to contribute heavily to the expected business-to-business boom in e-commerce over the next five years.

Europe clearly is the next largest e-commerce market after the United States, given the high penetration of PCs and Internet usage, particularly in such areas as Scandinavia. But while the European Union is nominally a seamless economic entity, variations among countries hold back faster growth there, one consultant reckons.

In Asia, where cellular telephone and personal digital assistant use has a very high per capita penetration, there also will be big growth numbers in some e-commerce segments. Countries with mobile phone capability in much higher concentration, such as Singapore and Hong Kong, are driving the demand for information and the kinds of services likely to be provided in the wireless protocol.

Government support in some Asian countries is also fostering land-line-based e-commerce. In a number of countries in Asia, government-led investments are trying to push the envelope quickly with low-cost technology infrastructure, not necessarily for the populace, but so that at least business can take advantage of the electronic pipeline to be part of the international business Internet play. That's creating a tenfold opportunity in the business-to-business channel.

In Latin America, too, there are a few countries leading the regional push into e-commerce. Brazil is the biggest, fastest-growing market far and away, because of the telecom infrastructure, the penetration of

---

Euro View

IDC's recent study, entitled *European Internet and eCommerce: Ready for 2000*, finds that 25 percent of Europeans now have access to the Internet and that 5 percent have made online purchases. The survey polled 10,600 Internet users in the 12 largest European markets.

The study points out the extremes in usage that still exist across the region. For example, Sweden's penetration rate is 60 percent, but France's is 16 percent. Furthermore, over 25 percent of UK users have purchased something online, but only 1 to 2 percent of Spain's users have.

A chief factor inhibiting growth of consumer e-commerce in Europe is lack of confidence in online security. Europeans remain ill at ease when it comes to using credit cards over the Net.

The study also notes that Europeans tend not to surf as much as Americans but rather visit particular sites. Because of high phone rates, only 25 percent of users go online for more than 30 minutes a day.

PCs, and the acceptance of the Internet. Mexico, because of its ties to the United States, Argentina, and Europe, is experiencing rapid growth as well.

One tactic that some U.S. e-businesses are using until the global e-commerce picture clears is a hedging strategy featuring overseas offices on several continents. "We have staffed offices in Hamburg, Paris, London, and Sydney and are concentrating on building international operations, [but we] are still in the process of deciding what countries to focus on more than others," says Linda Darling, the financial solutions marketing director at Vignette Corporation, a California-based manufacturing company.

Around the World

Some countries are embracing e-business tighter than others. Here's a rundown of some hot global e-commerce venues:

Australia: E-Biz Down Under

Australia's gross domestic product will grow by an extra 3 percent by 2007 if it adopts e-commerce, says a recent report by Australia's National Office for the Information Economy (NOIE). The report also categorized the impact on 340 different occupations, with health, education, tourism, business, IT, finance, accounting, and law benefiting from e-commerce. Printing, retailing, ground transport, and banking were portrayed as "losing industries." The report, which followed hard on the heels of an earlier six-month report card from NOIE, "E-Australia.com.au," demonstrates the importance the country places on e-commerce. Stuck out in the Southern Hemisphere, politicians refer continually to the "tyranny of distance."

But while the Australian government has done its best to promote the benefits of an online world, Australian business is facing the same problems as other countries. Small and medium-size enterprises (SMEs) too have been encouraged to get themselves online with the setting up of an independent, not-for-profit organization, the Australian Electronic Business Network, in partnership with industry.

Government initiatives include:

- The Australian Government has launched Online Australia, an initiative from the National Office for the Information Economy (*www.noie.gov.au*).
- The Office for Government Online in Canberra has a range of goals: to deliver all appropriate government services online by 2001; establish a single online point of access to government services; and move Commonwealth government business, procurement, and payments online.
- Government projects include implementing a project to enhance community access to government services in Tasmania with a view to a national rollout, introducing a new tax system, and developing a strategy for electronic procurement.

A range of industries are still coming to terms with e-business and e-commerce, but financial services are leading the charge. Organizations with strong brand names, such as Qantas, see an opportunity to attract e-business by using their well known names and offering better customer service and retention. But Qantas is reluctant to commit itself publicly to targets, unlike its international rivals.

Although there are opportunities to refocus supply chains through e-commerce, the geography of Australia has led to some quirks. For example, there are only two internal Australian air carriers—Ansett and Qantas—and only a limited number of flights to the United States.

The United Kingdom:
Slow Acceptance on the British Isles

In general the UK is still working out how to organize e-business and is toying with e-units and e-subsidiaries. Many company directors, aware of electronic commerce, have failed to see it as a driver for restructuring their business. Of UK manufacturing, retailing, and distribution companies, only one-fifth are believed to have an e-business strategy in place.

The British government's first report into electronic commerce in 1999 came up with 60 recommendations, including the appointment of an e-minister and e-envoy. But by and large, government structure in the UK has yet to be properly organized for e-commerce. Targets for electronic provision of government services—25 percent by 2002, 50 percent by 2005, 100 percent by 2008—are certain to be revised. Similar question marks remain over how quickly a national public infrastructure can be put in place.

Although UK small businesses admit they are aware of electronic commerce, they remain wary of the effect it could have on their operations. Some are afraid that it could put them out of business if they were unable to satisfy demand. They are wary of the technology, and even more wary of suppliers offering to get them connected for a cut of their business.

The government admits it is concerned over the e-commerce of small and micro UK companies, saying it lags behind other European economies, the United States, Canada, and Australia. A "multichannel marketing strategy" for SMEs is to be fully running by the end of June 2000. Despite this, there are success stories, such as lastminute.com and qxl.com.

India: No Sacred E-Cows

In India, the Internet is considered a technology that has revolutionized and redefined traditional trade. In 1999, e-commerce transactions in India tallied $31 million, far behind the United States but enough to show promise. Of that $31 million, $28 million was earmarked for B2B e-commerce. India's National Association of Software estimates that by the end of 2000, overall e-commerce sales will reach $71 million, with about $60 million falling into the B2B category.

Industry growth leaders, the NAS adds, are led by IT companies and banks, with manufacturers close behind. The government is helping companies who want to launch e-businesses in India find private funding and sales channel partners as well.

The problems with growth of e-business in India are primarily IT-based: low telecom density, poor telecom connections, substandard Web infrastructures, and an absence of legal and technical frameworks for companies to use as blueprints.

Saudi Arabia: Sand in the Gears?

The Internet is revolutionizing the way business is done, but the Arab countries have a lot of catching up to do in order to be part of the World Wide Web. Electronic commerce and use of the Internet require a highly developed telecommunications network, widespread use of personal computers, and an expansion in the use of credit cards. It also requires governments that are not obsessed with the control of information and are ready to embrace the global movement.

Arab consumers have shown a healthy appetite for the services available on the Internet, and most governments have accepted the fact that the Web economy is here to stay. Today, it is estimated that around 1 million out of a total Arab population of 272 million are online, but no country has more than 5 percent of its population connected to the Internet.

Saudi Arabia, the largest market for personal computers in the region, launched direct Internet services at the beginning of 1999 through a government-owned Internet service provider. Syria started offering Internet service in the latter part of 1999 to an estimated 3,000 subscribers.

Qatar and the United Arab Emirates have the highest percentage of Internet users, at around 5 percent of their population, followed by Bahrain and Kuwait at 3 percent, Lebanon at 2.3 percent, and Oman at 1 percent, with the remaining Arab countries below 1 percent. In contrast, the number of people using the Internet in the United States is put at 80 million, or 30 percent of the population, compared to 10 percent in Europe. The only countries in the Middle East region that do not yet offer direct Internet services are Libya and Iraq.

The value of e-commerce in the Middle East and North Africa still represents a fraction of that in developed Western markets. Nevertheless, it is expected to grow to $1 billion in 2003 from around $50 million in 1998.

Retailers in the region are already offering products on the Internet, ranging from books and software to jewelry and beauty items. However, the small number of Internet users in the region and their worry about using credit cards for Internet transactions have dampened the growth of e-commerce in the Arab world.

Scandinavia: Fjords Have a Better Idea

It's a Nordic invasion. All of a sudden, Scandinavian Internet companies that have thrived in their home countries are making aggressive plans to spread south to the great, largely untapped cybermarkets of Germany, France, and Italy. Already, Sweden's Boxman is selling music CDs all across the Continent, and Finnish e-brokerage eQ Online is preparing to offer stock trading in Germany. The prize is a big piece of pan-European e-business, which International Data Corp. projects will grow from $5 billion to $197 billion in 2002.

The Scandinavians are betting they can quickly come up with customized products for their neighbors, putting up Web sites geared to local tastes and languages. They hope to offer multilingual and multicultural alternatives to the Web, which is dominated by the Americans and English. In the process, their efforts should spur e-business growth in Europe, bringing the Web far closer to fulfilling its promise as a medium for connecting all of humanity. The Scandinavians already are starting to face American Web giants turbopowered by fabulous stock valuations. Amazon.com Inc., the American shopping site, and online auction pioneer eBay have both established e-commerce sites in Britain. Meanwhile, the Western Europeans, who so far haven't done much beyond starting Internet access services, are constructing e-commerce sites of their own. So intent are they on getting a head start that many Nordic Netrepreneurs are even skipping their normally sacrosanct month-long July vacations as they race to colonize Europe.

And why would Scandinavian sites have an inside track? It's simple. Unlike many Europeans, the Nordics are already online and have been for years. Indeed, Scandinavia boasts the highest Web surfing population per capita in the world, with Finland, Norway, and Sweden all topping 30 Internet users per 100 adults, while the United States trails with 28. The Scandinavians have plenty of e-commerce expertise, too. Pioneer shopping sites like Sweden's Torget have been operating since early 1996, when Amazon was still known principally as a jungle.

In the race to win with e-commerce, the Scandinavians have another crucial advantage: world leadership in mobile telephony. If they succeed in creating winning Web applications for the phone, they'll be positioned to sell to a vast cell-phone market in Europe, all operating on a single standard, something that American Webmasters can only dream of. Cell phones—in effect, pocket-sized computers—now number 115 million in Western Europe and are growing at a 50 percent per year clip. Soon, Euro Web merchants will be able to reach a continent of consumers in their pockets and purses. If the Scandinavians can master these mobile Web applications, they could be titans of the post-PC era.

Ya Ya, Canada

Canada is second only to the United States in developing a substantial Internet economy, concludes a report by the Canadian E-Business Opportunities Roundtable organization. The report, entitled *Fast Forward: Accelerating Canada's Leadership in the Internet Economy*, says Canada has the highest share of global electronic-commerce revenue after the United States, with an Internet economy currently valued at $28 billion Canadian dollars (US$19.3 billion) in revenue and employing 95,000 people nationwide.

The report forecasts that Canada's e-commerce could grow to C$155 billion in revenue by 2003 and create a total of 180,000 "high-value jobs." This, in turn, could help bolster Canada's overall productivity and international competitiveness, the study adds.

The Internet industry leaders who commissioned the report conclude from the findings that Canada is well positioned to take advantage of the burgeoning e-business opportunities but so far isn't aggressively rising to the challenge. Saying Canada's e-commerce industry is at a crossroads, the report from the Canadian E-Business Opportunities Roundtable identifies several hurdles that are slowing Canada's e-commerce development and the adoption of the Internet among Canadian businesses. These hurdles include:

- A lack of urgency among many Canadian business leaders, for whom the Internet simply isn't yet a strategic priority.

- The fact that Canada is a small market with a limited number of online customers.
- A shortage of talent to fill critical Internet technology positions.
- A false sense of security among Canadian retailers who have been sheltered from U.S. competition by the high costs of cross-border shipping and other barriers.

Global E-Business Software Options

Here are some of the more prominent and popular e-business globalization software packages available, with prices:

Global Site Ambassador
Global Sight Corp.
www.globalsight.com
Pricing starts at $100,000

Passport Enterprise
WorldPoint Inc.
www.worldpoint.com
$35,000 for one master enterprise user account, one master user account per Web site, and unlimited user accounts

Digital Island Inc.
www.digisle.net
$25,000 per year for the software license, monthly subscription, and support

Uniscape.com
Uniscape Inc.
www.uniscape.com
No up-front costs for this e-services translation portal; customers pay per-word charges (translating a 500-page Web site into five languages would run about $100,000)

WorldServer
Idiom Technologies Inc.
www.idiomtech.com
Priced from $75,000 to $200,000, depending on the number of languages, number of Web pages, and frequency of content update

WorldWeb Services
International Translation & Publishing
www.itpusa.com
Pricing not available

Source: *Information Week*

chapter ten

To Market, To Market

Positioning your e-business in the best light (i.e., attracting the right customers), creating the best selling opportunities, and convincing buyers to return to your site again and again, isn't that much different than it is in the brick-and-mortar world. Sure, the tools might be different, and yes, customers' attitudes about buying online can sometimes be a barrier; but in the end, you still have to build customer trust.

That wasn't an easy task in the early days of B2B e-commerce. The technology suffered at first compared to the retail e-commerce area because the retail sector was easier to implement. New start-ups didn't have to strategize with integrating online systems and legacy computer networks, which was B2B's biggest hurdle. Brick-and-mortar shops had an advantage over B2Bs because they had catalog sales. But, because of higher dollar volume with each transaction, B2B is thriving today.

On a broader level, the Internet is manna from heaven for marketing executives. The Internet lets you deliver specific, targeted messages to customers and prospects efficiently. It even has a built-in feedback mechanism. The challenge for marketing professionals is to recognize that each customer's needs are different, and targeting the right information to the right customer is the name of the game.

Attracting Customers

In the lightning fast world of e-business, where unprepared companies can lose customers to competitors at the click of a mouse, what's the key to attracting—and keeping—customers? The answer is not complicated. Give them a good reason to buy from you and they will keep buying from you. Take Dell Computers. Customers return again and again because Dell has figured out how to make loyalty more convenient than shopping around. A consumer tells Dell what he wants in a computer, and Dell configures a computer to his order and then remembers what he bought the next time he calls in. Dell does the same thing for the business customers, who account for the majority of its sales, making it easier for a company to reorder from Dell than to respecify its needs with a competitor.

But Dell doesn't stop there. The company's site also offers customers access to its "E-Value" program that takes customers to an online configurator where hardware can be purchased, as is or customized. It also gives specific information on each system, including the specs on the monitor, say, or the latest price. Another example is Dell's "Product Evaluation Center," which offers product information, product awards and reviews, and technical white papers.

Other companies are borrowing a page from the Dell playbook and doing new things to grab customer's attention. Things like preparing your bill any way you like it—on an Excel spreadsheet or with software your company uses. Or making information accessible to customers 24 hours a day via a secure Web site. Or guaranteeing next day delivery, offering discounts for ordering online, or providing free customer service.

As always, the idea is to keep customers coming back. The idea is to create an e-commerce model based on remembering individual customers from one visit or transaction to the next. Make it easier for a particular customer to do business with you, and you'll create a loyal, long-term customer.

Integrated Marketing

That's where an integrated marketing campaign comes in handy. An integrated marketing strategy marries the best of online and offline advertising and promotions, with an effective use of public relations and direct marketing. A company can elicit customer satisfaction through greater transaction speed and security, cost savings, incentives, and added value to products and services.

Beyond implementing the right technologies and solutions, the key that can unlock success in online retailing is a dramatic change in mind-set. The necessary marketing ingredient for an e-business is the willingness to experiment, accept failure, learn, and improve. Additionally, speed, focus, and superior execution are also vital characteristics for the Internet economy.

As e-business advances, personalized transactions that put a human touch on purchases will become more and more important with business-to-business sites automatically reminding clients when they need to restock or suggesting alternative products or services. Extending the human element, cyber-marketers will also emphasize other services such as attention to user control and personalization, simple pricing models, licensing deals that are prenegotiated and transparent to the user, secure and easy-to-understand account management and buying and check-out procedures, and an option for buyers to preview footage.

At the end of the day, the buyer has to be convinced that he or she is getting greater value. That means better selection, easier access, better pricing, using corporate discounts across multiproduct and service sites, and a guaranteed high level of service anytime, day or night.

One-to-One Marketing

E-business is a very fluid and dynamic enterprise. Although only a few years old, e-business is already changing, morphing from standalone Web sites to portal partnerships, extranets, and digital marketplaces. Pressure to cut costs, boost productivity, reduce cycle times, and improve relationships with channel partners and end users fuel such changes.

The one constant in the e-business equation is the use of technology to further your means. Cyber-marketing has only recently become practical and cost effective on a large scale because of what the computer now makes possible. Database technology allows an enterprise to track its customers and tell them apart individually. Interactive technologies—not just the World Wide Web but also call centers, sales force automation tools, and point-of-purchase systems—provide an automated connection between the customer and the business, enabling a company to receive feedback, including product and service specifications, from its individual customers. And mass customization technology permits a firm to configure its offering digitally, in effect mass-producing a product in lot sizes of one.

It's what e-business marketing experts Don Peppers and Martha Rogers, Ph.D., cofounders of the Peppers and Rogers Group, call "one-to-one" marketing. "Simply stated, one-to-one marketing involves tracking an individual customer's patronage over time, managing a continuing series of interactions with that customer, and then measuring that customer's business across different groups of products and services," write Peppers and Rogers with co-author Bob Dorf in their book *The One-to-One Field Book.* "The idea behind one-to-one marketing is that rather than sampling a 'market' of potential customers to determine what the average customer in the market needs, the one-to-one marketer focuses on one customer at a time." Peppers and Rogers's point is that by using these three types of computer technology—the database, interactivity, and mass customization—the marketer can set up a relationship that goes like this: "I know you, you're in my database. You tell me what you want, and then I'll make it for you. Next time, we'll start where we left off, and I'll make it even better."

The basis of a one-to-one relationship's advantage for an enterprise is the customer's own participation and involvement in it. When the customer actually contributes some effort or initiative and sees a corresponding action on the enterprise's part, then a true one-to-one relationship is developing, which brings us to another important point: Just because we call it one-to-one marketing doesn't mean you have to create a million product variations for a million consumers. Rather, the idea of one-to-one marketing is based on the simple notion of encouraging a customer to engage with you in a continuing one-to-one process of making your product or service better for that customer.

It is important to think through the organizational and business differences between one-to-one marketing and traditional marketing in order to fully understand the difficulty of launching a successful e-commerce initiative. While the key metric of success for a traditional marketer is market share, measured in one product category at a time, the success metric for the cyber-marketer is share of customer, measured one customer at a time. Traditional marketing can be done in a "silo" department, more or less independently of other nonmarketing functions at a firm. This can be problematic for any e-commerce program. For instance, who will "own" the business rules that determine at your Web site whether Customer A is offered a discount or a premium service? And who will you hold accountable for the sale of products from several different categories to a particular customer? For most companies planning ambitious e-commerce programs, issues like these create the biggest obstacles, while the technology poses little problem at all.

Day-to-Day E-Business Marketing

Enough of the big picture stuff. Marketing your e-business also requires you to dig in and get your hands dirty. Whether it's trying to get your site on the leading Web search engines or deciding whether to use ad banners to trumpet your business, there are a lot of day-to-day decisions to be made if you're going to maximize the visibility of your e-business Web site. Here's a laundry list of things you'll need to know as you strive to meet that goal.

Search Engines

Customers normally use Web search engines—those gateways to the meat and potatoes of the Internet that break down information and show Web users where to go—to find the stuff they're looking for. One of the most popular search sites is Yahoo, which organizes Web sites into categories. Try submitting your Web site to a leading search engine site like Yahoo. You'll find instructions on how to do this at *docs.yahoo.com/info/suggest*. It's free.

Unlike Yahoo, general Web search engines such as HotBot and AltaVista depend entirely on keywords. Search engines will eventually find your pages and add them to their indexes, but you can speed the process by submitting your home page URL to the search engine. Submit your site to AltaVista at *www.altavista.com/av/content/addurl.htm* and to HotBot at *www.hotbot.com/addurl.asp*. Most of the other major search engines have similar pages. Once you submit your page, don't

---

Search Engine Help

The first step to setting up an e-commerce site is making sure potential customers can find you. Here are the URLs you'll need for submitting your site to the major search engines. Most search engines have similar pages.

AltaVista: *www.altavista.com/av/ content/addurl.htm*
HotBot: *www.hotbot.com/addurl.asp*
Yahoo: *docs.yahoo.com/info/suggest*

expect immediate results; it can take a few weeks before it shows up in a search.

As you probably know, most queries generate dozens of pages of links. The higher up your site appears in those links, the greater the chance customers will visit your site. Here's a way to move your site up in the rankings: First, come up with a list of about a dozen phrases someone may use to find the products or services you sell. Don't forget to include popular brands, model names, and abbreviations.

For each phrase you came up with, create a page on your site with that phrase as its title. (Most search engines give a higher ranking to a page if it matches words in the title.) Make sure the new page has a link from an existing page on your site so the search engine can reach it. Also make sure the page has links to the parts of your site that provide information pertaining to that particular search.

Server log file analysis programs, such as WebTrends (*www. webtrends.com*), can tell you which search engines your visitors use most often and which keywords they used to reach your site. Your ISP may provide this or a similar tool as part of your service package. If not, you can usually get a copy of your log file from the ISP and analyze it with one of these programs. However, don't depend on this information to give you a complete picture of keyword searches. This represents only the people who used those search terms and made it to your site. You need to be just as interested in the people using other search terms who aren't getting to your site.

Specialized Shoppers

Even though many people use general search engines to shop for products, they're not very effective. Too many of the pages they find have nothing to do with buying products. Fortunately, specialized search sites for shoppers—such as Shopfind, Price Watch, PriceSearch, and bottomdollar.com—are gaining popularity. If you search for "phone" at these sites, you'll be directed to pages from stores that sell products with the word "phone" in their descriptions.

Two sites—BotSpot and SmartBots.Com—provide a list of these shopping search agents. Many sites specialize in a small set of products, such as computer equipment. Some will add your company to their listings at no charge, but you may need to do some technical coordination with their sites to make sure they obtain the correct

Search Engines for Shoppers

If you want to reach those who are ready to buy, consider a specialized search site.

Bottomdollar.com: *bottomdollar.com*
PriceSearch: *price-search.net*
Price Watch: *pricewatch.com*
Shopfind: *shopfind.com*

Want more? These sites provide listings of shopping search agents.

BotSpot: *botspot.com*
SmartBots.Com: *smartbots.com*

product information and price listings. Some sites charge a flat rate or bill you on a per-purchase or per-referral basis.

Banner Placements

Only a few years ago, banner advertising was about the only kind of advertising on the Web. And although paid placements and other promotion techniques have grown in popularity, banner ads are far from dead.

In keeping with the "get it for free" spirit of the Internet, you can do quite a bit of advertising without spending a dime. Just sign up for membership in a banner exchange program offered by companies such as MSN LinkExchange or HyperBanner. (Search Yahoo or Alta Vista for "banner exchanges" to get an extensive list.) When you join one of these programs, you agree to display banner ads from the network on your Web site. In return, the network will display your banner ads on other participating sites in the network. Typically, network members display one of your ads for every two you display on your site. Why the disparity? The banner exchange program sells the extra ad to a paying customer; it's what keeps the program free to participants.

It's a breeze to join most banner exchange programs. Just visit the Web site and submit a form to register your username and password. You may be asked about the categories your site fits into. Then you'll be given a set of HTML code to put into the pages on your site to display banners from the program. Once you put the HTML onto your pages, you'll get credit to your account each time your page is loaded. Next, create a banner ad for your own site and submit it to the network to be displayed on other sites. The banner exchange programs provide

Banner Exchange Programs

Here's a free way to get your ads on   HyperBanner: *www.hyperbanner.net*
others' sites. For more, search Yahoo   MSN LinkExchange:
for "banner exchanges."   *www.linkexchange.com*

specifications for the size and content of the ads, and many offer online banner creation.

When choosing a banner exchange program, read the agreements carefully. Some programs have specific rules about where you have to place the banners, and that may affect the design of your Web pages. Some require their service to be the only one you use on your site, so you won't be able to sign up for multiple programs. Even if you are allowed to display multiple advertising banners on your Web page, remember that advertising graphics can take time to load. Be careful not to drive your customers away by making your Web store too slow or too cluttered with advertising.

Web Advertisements

Although the Internet has opened up the buying process for many commodities, advertising isn't one of them. If you try to research the cost of ads at most sites, you'll be instructed to contact the advertising department by e-mail and ask for a quote. A few advertising networks, such as the Adsmart Network (*adsmart.net*), do provide online information about their participating sites, but it isn't enough to help you make a decision.

For paid advertising, most Web advertising banners are sold using the cost-per-thousand-impressions (CPM) rate. A CPM of $40 means you'll pay $40 for 1,000 people to see your ad banner on the top of a Web page. However, many Web sites, especially the larger ones, don't accept an ad campaign that small. You'll usually need to contact the Web site representatives for an explanation of their rates and requirements.

For a small company, the cost of a minimum ad buy for a large site can be a burden. Fortunately, there's still a way for small businesses to advertise on these sites. If you'd like to reach the audiences at Yahoo or other sites but only want to do a small campaign of $100 or so, check out the AdStore service run by LinkExchange.

Order Processing

Order processing simply means having the software or services in place to accept orders through the Internet. In most cases, as buyers browse your site they'll collect merchandise using shopping cart software. Many ISPs offer this software as part of an e-commerce package, and there are many third-party shopping cart applications you can buy. Prices range from free for simple cart-only scripts such as PerlShop or GTA NetOrderForm to $369 for a 12,000-order version of the JustAddCommerce plug-in for FrontPage sites. Many database-oriented commerce software packages have integrated shopping carts. You don't need to be concerned about security during this part of the process because the buyer hasn't provided any personal information yet.

When it's time to complete the purchase, the software sends the buyer to a page that uses the secure HTTP protocol to encrypt information that comes from the browser, such as credit card or purchase/invoice numbers. A closed padlock on the status bars of both Microsoft Internet Explorer and Netscape Navigator indicates a Web site is using the secure protocol, as does an "S" after the http in the URL ("https://...").

Next, the order goes to the Web server. Most e-commerce packages let you retrieve orders via a Web page interface. This should be done via secure HTTP as well because it includes the buyer's payment information.

Of course, you can use a service to handle most of the details. When customers are ready to check out of your store, you send them to the service bureau's secure server instead of handling it on your own site. The service bureau collects the credit card information, performs real-time authorization, and gives the customer a confirmation number. It then gives you a secure way to retrieve these approved orders, typically through a secure Web page.

The most hassle-free way to run your Internet store is to use a provider that offers the shopping card and secure transaction features to host the Web site. Some, such as Yahoo Store, sell their services directly to merchants. Others, such as Virtual Spin, sell through ISPs and other resellers. Try a variety of services before you commit to one because it's harder to move once you've set up your store. Most services make use of templates to simplify store setup. Make sure there's a template that works for your type of store.

Web Hosts

These sites manage your e-business site for you.

Virtual Spin: *www.virtualspin.com*
Yahoo Store: *store.yahoo.com*

Shopping-cart scripts and software:
PerlShop: *www.arpanet.com/PerlShop/ perlshop.html*
GTA NetOrderForm:
www.shoppingcarts.cc/

JustAddCommerce plug-in for FrontPage sites: *richmediatech.com*

Credit-card authorization/service bureau:
The Processing Network:
www.processing.net
Open Market's ShopSite:
www.openmarket.com/shopsite

Order Tracking

Once they've made a purchase, buyers want reassurance their order is being processed. Since they bought via the Internet, you should provide some way to track the order through the Internet as well. At a minimum, you should offer quick replies to e-mail inquiries about order status or requests for returns. Better yet, answer the questions before they're asked. Once you ship the order, use the package carrier's Web site to provide order information to your customers. E-mail the tracking number to the customer, along with instructions for using the carrier's online tracking feature. If possible, offer your own Web-based tracking so customers can track their orders in real time at your site.

E-Mail Services

E-mail advertising is one way to get customers to come back and shop at your site—if you use it right. Sending unsolicited e-mails, known as spamming, can turn customers off. If you do offer an e-mail newsletter, make it an opt-in program, whereby customers can consciously decide whether they want your mail. Give them a reason to want it by offering exclusive sales, specials, or promotional items.

For a small list—fewer than a hundred people—you can manage the list in-house using standard e-mail software. Beyond that, it becomes unwieldy to send out hundreds of e-mails using a standard mail client. Some ISPs offer mailing list software as part of their services, or you can purchase your own software to manage the list.

> **Mailing List Management**
>
> Keep your business in the minds of your customers via e-mail. You can manage the lists yourself using software or give the job to a list manager.
>
> Software:
> L-Soft: *www.lsoft.com*
> Lyris: *www.lyris.com*
>
> Mailing list managers:
> Biglist: *www.biglist.com*
> eGroups.com: *www.egroups.com*
> Mail-list.com: *www.mail-list.com*
> ONEList.com: *www.onelist.com*
> PostMaster General:
>   *www.postmastergeneral.com*

Another alternative is to delegate the entire chore to a mailing list management company. This being the Internet, you can find a company that will run your mailing list for as little as—you guessed it—nothing. But there's a catch. The company places ads in your mailings, and they come with the same caveats as banner exchanges. In this free service category, ONEList.com and eGroups.com offer a good selection of features for managing lists with a few hundred subscribers.

If you'd rather your lists include only your own content, but you still don't want to manage the list yourself, you can pay a company to manage your lists for you.

Using Newsgroups

Educating customers is a key tenet of good marketing. One easy and inexpensive way to do that is to offer advice related to the products or services you sell, which can translate into increased sales. Just make sure the messages you post aren't merely advertisements for your products or services. They should address the question the author poses, and mention your company only if it's applicable. Be sure to include your Web site URL in your signature.

It's just as important to participate in newsgroups for defensive reasons. Many prospective customers use services such as deja.com to research products, services, or retailers. If your company gets a bad reputation in newsgroups because of some vocal dissatisfied customers, it may scare off potential customers. The best way to deal with these types of problems is in private via e-mail, but if a disgruntled customer posts disparaging remarks, you should address them publicly. Be conciliatory, but be direct in addressing any issues raised by the customer.

It's nice to be able to leverage things like newsgroups and e-mail software to reach customers, but, in the end, remember that it's the human element that can spell the difference between retaining a good customer or not.

E-Marketing Success Stories

Grabbing customers' attention and convincing them to buy from you again and again is the goal of any e-business marketer. The trick, experts say, is to make it as convenient as possible to do so. According to e-business experts Don Peppers and Martha Rogers, these companies are at the top of the list in doing so.

- **Amazon.com**
  (*www.amazon.com*):
  According to a recent *Business Week* article, the repurchase rate of Amazon.com's customers is 64 percent, more than double that of a typical brick-and-mortar bookstore. This means that, at any given level of sales, Amazon's customer base is worth three to five times the customer base of a traditional bookstore. And Amazon has some 10 million customers all over the world. Are you an Amazon customer yourself? Why do you go back? Could it be that you've already stored your address and credit card number with them and you can obtain a book with one click of your mouse? Or is it the book recommendations Amazon makes, tailored to your own previously expressed interests? Barnesandnoble.com has the same basic book recommendation and one-click-ordering capabilities. But if you are already buying from Amazon, do you really want to go

to the trouble of reinventing your relationship with someone else?

- **American Airlines**
  (*www.aa.com*):
  The airline giant renders dynamically customized pages to accommodate more than a million registered AAdvantage members, including upward of 25 percent of the elite level Gold, Platinum, or 1K members. The site is highly customized to the individual user, including seating preferences, amenities, home airports, and other flying habits. Sign on to AA.com and your home page might contain suggestions for travel to your favorite type of leisure destination—beaches, ski resorts, historical sites, or whatever—with a special discount offer applicable during the week when your children have time off from school in the school district where you live.

- **RS Components**
  (*www.rswww.com*):
  One of Europe's largest electronic components distributors, with more than 100,000 products, RS Components used to sell its wares only in catalogs—big, thick, cumbersome catalogs. But now a customer can shop online from RSWWW.com, storing 13 months' worth of its own product purchase records and technical data sheets

(continued)

E-Marketing Success Stories *(continued)*

at the site, which can compose and save lists of the components needed for particular events, like changing up an assembly line or bringing down a big piece of machinery for maintenance. The site can also customize the authorization levels for expenditures according to the customer's corporate hierarchy.

- **1-800-FLOWERS**
  (*www.1800flowers.com*):
  1-800-FLOWERS made a name for itself early in the e-commerce arena by recognizing that one of the keys to success is providing convenience and service to its most valuable customers—those who come back again

and again to make purchases. The company provides a convenient way to store the names and addresses of those you send flowers to on a regular basis, as well as e-mail reminder services so that you never forget an important birthday or anniversary. Remembering customer-identifying information and preferences can give online florists a tremendous advantage over their offline competitors, for sure. But equally as important is that such a competitive model gives an online florist a similar advantage over any other online florist! One customer at a time, customer relationships like this create a virtually unlimited barrier to competition.

So go ahead use the great new technology tools we're seeing these days, but don't stop using the human touch. Phone calls, on-site visits, even birthday cards are still formidable weapons in the market's arsenal. After all, marketing is about building relationships, and people can do that a whole lot better than a computer can.

Marketing Automation Tools

There's a new sheriff in town in the marketing software game that's offering superior methods of tracking the results of Web advertising, e-mail campaigns, and even the administrative details of traditional ad campaigns. Called "marketing automation" applications, these software tools are built to manage electronic marketing campaigns and measure the success of those campaigns, as well as electronically organize marketing materials such as brochures and presentations so that they are readily available via the corporate intranet. Some of these marketing automation tools can even be configured to keep tabs on the competition by using intelligent agents to crawl competitors' Web sites.

Marketing automation software usually operate as front-office components, integrating with corporate Web servers, e-mail servers, and databases to collect and disperse customer data. Typically, the tools run as Unix or Microsoft Windows NT application servers, with Windows or Java running on client desktops.

By slicing and dicing the customer database, the tools automatically segment the campaign's target audience based on parameters marketing professionals select. Once the campaign is designed and executed—via either direct mail, Web banners, or e-mail—marketing folks can measure results by recording and tracking responses to the campaign. The software lets you track responses not just according to volume but also by demographics and other criteria.

Naturally, each marketing automation tool has its own strengths. Some tool suites let marketing professionals define and execute campaigns from their desktops so that IS doesn't have to write e-mail scripts for electronic campaigns (which isn't to say there aren't integration challenges, which are discussed later). Such tools use a graphical program editor to lead marketing professionals through the task of defining media channels, creating special offers and promotions, managing customer lists, and generating instruction lists for service bureaus such as printing houses.

Other new developments include new sales lead management software. Typically, leads have to be collected from a number of sources, such as corporate Web sites, trade shows, phone calls, and salespeople themselves. These leads must then be distributed to the appropriate salesperson, who in turn must follow up on them until they become sales or dead ends. With the new lead management software, sales opportunities are automatically compiled from different sources and sent directly to the appropriate salesperson, who can follow up on a lead that was generated only minutes before—all online.

Gauging ROI on Your Online Ad Campaign

To the Web marketing gurus at 3M, creating a site that fairly shouted its supremacy as the number one venue for premium multimedia was hardly a snap. In fact, directing new top-tier video camera buyers, willing to pay $7,000 for a projector, to the company's glitzy Web site left the company seeing double, DoubleClick, that is.

DoubleClick is one of a growing number of online advertising companies that are helping companies build their brands on the Internet and figure out how their Web marketing campaigns are panning out. DoubleClick's idea? To position 3M's Web ads where video camera buffs hang out and to embark on a database-building campaign that targeted prospects in a market segmentation campaign in likely venues such as the Internet, media, advertising, marketing, publishing, and training companies. In addition, targeted creative banner ads were directed at the different audiences that DoubleClick was able to locate.

Bingo, bango, bongo. In the first month of business, 3M's online ads generated 1,850 leads; 78 percent of them were qualified Web-generated leads, with over one-third of the leads categorized by 3M as "quality" leads. Best of all, the cost per qualified leads for the campaign averaged $70 per lead (versus an average of $138 for print), with a relatively low 41-cent cost-per-click to 3M.

"Any time you derive increased performance and reduced costs from a campaign like that you're doing great," says Scott Campbell, Internet services manager at 3M.

Analysts also say that the two dominant benchmarks that companies will use to track their online ad campaigns will continue to be cost per thousand viewers (CPMs) and click-through rates. Through 1999, CPMs and click rates topped the leader board in Web ad evaluation tools. The median for CPM for the first half of 1999 was $25, compared to $28 for the same period in 1998. The median click rate declined as well, falling to 1.5 percent in 1999 from 2.0 percent in 1998.

As far as costs for vendor packages used by companies to track online Web advertising campaigns, they vary depending on things like click-through rates, report clicks, sales, repeat purchases, and revenue. Straight Up! Software Inc. sets a monthly rate of $2,500 for its Internet tracking and reporting software, but that fee fluctuates on customer usage.

Other vendors set licensing fees for their Web advertising tracking software that, among other criteria, are based on issues like the number of company servers used to gather, store, and disseminate data. San Diego–based Accrue Software uses this fee method, charging $17,000 per license.

That number isn't so bad when building an in-house tracking system can cost a company anywhere between $250,000 and $500,000. "I don't think companies have any problem spending money to create and track online ads," notes Jay Friesel, vice president of sales and marketing at 24/7. "But the key continues to be keeping the competition in the dark as to how you're doing it."

This Brand Is My Brand, This Brand Is Your Brand

More brand-name newcomers than ever are getting into the online advertising act. Consider the Hard Rock Cafe. Despite the strong brand-name recognition of their offline chain, Hard Rock Cafe had never conducted an online advertising campaign until recently.

Using Excite@Home's Enliven online ad creation, maintenance, and monitoring tool, the campaign set out to increase foot traffic to Hard Rock Cafe's brick-and-mortar locations, increase site traffic to *www.hardrock.com,* and be among the first cyber-advertisers to drive offline sales.

To grab consumer interest, Hard Rock designed a trivia quiz about musical artists and rock history that allowed consumers to play directly within the banner space. After successfully answering a question, the consumer could move on to the next question or visit *www.hardrock.com.* At any point in the ad, a prominent call to action directed consumers to print a coupon redeemable for discounted Hard Rock Cafe merchandise purchased on *www.hardrock.com* or a free dessert when they visited participating Hard Rock Cafes.

The results were more than the restaurant chain hoped for. Altogether, the banner produced a 22 percent interaction rate, doubling the company's predicted rate, with nearly 11,000 coupons printed. The average number of clicks within the ad was over eight clicks per view. And site traffic on *www.hardrock.com* increased by over 10,000 hits over the ad's four-week run. "We saw the industry-wide decline in click-throughs, so we decided to jump straight into rich media so we could capitalize on its interactivity," explains Dave Watta, executive site producer, at Hard Rock Direct.

What worked with Hard Rock, Watta says, was that its younger audience was more inclined to play interactive trivia games than, say, senior citizens would. Hard Rock simply took advantage of its main consumer audiences' propensity to play online on a brand-name site they consider to have cachet.

Cracking the code on what Web ads work and the resulting return on investment (ROI) is the Holy Grail for Internet marketers, from Boston to Bombay. The sooner the better, as online advertising spending is expected to reach $9 billion annually by 2002, according to Jupiter Communications.

"I'll make you a bet," says Eric Ward, an ad industry consultant who launched one of the Web's first awareness-building services for Web sites back in 1994. "If two seafood distributors operate online stores and one undertakes these ROI activities and one does not, in several years the one that does not will be selling less seafood than the one that does."

That's one reason everybody, it seems, is getting into the act. In its inaugural AdRelevance Intelligence report, which it labeled "Web Advertising Goes Mainstream," the Seattle-based company says that it found 61 of *Advertising Age*'s top 100 "megabrands" were being promoted online during a survey period in August 1999. But not all are successful.

The AdRelevance report stated the Web Media category accounted for approximately 36 percent of online advertisers spotted. Within that category, it said, major "portal" sites were behind 44 percent of online ads. That means twice as many ads were appearing on company Web sites than on portals like Yahoo or Lycos.

Ad Sponsorship Strategies

According to the Internet Advertising Bureau, sponsorships are the second most predominant type of online advertising; and 35 percent of companies surveyed reported that the association of content with the advertiser is the main reason they have become so popular. While sponsorships cost less than traditional media campaigns, it does not seem to be a major factor in their growth. Only 12 percent of companies maintain that lower costs have affected sponsorship popularity. The ability to build brand awareness was the second most cited reason for their growing popularity.

Combining lower costs and greater brand awareness was a major goal for Bristol Myers. The company's Excedrin brand is known coast-to-coast, particularly to the mothers of young children.

Aiming to build a database of potential customers with lower costs per lead than traditional media, the company decided to create a banner ad campaign and a micro Web site that offered free samples to cyber-consumers. In a self-help operation, the company enlisted the aid of DoubleClick to teach it how to track user activity after the click and determine which click-throughs led to leads. To show that Excedrin had a sense of humor, company officials decided to launch the new ad campaign during tax season.

Excedrin didn't have to wait long for the results. The site tripled marketing managers' expectations of registered names and achieved cost-per-lead (CPL) acquisition that was 50 percent less than the traditional ad media channels the company had used before, says Peggy Kelly, vice president of advertising services at Bristol Myers. Overall, a whopping one million users saw the campaign with 15,948 click-throughs.

"I think our online campaign demonstrated the power of the Web as an efficient and cost-effective marketing tool," says Kelly. "We were able to reach a vast audience and then calculate the effectiveness of our campaign."

chapter eleven

Success Stories

E-business success stories are being written every day in ways that few thought possible only a year or two ago. Consider the case of Hong Kong–based Alvis International Enterprises. Not too long ago the company had a problem common to many manufacturers worldwide. A customer canceled a purchase order, leaving the manufacturer with 40,000 units of 35-mm cameras. With limited management resources to dedicate to solving this problem, Alvis turned to a business-to-business Web site company called Liquidation.com for a solution.

Liquidation.com today is a new Web site and service offering tailored to meeting the needs of business-to-business liquidation customers. By bringing together buyers and sellers in a professionally managed, trusted trading network, the company has developed a reputation as a dependable online resource to buy or sell a variety of surplus assets, excess inventory, and closeout merchandise. Liquidation.com's total assets featured for sale through its online marketplace topped $75 million in early 2000, based on sellers' reserve prices. Liquidation.com also says that its business-to-business marketplace currently offers buyers nearly $400 million in potential wholesale savings.

Liquidation.com designed a sales program for Alvis International Enterprises, and within a few weeks completed the sale of over $2,500 of merchandise and has received additional buyer interest and further transaction activity.

Or how about Global Exploration Corporation? The Vancouver-based diamond mining giant recently entered into a partnership agreement with an African-based diamond mining property owner, HAGA Group, to build a business-to-business Web site (*www.africaresources.com*) geared toward global jewelry wholesalers. Under the terms of the agreement, Global Exploration Corporation purchased 1,000 carats of uncut high-quality diamonds and purchased a 49 percent interest in two diamond concessions in Africa.

GEC's diamonds are now delivered to a Los Angeles company specializing in diamond cutting and polishing. The finished stones are offered exclusively on the company's Web site for sale to retailers around the world. The B2B site, the first one to offer diamonds direct from Africa to retailers via the Internet, provides photos, specifications, industry recognized professional evaluations, and appraisals to customers. In addition, the site offers multiple payment and shipping options along with a quality guarantee/return policy.

Then there's Alcatel, the largest manufacturer of telecommunications equipment in Australia. Key offerings range from telephones and PBX systems to undersea cable networks, digital mobile infrastructure, and data communications equipment.

Alcatel's new secure e-business Web site allows customers to determine the status of orders, contact appropriate personnel, and research catalog information via the Internet. By offering this "self-service" capability, Alcatel eliminated the back-and-forth faxing and telephone calls that used to be required to answer customer inquiries. Alcatel has seen a 90 percent improvement in response time, going from hours to minutes, and sales, marketing, and other departments have been freed up to focus on more value-added activities. Both Alcatel and its customers benefit from a consistent view of the same data. And the around-the-clock availability of the e-business solution benefits customers outside Australia who cannot always call during Sydney's office hours.

Alcatel also established an order status inquiry system that allows customers to quickly and easily investigate order information over the Internet. Because the system is securely linked with applications on Alcatel's IBM S/390 enterprise server, the foundation is in place for future enhancements that will help reduce customer inventory requirements and lead to "open-book" relationships.

More Success Stories

E-businesses that succeed usually do so by applying a blend of business and technology strategies to their Web commerce sites. Here's the result of some of the more successful efforts we're seeing on the e-business landscape.

- FedEx saves $20 million annually by providing customer service, including package tracking information and shipping management, via the Web. By making it easy for companies to place their catalogs online—and ship the resulting electronic orders via FedEx—the company has combined electronic commerce and shipping to become the fulfillment leader for the Internet economy.
- Ford Motor Co.'s worldwide corporate intranet enables product design and engineering teams to collaborate around the world and around the clock. Sharing information this way has reduced the company's new product development time from three years to two. Ford also uses Internet technology to manage products from 60,000 suppliers and to interact with its 15,000 dealers.
- Charles Schwab leads the electronic trading industry with 1.3 million active online accounts—a 33 percent share of this brand-new market focused on low cost, convenience, and ease of access. Electronic trading represents almost 40 percent of Schwab's trades, and the company expects, with this capability, to capture as many new accounts over the coming year as it did over the past thirteen.

Rewriting the Rule Book

What's up with these companies, anyway? With e-business, visionary companies like the ones listed here are using the Internet to cost-effectively apply the benefits of computing to all facets of their business. They're using the Internet as a global network that provides a standard means of efficiently connecting with not only every employee but also with end customers, partners, suppliers, vendors, and channel partners. In this context, employee intranets streamline internal processes such as communications, planning, program management, and training. Extranets allow trusted suppliers, vendors, and customers to become part of a company's information system's inner circle.

Technology-wise, these success stories are happening now because of the maturity of e-business building blocks. Powerful PCs are easy to buy and install. The Internet has made what used to be expensive electronic connections between businesses and buyers practically free, while providing the standards needed to make communications with anyone, anywhere, easy and individualized. The price-to-performance ratio of Web servers continues to rise, and standard high-volume

(SHV) server platforms based on cost-effective technology make it easy even for small businesses to interconnect their employees as well as connect to other businesses and consumers via the Internet.

In addition, the broad distribution of low-priced browser technology has enabled both an appealing application environment and widespread access to critical systems. Today's advanced browsers provide robust infrastructure for e-business client applications. Many of the Web-enabled software applications needed to put e-business solutions together are available off the shelf. Newer browsers and tools will provide key infrastructure (push, multimedia, application sharing, integrated full multimedia support, networked application sharing, video conferencing) for building next-generation e-business applications. In addition, N-tiered software architecture and component software technologies allow companies to easily integrate new e-business solutions into legacy back-end systems, enabling broader access to critical data. Also, Intel Pentium II and III processor-based systems have brought users the performance needed to run this new class of applications.

The Cisco System

How are e-businesses leveraging this new era in network computing that's upon us? Quite simply, actually. Recognizing that the Internet is fundamentally changing customer value propositions, product cycle times, industry service and fulfillment models, and cost structures, visionary companies—seizing the opportunities now available—are making the transition into what Cisco Systems calls "global e-business."

Cisco has put its money where its mouth is with its own corporate e-business site (*www.cisco.com/ibsolutions/se-com*). Cisco now receives more than 50 percent of its product orders via the Internet—more than $20 million in business a day. Cisco has also improved customer satisfaction by 25 percent while reducing the use of customer service engineers and lowered its cost of doing business more than $560 million per year—while growing at an annual rate of 400 percent for the past five years.

"Since we went live with our e-commerce system, the business that comes over the Internet went from 2 percent to 80 percent of our $12 billion revenue," says Peter Solvik, CIO at Cisco. "It's grown about 300 percent."

Much of the company's Web business to date has been from about 30 large customers that have direct access to Cisco's networks through a server at the customer site. But Cisco is looking to expand that with a new multitier distribution channel that's accessible via the Web. Under this scenario, if a reseller wants a Cisco product, it can go to a Web site and choose the product. The reseller then uses Extensible Markup Language, an e-commerce application development language, to go to various distributors who present offers. From there, the reseller can select whichever distributor it wants to use.

Employee Options

Cisco believes that its e-business site can't succeed unless all its employees are on the same page. To train employees in the use of new products or in new areas of expertise, for example, most courses require them to travel out of town for a week at a time. But Cisco has a program in place to let employees take training courses when and where they want to. If, for example, an employee wanted to take a course Cisco offered, that person would make a request over the company intranet, and the corresponding training module for that course would be transmitted overnight when network traffic would be least affected. Course information and employee data are automatically fed into the human resources database. This allows Cisco to keep track of which employees have particular skills.

With just-in-time electronic learning, employees can take courses a few hours at a time, when they need them. Not only does this help reduce travel costs for the company, it improves employee retention. That's a critical need considering today's IT skills shortage.

Although keeping employees happy is important, keeping customers happy is another top concern, one that is well served by Cisco's online efforts. Cisco is providing about 80 percent of its customer service over the Internet. Customer connections are provided through a private extranet to ensure security. The company is also working to offer more direct connections for its customers, although nothing is ready to be tested.

No Big Secret

The reason Cisco and other companies have been able to streamline business so successfully is twofold: they are using technology in a way that's aligned with their business needs, and they established a technology foundation that allows them to easily build iterative applications.

That means examining your business as a whole, including internal interactions and interactions with prospects, partners, customers, and suppliers. Think about the kinds of collaboration, communication, and transactions that could be done differently, and consider whether you have the technology and network infrastructure necessary to make that happen.

At Cisco, cross-functional teams abound. These teams, with constituents from different divisions and even different enterprises, include representatives from both the technology side and the business side of the organization. Over time, the team members begin to assimilate one another's skills, and it becomes easier to align technology efforts to business goals.

The Technical Side

In technical terms, Cisco's global e-business is an organization whose open network infrastructure and standards-based technologies facilitate communication, collaboration, and the sharing of knowledge with prospects, customers, employees, partners, and suppliers.

The tools and technologies of the Internet revolution—a common foundation, standards-based tools, platform-independent browsers, and network-facilitated communication and collaboration—made it possible for Cisco to build a global e-business.

The company used a two-pronged IT approach to building its e-business. Networked applications address the business goals, offering a discreet set of functions accessed via the network for authorized users such as employees, customers, suppliers, or partners. Cisco also used enabling technologies—the set of tools and technologies that facilitates the building of other processes and applications.

Such a "prerequisite system" combination produced a seamless network of structured data and business logic, sometimes wrapped in an application, that exposed information as requested or directed. Here's what Cisco's e-business included:

- Networked Applications Account Planning
- Customer Profile Management

- Human Resources Management
- Internal IT Services
- Business Operations Management Training
- Corporate Communications
- Commerce
- Demand Management
- Legacy Data Transformation
- Work/Document Management
- Knowledge Tools and Order Information
- Product Information
- Call Tracking
- Customer Information

What Cisco Is Doing with Its E-Business

Over the last several years, Cisco has developed a variety of network-based, self-service applications that have enabled it to interact more effectively with its prospects, customers, suppliers, partners, and employees. The use of customer service, commerce, supplier, marketing and internal applications, running over or connected to a corporate intranet, has allowed Cisco to sustain high growth, assimilate numerous acquisitions, and control costs—all while improving customer satisfaction and gaining market share.

With the Cisco e-business site, customers submit support requests and find answers to frequently asked questions within seconds. In addition, they can download software updates and diagnostic tools, get help in an electronic forum, communicate electronically with support staff, and register to receive automatic notification of software bugs and updates.

Cisco has also been able to grow its business and improve the quality of technical support while reducing support costs and increasing customer satisfaction. With immediate access to a variety of support information and tools, customers can choose what they need. Customer support representatives can focus more time on the most challenging problems.

By not having to hire and train engineers to provide technical support, Cisco saves $75 million annually. Providing the same access for nontechnical support saves $8 million. Electronic commerce customers can use Internet applications to price, configure, validate, and order products. They can also use the Net to get copies of invoices, review shipping schedules, and receive notifications of shipments or changes. The applications are linked to centralized internal systems that share new product information and engineering change orders with various satellite applications to coordinate the entire supply chain.

Cisco has been able to lower the overall cost of taking orders and also reduce errors in product configuration and ordering, thus reducing the expenses as well as the customer frustrations associated with product returns caused by configuration errors. Cisco customers report that their own purchasing productivity has increased because they have 24-hour access to an easy-to-use, self-service system.

By automatically trapping errors at the configuration stage, Cisco has reduced, from 15 percent to 2 percent, the orders that require reworking. With the increased accuracy in ordering, product delivery lead times have been reduced by 2 to 5 days. And Cisco's sales personnel, now freed from most order-related administrative tasks, can concentrate on proactive account management. Distribution software, including upgrades and beta versions of new releases, are available via Cisco's Web site. A feedback form encourages comments from users. Cisco saves the cost of software distribution, and customers have immediate access to new versions and upgrades. Cisco also gets valuable customer feedback on prereleased software.

By distributing 90 percent of its software electronically, Cisco saves $250 million annually in production and shipping costs. Employees file expense reports electronically, using a networked application that is linked to internal finance and human resource systems, and to American Express. The application checks submissions immediately, flagging policy violations and paying approved expenses within four days. Cisco pays American Express directly, on the employees' behalf, for AmEx charges assigned to the expense reports. Only exceptions are handled outside the automatic system. Cisco reduces the cost of managing expense reports. Employee satisfaction is higher because of the fast turnaround, and employee productivity is higher because expense reporting now takes less time. And, because fewer reports are late, Cisco can track expenses more closely.

By using this networked system that requires only two auditors for more than 12,000 employees, Cisco saves the cost of the ten additional people typically dedicated to auditing expense reports in a company of its size. Cisco's electronic commerce application automatically notifies suppliers when incoming orders deviate from forecasts. Cisco has been able to increase responsiveness to customer requests while lowering inventory costs and reducing product delivery lead times. Cisco has also been able to improve its inventory tracking and to respond more quickly to component shortages by transferring inventory between suppliers.

By increasing responsiveness to customers, Cisco has been able to increase revenue capture by $100 million annually. By integrating suppliers earlier in the ordering process, the company has reduced lead times from an average of 40 days to 7 to 21 days. In total, Cisco's supply chain initiatives save over $70 million annually.

Putting E-Business Policies into Action

Many companies are following the Cisco blueprint. In doing so, they're trying to anticipate customer needs in the nascent world of e-business, rather than react to it.

That's what happened with Pacific Gas and Electric Company (PG&E), one of the nation's largest utility companies. With a goal of improving product search and selection processes with its suppliers, PG&E implemented in 1997 a new real-time electronic procurement Web package linked to a multi-supplier catalog.

Linking PG&E directly to its suppliers in realtime allows PG&E's requisitioners and purchasers to select products easily and quickly from contracted suppliers and compare offerings. The electronic procurement infrastructure and knowledge base also acted as a jumping-off point for the deployment of an enterprise-wide electronic commerce solution that the company built in 1998.

Computer technology reseller Mushkin, Inc. tells a similar story. The company is a virtual shop only, with no retail locations. Hosting its e-business site on Intel Pentium Pro processor-based servers, Mushkin started off with a Web page and an online catalog, but orders came via telephone and fax. Mushkin evaluated e-commerce solutions through the computer industry press, with a special interest in store-front creation software, to determine the most cost-effective method to develop an online solution with the features necessary to create a long-term strategy for the Internet.

The company's solution? To build its own virtual storefront. Mushkin, Inc. did all the work themselves, with the exception of some graphic design efforts and HTML coding, which they outsourced. Mushkin is able to take care of all hardware support in-house but relies on companies like Intel for software support. Now through its e-business site, Mushkin takes orders 24 hours a day. Their Web page contains detailed product information and news of special promotions. Traffic initially averaged 1,200 hits a week; today it is a whopping 1,000 visitors a day. Mushkin, Inc. estimates that growth due to the e-commerce aspect of their site has contributed to an increase in revenues in the latter part of 1996 by 500 percent. They project an additional 150 percent increase in the current year.

Companies like PG&E and Mushkin, Inc. get e-business. They understand that e-business means making buyers come to businesses. They're intelligently seeking out buyers based on profiles buyers post on the Internet, potentially a more effective process. The concept of mass customization is also maturing. Businesses are now customizing

---

Things to Consider in Building Your E-Business

Today's use of Internet technologies has created opportunities for innovation and increased efficiencies in the implementation of network-based business solutions. Technology standardization, from networks to applications, has reduced complexity resulting in shorter development time while reducing variable costs. Once foundation technologies are in place, the cost of incremental applications is low compared to previous proprietary systems, and ROI is high. So companies that develop the necessary infrastructure will quickly be able to use their networks competitively for communicating, collaborating, and transacting business.

The following business functions are good candidates for a potential global networked business to address:

- Customer service—Call-center management, customer self-service, diagnostics, and trouble ticket reporting
- Sales—Customer relationship management, product information, configuration, pricing, ordering, scheduling, order status, invoicing, and field-product training
- Marketing—Publication and distribution of product and company information, event registration, and delivery of training
- Engineering/Manufacturing—Legacy system integration with engineering and bill-of-material systems, engineering documentation, product documentation, and product design collaboration
- Human resources—Insurance enrollment, benefits enrollment, employee requisitions, training registration, distance learning, and expense reporting

each individual's experience on their online sites, notifying customers when new products in their favorite categories arrive, and responding to buyers' advertisements, rather than vice versa, to make a sale.

E-business customers also stand to gain by putting technology to work in order to locate the best products and services. Online services and the spread of intelligent agents (information-gathering software programs) are allowing consumers to comparative shop among hundreds of suppliers to find the best value, often directly from the original manufacturer. Many firms grant discounts to customers who order online rather than over the telephone or through a physical outlet. New consumer services are available from leisure agencies and information retrieval services as the Internet allows small businesses to personalize their service options for consumers.

Building Partnerships

Many of these companies aren't doing it all alone. Industry consortiums and partnerships are popping up all over the place that give customers one-stop online shopping.

Take e-Chemicals, the chemical industry's first online store. For large chemical manufacturers in the $250 billion U.S. chemical industry, 20 percent of the customers typically generate 80 percent of the revenue. The rest of the customers buy in smaller volumes, so manufacturers have found it difficult to serve them cost-effectively.

But no longer, because e-Chemicals is bringing the efficiencies of business-to-business e-commerce to the chemical industry through the Web's first online chemical store.

Bringing aboard leading manufacturers, including DuPont and Elf Atochem, www.e-chemicals.com has an inventory of several hundred chemical products, which it supplies to its customers at up to a 20 percent savings compared to traditional wholesale channels. Developed with an e-business solution from IBM, the Web site averages 7,000 hits each week and that number is growing rapidly.

Several hundred businesses have already registered as customers with the online store. For chemical manufacturers, e-Chemicals presents a cost-effective means to broaden their market base. "Most customers buy in small volumes, so one of the toughest challenges for chemical manufacturers is finding the least expensive means to reach markets of all sizes," says one consortium executive. "Because we are such a streamlined business, e-Chemicals is the perfect way to do it."

E-Chemicals has tailored its Web site to the unique requirements of the chemicals market, providing a shopping cart, an easy-to-search electronic catalog, as well as facilities to view order histories and track order status. A software suite that supports industry-standard, 128-bit Secure Sockets Layer (SSL) encryption, provides security for purchases.

When a customer submits an order, it is transmitted through electronic data interchange (EDI) to SunTrust for credit authorization. Once validated, the order is routed to the nearest manufacturer and an advance shipping notice is sent to Yellow Freight, e-Chemical's shipping partner.

The system's database stores the product catalog, giving e-Chemicals the flexibility and scalability needed to further customize its online store. For example, because chemical pricing is in decimals, not dollars and cents, a relational database that allows such field changes is essential. E-Chemicals can also easily keep its online product catalog current. E-Chemicals also recently deployed a Lotus Notes tool that chemical manufacturers will use to update shipping lead times and prices from a secure page on the e-Chemicals Web site.

E-Chemicals now has several thousand customers choosing from among 1,000 products produced by 100 manufacturers. Currently, the company is getting a glimpse of customer browsing and buying habits using some new business intelligence software.

Consolidating Procurement

In the business world, it often takes a multitude of companies to manufacture and distribute just about any product: suppliers of parts, servicers of equipment, the manufacturer and distributors, to name just a few.

General Electric's Lighting division is no stranger to the partnerships that lead to successful manufacturing. Production lines in the Cleveland-based light-bulb manufacturer's 26 assembly plants run 24 hours a day as machines such as those that shape glass and stamp metal crank out hundreds of different light bulb models. If a single part in any one of those machines fails, it can mean lights out for the entire assembly line. The company used to deal with the problem the old way, placing special rush orders with machine-tool suppliers when part failures shut down production. But today, GE Lighting is viewing the problem in a whole new light: It is using the Internet to create close alliances with its business partners and thereby keep its operations from burning out.

For many industries, tight supply chain integration with other businesses is no longer a competitive advantage—it's a competitive imperative. It used to be Company X competing with Company Y. Now it's supply chains competing with supply chains.

Today, electronic commerce (EC) can be the means to end-to-end supply chain management. Using the Internet as a universal networking standard, business partners can create seamless, automated supply chain systems that function as smoothly as if the organizations operated as one entity. That creates faster order processing, improved inventory tracking and management, more accurate order fulfillment, support for just-in-time manufacturing, and improved customer service.

At GE Lighting, for instance, electronic commerce was the key to creating a streamlined procurement system that is integrated with the firm's 55 machine parts suppliers. Until recently, the requisitioning process from the plants was initiated electronically via the existing purchasing system. The purchasing agents would review daily requests and initiate the price quoting process. The engineering drawings of the part and an electronic quote form were requested, and the packages were prepared. Simply fulfilling a request for quotation could take several days, and the division typically issued 100 to 150 such requests a week. The company then mailed the completed requests to suppliers. In fact, some people in the machine parts unit were basically just stuffing envelopes all day. In all, GE Lighting's procurement process used to take as long as 22 days.

Today, however, GE Lighting is transforming that time-consuming process into a streamlined one that takes about eight days. How? It started using the Trading Partners Network (TPN), an extranet developed by sister division GE Information Services (GEIS), a Rockville, Maryland–based provider of electronic commerce services. By integrating TPN into its legacy procurement system, GE Lighting gained the ability to let suppliers view the requests on the extranet shortly after buyers in the worldwide sourcing division post them. Suppliers can then post blind bids using TPN.

Here's how it works. Plant personnel request parts using an IBM mainframe ordering system. Once a day, those requisitions are extracted in a batch process that automatically matches them with the corresponding drawings stored on an optical jukebox. A Unix system interfaces with the mainframe and the jukebox to match TIFF drawings with codes for the parts, and Autoload, a Windows-based desktop tool, automatically posts the request on the network. Suppliers enter bids on TPN forms from their Netscape browsers, usually within seven days of the request's posting.

For several years before the advent of TPN, GE Lighting could receive bids from suppliers on the GEIS network. Because TPN is an Internet solution, now suppliers need only have a Web browser, which opens up the process to new suppliers. For example, GE Lighting recently received a bid from a Hungarian company that underbid the competition by 20 percent. In years past, the Hungarian company wouldn't have had access to GE's order and therefore wouldn't have had the opportunity to make a bid.

GE Lighting's project to integrate procurement systems with TPN took six IS people about three months to complete. Though IS had to do some C coding, the most challenging part of the project was coordinating the new process because so many people—buyers, engineers, and suppliers—needed to give their input. Working with suppliers to make sure they were comfortable with the TPN interface prototype was a key success factor. GE Lighting had close relationships with suppliers before, but with the network, those alliances have become even stronger. For example, it is not unheard of for the GEIS technicians to drive through snowstorms to reload Windows on a supplier's TPN PC just to get the supplier back online so it can make bids.

By using TPN, several General Electric divisions, including GE Lighting, have, on average, cut procurement cycles in half, reduced procurement processing costs by 30 percent, and induced suppliers to reduce prices due to online bidding.

Winning the Sales War

Forward-thinking e-business are also using their Web sites to change their corporate cultures—for the better.

At airplane parts supplier Aviall Corporation, sales staffers have been transformed from product brokers to ambassadors of e-commerce and customer care. That's because Aviall developed a Web-based self-service order and distribution center that lets customers handle routine questions themselves. That doesn't take business away from the remote sales force; it frees them from having to handle some of the mundane tasks.

The company's strategy? If it could get the small brokers and customers to use the Internet, salespeople will still get their commissions and then focus on what they do best—customer service. The company was right on target. Two weeks after it launched, the site did so much business that Aviall officials forecasted that the company's online sales would top $10 million for the year. In addition to an impressive sales volume, Aviall expects to save $250,000 yearly by having customers obtain quotes online.

While the sales department saw the e-business site as a threat to their livelihoods, company managers were successful in convincing them that the benefits of selling over the Web are too great and that the company couldn't be successful without buy-in from the sales force. Aviall educated the sales force in the ways Web marketing could boost the company's revenue stream, help it expand into new markets, solidify existing customer relationships, and expand ties with business partners.

Of course, selling salespeople on a new idea is easier said than done. Salespeople may be far-flung and rarely seen at the home office—or even in the remote offices—since many are mobile as well. Still, they are often the enterprise's closest link to customers, presenting the first and often the only face a customer knows.

Like other companies, Aviall found that IT had to be more involved in the development and support of the sales force if the company was to truly get a solid ROI from its foray into the Internet business. One Aviall manager says her experience has taught her that CIOs and upper IT management should take on a significant role to ensure that technology supports and encourages the changing sales force. "It's our responsibility to sell the technology; it's not the job of the director of sales. We had to work together to show [sales] the benefit of technology to the customer," she said.

The company also made a concerted effort to walk the sales staff through the basics of business-to-business e-commerce and the projections on sales from such transactions. Aviall also schooled the sales force in spotting new opportunities for the company. The company showed them that e-commerce is more than just selling parts over the Internet.

Aviall also challenged its sales reps to look for ways to leverage the company's huge IT investment. Two possibilities came out: Aviall could help customers trace airline parts or add bar codes to products.

Ultimately, sales reps stopped worrying about losing business and began looking for ways that Aviall could help customers with their problems.

The Bottom Line

What do all of these successful e-businesses have in common? They understand that if you can't do business online, the customer doesn't want to do business with you at all.

"People are telling us they don't want to fax us anymore, and they don't want to call us anymore," says one manufacturing executive. "Consequently, we saw the light and began singing the same tune. Now, we only want to do business with someone we can deal with electronically."

If that recurring mind-set doesn't spur you into action, what will?

chapter twelve

Vendor Magic: The Top E-Business Players

L ooking for the right e-business vendor is like shopping for a new car. Like auto dealers, a lot of e-business vendors will promise things they may not be able to deliver. And if you're not careful, you'll discover that some vendors will nickel and dime you to death by adding costs that far exceed the sticker price. By and large though, you can get a square deal from most e-business vendors if you know what you're doing, specifically, if you know what you're looking for.

The primary characteristics of a good e-business vendor are honesty and a good track record. Beyond that, your e-business vendor should demonstrate solid technology functionality, a sterling ability to execute, and a shared vision of where your e-business is going.

Unfortunately, vendor evaluation in the e-business market takes place in an atmosphere filled with vendor hype, unrealistic expectations, and internal political agendas. To thwart these and other barriers, it's a good idea to adopt a best-practices approach to vendor selection, using a statistically valid vendor evaluation process and a best-of-breed selection methodology, ensuring that the user organization's needs are appropriately matched with the vendor of choice.

Choosing Wisely

Unfortunately, developing good business practices isn't easy. As Reed Cundiff, research director of Decision Drivers, Inc., says, many organizations do not have a formal process for vendor selection. "In many cases," writes Cundiff in his white paper *Choosing the Right E-Business Vendor* that was recently released by the Gartner Group, "the final vendor selected is at best a coin flip, adding significant risk that the product will not meet IS, management, or end-user requirements. Most often, the net result is a tactical purchase that merely delays another acquisition due to inevitable vendor financial difficulties, service and support problems, or differences in corporate/ product vision that were unaccounted for during the product evaluation process."

In the report, Cundiff identifies four major stumbling blocks to successful vendor selection:

Time: IS routinely reports that the selection process can consume the time and resources of up to 20 employees for up to 12 months, with much of the effort spent identifying the key evaluation criteria and collecting data on the alternatives.

Cost: Though the cost of making a decision is largely hidden, it can account for as much as 30 percent of the acquisition cost. Costs associated with making the decision include criteria definitions, RFP development and distribution, data gathering, data validation, vendor interviews, travel, and people time.

Objective data: Clients reported that they lacked objective, validated data on vendor products and services, and are often forced to rely solely upon vendor RFP responses, presentations, or marketing materials to make their final decision.

Lack of a structured process: Many clients, lacking a rigorous selection methodology, either focus on a very limited set of criteria (often 8 to 10 total) or cave to internal political agendas, rules of thumb, or gut feelings.

Cundiff also points out that the most successful organizations have implemented a best practice vendor evaluation methodology that incorporates five primary criteria: functionality, cost, service and support, ability to execute, and vision. Typically, IS focuses more than 90 percent of its attention within the tactical criteria of functionality and cost; however, a best practice approach suggests that IS should also incorporate the strategic criteria of ability to execute and vision, as well as the intermediate criteria of vendor service and support.

Functionality: What critical features separate the contenders from the pretenders? This is usually the primary (and often exclusive) focus of IS's evaluation, but best practices suggest it should ideally represent less than one-third of the total decision importance. Criteria should be decomposed in a "family tree" structure into their component pieces, down to a feature-function level of detail. In this example, we outline the critical areas for evaluation for developing a Web-commerce server focused on "front-end" merchandising.

Criteria include:

- Product Content—What capabilities does the product have to ensure that organizations can view and maintain catalog information on our goods and services? They should include tools to present content electronically, configurators to easily target different vertical and geographic markets, and the ability to incorporate new media formats.
- Product Pricing—Must have functionality such as complex pricing capabilities, administration tools to enable automation of pricing functions, and promotional and bundling capabilities.
- Customer Outlining—Can I interface with my customers' e-commerce applications? Can my customers maintain their own profiles? Is my outlining information secure?
- Shopping Cart—Can my customers add, delete, and edit items from their shopping list at any time in the session? Is security available at all levels of communication?

Cost: What is the total cost of the product? Initial cost is almost always (incorrectly) one of the most heavily weighted evaluation criteria in the service desk application selection process. Cundiff's research has shown that the initial cost often accounts for less than 25 percent of the total life cycle cost of a given technology, with the great majority of the cost hidden within product training and customization. Our research suggests that the cost discussion should be expanded to include not only initial product license costs, but also knowledge tool license costs, installation and maintenance costs, help desk gateway costs, ongoing education and training, and professional services such as customization and integration.

Vendor vision: Where is the puck going, and which vendors will skate to it successfully? The strategic nature of the electronic business decision calls for a strenuous examination of the vendor's stated and realized development plans. In a generic sense, "vision" has four components:

1. Does the vendor have a vision or a strategic plan?
2. Is this vision in line with industry and sector trends?
3. Does this vision map to the strategic direction of your IS organization?
4. What is the target audience of the vendor's vision?

With those four overall factors in mind, IS should decompose vendor vision into five key components:

1. Technology Vision—How will the vendor incorporate and utilize new and emerging technologies into its product architecture?
2. Functionality Vision—How will the vendor evolve its current product and add to or enhance its current functionality?
3. Support Vision—What is the vendor's strategy to evolve its general and professional services support?
4. Financial Vision—How will the vendor fund its vision?
5. Sales Vision—What is the vendor's channel and alliance strategy?

Service and support: How does the vendor treat you once they have your wallet? Service and support should examine two core components:

1. Quality of General Support—This should include criteria such as the vendors' product installation capabilities, its ongoing product support, vendor service availability, geographic availability, and quality and timeliness of help desk service.
2. Quality of Professional Services—According to client surveys, this criterion consistently scores among the top three client requirements and represents a weak spot for many vendors. Organizations should evaluate providers for project management, systems integration, and business consulting skills, and aggressively demand references that closely match both its industry focus and project scope.

Ability to execute: Where is the vendor going—to the morgue, altar, or nirvana? Given the fragmented state of the market and the strategic importance electronic commerce has in an organization, the financial well-being of a potential partner cannot be emphasized enough and is often the single most important criterion in an evaluation. This criterion is especially critical given that Cundiff believes that the maturation and intense competitive nature of the electronic commerce market will reduce the number of vendors by more than 40 percent by the year 2000. One needs to determine with relative certainty whether potential suitors are traveling on the road that will lead them to the morgue, the altar, or nirvana.

Criteria for ability to execute include:

1. Financial Viability—This should stress the use of both qualitative analysis and traditional Wall Street metrics to examine the vendor's financial viability in both absolute and relative terms. Differentiating metrics could include: revenues, growth, margins, sales and marketing investment, quick ratio, and so on.

2. Technical Execution—This section should stress metrics that reveal the relative quality of vendor personnel within key departments (sales, development) and their ability to meet industry milestones. Is there a history of timely completions? What historically has been the difference between what was promised and what was delivered? How do vendor R&D capabilities compare to those of other players? Is there a trend of high turnover among talented people?

Selection Methodology

After the appropriate criteria and structure have been created for an evaluation, organizations must have an effective selection methodology to walk them through each step in the selection process. Cundiff has outlined three major phases in the selection process: internal needs assessment, vendor evaluation, and negotiation/ultimate selection.

Phase One: Internal Needs Assessment

Internal needs assessment involves project-scope definition, internal requirements gathering, market research, and analysis, and culminates with the issuance of an RFP to the appropriate vendors.

Good Traits

How easily a company slips into an e-business strategy—and how well it handles the myriad changes e-business brings about—depends on a number of factors. According to the Extraprise Group, companies that succeed in e-business share a few common traits: They support or rearchitect internal business processes, have a measurable business objective, have top-level management committed to the program, and make a long-term investment in operations. They also integrate the initiative with existing sales and customer support programs.

Steps included in Phase One include needs identification, requirements definition, long-list creation, RFP issuance, and holding a bidder conference.

Phase Two: Vendor Analysis

In this phase, the needs determined in Phase One are mapped to the capabilities of the vendors. Ultimately, this phase results in a short list of appropriate vendors. Typically, two or three vendors are asked to move into the final phase of negotiation and selection.

Steps included in Phase Two include RFP validation, vendor comparison, short-list creation, scripted scenario creation and presentation, and group review of demonstration results.

Phase Three: Negotiation and Selection

In the final phase, the selection team prepares their negotiating strategy, develops critical terms and conditions for the contract, and negotiates with the vendors.

Steps included in Phase Three include strategy development for negotiation, navigating through rounds of negotiation, group review of options, documentation creation, presentation to management, and creation of final terms and conditions.

"An effective selection methodology ensures that the project team outlines appropriate evaluation criteria, gathers the most objective industry data possible, and evaluates that information in a structured format," concludes Cundiff. "Often, even more importantly, it facilitates a well-documented process, and allows the project team to properly enunciate exactly how and why they selected the vendor of choice. Organizations can standardize on a best-practices selection process to ensure that they work with the optimal strategic partners to make their electronic commerce vision a profitable, secure reality."

The Top Players

So who are the best strategic partners out there? Who can give your e-business a "profitable, secure reality"?

There are literally hundreds of e-business providers who claim they can, but not all do. Every vendor has its own vision, its own way of handling e-business development.

"You need a partner, not just a software vendor," said Pete Hitchen, senior Internet analyst at the research company IDC. "You need a partner who'll keep pace with the trends. You just can't buy brand-name software. You have to buy from someone who knows your industry."

That could mean big brand names like Microsoft, Hewlett-Packard, or IBM. Or it could mean an IT shop that you've have never heard of before, such as BroadVision, InterWorld, Open Market, InterShop, Sterling Commerce, or Ariba.

To get a better perspective on who these companies are and what services they can provide you, here is a quick overview of IDC's most popular e-commerce servers, using information taken from each vendor's respective Web site.

Oracle

URL: *www.oracle.com*

Server types: B2B, B2C

Key markets: Automotive, aviation, defense, communications, oil industry, financial, health, pharmaceuticals, public service, utilities

Summary: Provides end-to-end e-commerce enablement of its business applications, which, it says, transforms administrative processes into

E-Business Backlash?

Nearly two-thirds (61 percent) of the 250 IT executives surveyed by InformationWeek Research say e-business has prompted the re-engineering of the IT department. And 59 percent say business processes and functions had to be re-engineered. Most affected were technological skill requirements, employee training, and cross-functional job descriptions. But employee turnover and job satisfaction also changed as a result of e-business implementation.

self-service kiosks, exposes internal information to external stakeholders, and turns transactions into business intelligence. Also has a strong emphasis on customer relationship management, encompassing the centralized tracking of all interactions between a company and its clients.

Ariba
URL: *www.ariba.com*
Server type: B2B
Key markets: Consumer, oil industry, telecoms, public service, high-tech, financial, transport
Summary: Operations resource management is the buzzword Ariba uses to introduce the benefits of business-to-business e-commerce. It says paper-based processes are costly, time-consuming, and complex. The Ariba solution is to connect buyers and sellers through their operations resource management system to a standards-based online market. In this way buyers can be quickly united with sellers on a common IT platform.

InterShop
URL: *www.intershop.com*
Server type: B2C
Key markets: E-commerce solution providers
Summary: Sells three levels of e-commerce servers for "commerce service providers" (CSPs), which sell Web hosting services to companies wanting a commerce site without the pain of building it. A basic e-commerce site can be created by end-users with their e-page product, a "shared server" site with their "hosting" system and a dedicated server with their Merchant product.

BroadVision
URL: *www.broadvision.com*
Server type: B2B
Key markets: Retail, distribution, technology, manufacturing, finance, telecommunications, travel
Summary: Has a one-to-one concept of personalizing the experience for users using built-in rule-based management features. These are designed to reflect business workflows, such as contract fulfillment, and are claimed to be easily modifiable by managers with no programming expertise.

InterWorld

URL: *www.interworld.com*

Server type: B2C

Key markets: Manufacturing, retailing, and distribution

Summary: Pitches itself at high-end, global 2000 companies wishing to establish the Internet as a strategic channel for their products. A flexible architecture allows their commerce exchange to run in conjunction with a variety of databases, Web servers, and operating systems. The system is based on their process application server, which integrates business workflows and various IT systems.

Open Market

URL: *www.openmarket.com*

Server type: B2C

Key markets: Internet commerce service providers, individual corporations

Summary: Has three e-commerce server products. Transact handles the business issues of online customer authorization, order taking and tracking, tax and customer service functions. LiveCommerce is a standalone online cataloging system that integrates with Transact, and ShopSite is a merchant hosting server that can be used to sell e-commerce services feature by feature.

Sterling Commerce

URL: *www.sterlingcommerce.com*

Server types: B2B, B2C

Key markets: Banking, automotive, retail, health

Summary: COMMERCE and GENTRAN suites consist of a highly compatible S/MIME and traditional electronic document interchange messaging systems, which also can use XML for interorganization communications. The suites also have Web forms and Web data exchange components to securely link casual e-commerce and non-e-commerce-enabled users into the system. Sterling solutions are designed to integrate well into ERP systems from other vendors.

Netscape

URL: *www.netscape.com*

Server types: B2B, B2C

Key markets: Companies committed to generic open-standards systems

Summary: CommerceXpert suite revolves around its ECXpert and TradingXpert servers, which support interorganizational transactions and trading communities. Add-on products include BillerXpert, which allows customers to pay accounts over the Internet, while BuyerXpert offers paperless purchasing. MerchantXpert and SellerXpert provide business-to-consumer and business-to-business end user interfaces.

The Skinny on the Others

You noticed that in IDC's top e-business providers, big-name companies like Microsoft and IBM were nowhere to be found. What's their story? And what's the story with other bigtime IT companies looking to grab your e-business business? Let's have a look.

Microsoft

Microsoft's e-business philosophy is to provide customers with a common, secure e-business infrastructure that would let them make changes rapidly and cost-effectively, integrates well with existing packaged solutions, and allows customers to leverage existing skill sets. In addition, they wanted to exchange data electronically while incorporating business processes.

The Microsoft strategy revolves around three objectives: providing a platform for diverse commerce scenarios, creating strong partnerships, and ensuring interoperability.

The Microsoft open platform has evolved from Microsoft's broad experience with e-business. This includes Microsoft Internet properties such as Hotmail, MSN, Microsoft Investor, and Expedia, as well as working with customers that have chosen the Microsoft platform for their electronic commerce solutions, including companies like Office Depot, Dell, Tower Records, Spiegel, and CompUSA.

The breadth of Microsoft's product offerings include Commerce on the client (Windows 98, Internet Explorer), as well as a secure Commerce server platform, which includes Windows NT, Microsoft BackOffice products, and special industry-specific products such as the Microsoft Commercial Internet System and the Microsoft Internet Finance Server Toolkit.

Windows is at the core of the Microsoft e-business platform; the Windows implementations span from alternative form factors (Windows CE, Webtv, smart card technologies) to personal computers (Windows 98) to enterprise servers (Windows NT).

Windows NT and the Windows NT Option Pack are the basis for Microsoft Commerce solutions.

- Windows NT provides Web services and scripting capabilities with the Internet Information Server and Active Server pages.
- Microsoft Transaction Server is a distributed transaction coordinator that ensures thread pooling and synchronization, process management, and role-based security.
- Microsoft Message Queue provides reliability and resilience in disconnected environments, gives customers the ability to implement an asynchronous programming model, and is interoperable with other message queue technologies.

The company views e-business as being made up of four segments:

- Direct marketing, selling, and service: Market, sell, and service customers one on one via the Web
- Financial and information services: Delivery of electronic goods and services via the Internet—bill delivery and payment, online banking and investment, delivery of "soft goods" such as information and software
- Corporate procurement: Corporate purchasing sites of indirect materials (MRO: maintenance, repair and operations) from company suppliers
- Value chain trading: Extending business operations via the Web to streamline direct purchasing with trading partners

Microsoft's Site Server Commerce package is the cornerstone of its e-commerce enterprise. Site Server helps businesses engage customers and partners with the creation of cost-effective commerce sites and applications, targeted online advertising and marketing, and personalized promotion. Based on strong integration with Windows NT Server, it allows businesses to conduct online transactions with secure and scalable order capture, management, and routing. At the same time, businesses can easily integrate Site Server Commerce into legacy systems that may handle functions such as inventory, accounting, ERP, and EDI applications.

Company and contact information:

Microsoft Corporation
One Microsoft Way
Redmond, WA 98033
www.microsoft.com/worldwide

Hewlett-Packard

Hewlett-Packard calls its e-business strategy the "Electronic World"—a world supported by digital technology, and the Internet—providing access to information in our homes, on the road, in businesses, banks, hospitals, and schools. In its Electronic World, interaction between the consumer and business becomes more intimate and immediate. The consumer is empowered to influence the way products and services are delivered and the very nature of the product itself by providing immediate feedback and proactive recommendations on product and/or service requirements. In the field of online entertainment and education, for example, the consumer actually becomes an integral part of the product itself, as consumers interact with the information and each other online. Unlike the physical world, in the virtual world individuals slip seamlessly between their multiple roles of consumer, businessperson, parent, teacher, and so on.

HP's e-business philosophy involves conducting business using digital technology and the Internet. Companies developing and/or implementing e-business solutions often innovate existing business processes or develop entirely new processes to take advantage of the speed and efficiency of the Internet.

HP identifies three key business process areas in e-business: internal administrative processes, extended supply chain, and customer interaction. The extended enterprise infrastructure provides the technological foundation for e-business to occur. Within each of these process areas, a variety of activities occur.

- Internal administrative processes include Human Resources management, payroll and financial services, internal procurement, etc.

- Extended supply chain processes include supply chain planning, Web-based ERP, and supply/demand chain integration and collaboration.
- Customer interaction processes include large-scale commerce (both business-to-consumer and business-to-business), online financial services, and customer support (pre/post sales).

HP contributions in e-business include:

- HP Domain Commerce platform for deploying Internet commerce sites (*www.hp.com/go/domain*)
- HP Change Engine Architecture, supporting continuous business process evolution (*www.ebizsoftware.hp.com*)
- HP Middleware Applications for three key business processes (*www.ebizsoftware.hp.com*)
- Internal Administrative Automation
- Demand/Supply Chain Integration
- Customer Service Delivery
- Hardcopy—Digital Workplace
- Electronic Messaging Solutions (*www.hp.com/go/openmail*)

To fulfill the e-commerce requirements of business and IT managers, Hewlett-Packard has developed HP Domain Commerce, a comprehensive, highly scalable software platform that delivers the ideal infrastructure for deploying mission-critical Internet commerce applications. The HP Domain Commerce platform includes:

- HP ServiceControl, with HP's patented Web Quality of Service (QoS) capabilities, to prevent server overloads and prioritize customers and transactions. HP ServiceControl lets you provide predictable service levels by giving preference to your key customers or transactions.
- The HP Domain Management System, based on industry-leading HP OpenView technology, enables management of the system, network, and e-commerce applications from a standard browser, simplifying operations and lowering administrative costs.
- VeriFone vPOS, an advanced, flexible point-of-sale payment application that enables secure handling of Internet payment transactions. It supports direct transmission of payments, transaction

reporting and management, and such critical merchant processes as end-of-day reconciliation.

- HP OpenPix Internet imaging software, which enhances communications and collaboration for businesses that want to increase Web-based transactions through image-rich Web sites.
- Netscape Enterprise Server, a flexible, enterprise-strength Web server for business-class applications that provides Web publishing and document management capabilities.

Several leading e-commerce applications—including those from iCat, INTERSHOP, BroadVision, Open Market, InterWorld, and ClearCommerce—have been certified for the HP Domain Commerce platform. These HP Domain Commerce partners can satisfy a wide range of needs from simple electronic storefronts to robust transaction engines and complex global business systems. For more information on HP's e-business solutions, see: *www.hp.com/go/domain*.

Company and contact information:

Date Founded: 1939
Headquarters: Palo Alto, California
800-637-7740
Canada: 416-206-4725
Japan: 03-5371-1351
Latin America: 525-326-4400
Australia/New Zealand: 03-895-2895
Asia Pacific: 852-599-7777
Europe/Africa/Middle East: 41-22-780-81-11
www.hp.com

PeopleSoft, Inc.

At PeopleSoft, e-business is an umbrella term that incorporates many popular initiatives including electronic commerce, electronic data interchange (EDI), electronic funds transfer (EFT), and workflow. It also includes a new set of opportunities, such as electronic storefronts, self-service Web applications, and supply chain integration. The number of initiatives labeled "e-business" will continue to grow for several years. In order to better manage the opportunities relating to the various components of e-business, PeopleSoft has developed its strategy around five role-based "ecosystems."

In business terms, an ecosystem is a virtual information system that incorporates transactions, analysis, messages, and other content from enterprise applications, business partner applications, groupware, and various internal and external sources in relation to your organization. Business ecosystems are role-oriented, versus the process or functional orientation of enterprise applications. The need to recognize and manage business ecosystems is the result of a shift in focus of application deployment from functional experts to an expanded population of users that includes employees and managers—the work force ecosystem—suppliers, customers, and other business partners. While the Internet, intranets, and extranets provide a means for deploying Web applications to these user communities, ecosystems provide a contextual framework to manage access and usability from a user perspective. Since each of these ecosystems is interdependent, they require effective system management to maximize effectiveness and return on investment.

The Five Role-Based Ecosystems

PeopleSoft has identified five primary ecosystems supported by its enterprise applications. Three of these ecosystems make up the value chain—supplier, producer, and customer—and can vary significantly based on industry. The work force ecosystem, consisting of employees and managers, is dominated by human resource applications, while the executive ecosystem is dominated by financial applications.

PeopleSoft believes the deployment of an e-business strategy is critical to a company's long-term business success. However, because not all business partners will migrate to e-business in the same fashion, you must support several processing alternatives simultaneously. This requires a backbone system that provides the flexibility, control, and integration to accommodate new and varied e-business processes (including those that are not yet defined). Companies that implement a flexible enterprise software solution to support their e-business strategy will be in a stronger position to successfully manage change over time.

There are three primary issues that support PeopleSoft's "enterprise-backbone approach" to e-business application strategy:

Issue One: E-business is an addition, not a replacement. Though e-business has gained more attention the past few years, particularly among executives, the majority of today's business processing is paper- and fax-based. And despite the most optimistic projections of e-business adoption rates, traditional paper processing will remain part of our business activity for some time. This requires your company to support both electronic and traditional commerce processes with customers, suppliers, and business partners. A flexible, enterprise-wide system architecture is designed with this transition in mind.

Issue Two: E-business projects are often works in progress. E-business processes often incorporate traditional business applications such as accounting, human resources, and supply chain management. Typically, these applications are managed by separate departments with different priorities, resulting in incomplete or inconsistent e-business implementations. Companies may be required to support a single customer that wants Web-based order entry, EDI invoicing, and paper check payments—three different technology approaches for what many consider a single business process.

Issue Three: E-business is promoted for competitive advantage. Companies are increasingly leveraging "process differentiation" in their marketing programs for competitive advantage. Similar to product differentiation, process differentiation—e-business is a great example—will help a company secure loyalty with key customers. As an example, vendors that support EDI processing are winning business over those that don't. In the future, when EDI and other e-business applications become standard, vendors will then compete on whether certain management practices are supported, such as Vendor Managed Inventory. Likewise, certain data elements must be supported, such as number of units per case or amount before discount applied. Without an enterprise backbone to accommodate these variations, companies may lose key customers or critical suppliers to more responsive business partners.

PeopleSoft's Workflow package is the foundation of its e-business strategy. Workflow enables users to automate, streamline, navigate through, and control the flow of information across your enterprise. By integrating workflow throughout its applications, PeopleSoft aims to get the right information to the right person at the right time for more timely response.

PeopleSoft also supports both two- and three-tier transaction processing for reliable and superior performance over LANs and WANs.

Its e-business applications run on a variety of leading hardware and database platforms, giving users decent choices throughout the life cycle of their system.

Company and contact information:

Date founded: 1987
4305 Hacienda Drive
P.O. Box 8015
Pleasanton, CA 94588
Phone: 925-694-2152
E-mail: david_michaud@peoplesoft.com
www.peoplesoft.com

Compaq

Known for its high-performance PCs and servers, Compaq is trying hard to make a name for itself in the e-business world. Like Microsoft and HP, it has the brand name to get in the door. With a boost from its acquisitions of Digital and Tandem, Compaq has emerged as a driving force in the growth of the Internet and corporate intranets worldwide.

Compaq's e-business philosophy is that any form of commerce depends to a great extent on trust and the ability to establish a common set of business procedures for handling transactions. Security issues arise when companies make credit checks, establish credit limits, sign contracts, identify authorized signers, analyze product specifications, formulate product warranties and return policies, create payment schedules, and monitor payment histories. In addition, responsible companies work to diligently guard the privacy and protect the information and interests of all parties to a transaction in order to create a secure environment for business transactions.

But the company says that electronic commerce over the Internet poses a unique set of trading and security challenges, primarily because in most instances the buyer and seller are faceless and voiceless, known to each other only through their presence on the network.

That's where Compaq is headed—as a major player in supporting secure, reliable electronic commerce. With the help of recent acquisitions, such as Tandem and Digital, and other partnerships, Compaq has the expertise and deep pockets to deliver comprehensive solutions through products and services that simplify the deployment and operation of effective, cost-efficient, and highly secure electronic commerce solutions.

In short order Compaq has developed a framework that describes the electronic commerce marketplace and depicts the interrelationships and supporting structures within the market. That framework includes a series of platform products tailored to the requirements for e-business. These include powerful platforms that enable confident deployment of e-commerce and firewall servers using standards-based applications from Compaq's partnership with Microsoft and Axent.

Compaq's leading line of e-business products includes ProLiant E-Commerce Servers, ProSignia and ProLiant Firewall Servers, the iTP Payment Solution, iTP Virtual Store, iTP Certificate Security Solution, and iTP NetACD. The company also offers comprehensive systems integration services for reliable, secure electronic commerce solutions.

In addition, Compaq's E-Commerce Server, based on Microsoft's Commerce Server, can be extended to provide Secure Sockets Layer (SSL) standard support for e-commerce transactions, providing the simplest approach to protecting data as it flows from the browser to the Web server. Companies like Motley Fool, Auto-by-Tel, and Net Grocer rely on Compaq for business-critical e-commerce activities.

Other solutions incorporate the new SET (Secure Electronic Transaction) protocol. Compaq's iTP suite of solutions enable SET transactions for true end-to-end encryption from the browser through the Web server to the bank's Internet gateways. At each step in the process, information is protected as appropriate. For example, merchants do not need to see a buyer's credit card number; they only need to see that the purchase is within authorized credit limits. The bank, on the other hand, does not need to see the content of the transaction; it only needs to see the total dollar amount and the card number.

Compaq's electronic commerce solutions also support highly sophisticated features such as electronic wallets, digital certificates and cryptographic keys, point-of-sale payservers, and enhanced storefront functionality such as voice, video, and data capabilities.

Here's some more information on Compaq:

- Compaq platforms are used in nearly one-quarter of all Web servers installed in U.S. businesses. This is more than twice as many as the next closest Windows NT system-based competitor. Source: ZD Market Intelligence (*www.infobeads.com*), March 1998.

- In Secure Internet sites with third-party server certificates, 28 percent of Web sites using SSL are running on Microsoft Windows NT Server with IIS. This is nearly twice as large as its next closest competitor, Apache (with 16 percent). Source: Netcraft (*www.netcraft.com*; a U.K.- based consultant) survey, March 1998.
- Compaq was named as the server brand in use by an over-whelming 60 percent of large corporations. Source: CRN, March 30, 1998.
- More than 70 of the Premier 100 customer Web sites use Digital products and services. Source: *ComputerWorld.*
- Digital itself does more than US$1 billion in transactions annually over the Internet.
- Tandem's servers handle 90 percent of all securities transactions, 80 percent of all automated teller machine (ATM) transactions, and 66 percent of all credit card transactions around the globe.

Company and contact information:

Compaq Computer Corporation
20555 State Highway 249
Houston, TX 77070
Phone: 281-370-0670
www.compaq.com

GE Information Services

GE Information Services bills itself as an "internetworker" of com-panies through its e-business solutions. The company delivers a full suite of solutions that streamline the extended supply chain, including Electronic Data Interchange, messaging gateways, extranets, elec-tronic catalogs, and electronic marketplaces, all supported by a full range of professional services. Company e-business professional serv-ices include system integration, electronic trading community ramp and management, program management, and training. GE Information Services aims to create a competitive advantage for its clients by combining computers and telecommunications technolo-gies to link, integrate, and support the business processes of multiple enterprises.

GE Information Services' goal as a provider of electronic commerce solutions is to maximize both the extent of reach and richness of content of business communications, thus increasing the return on electronic commerce investments. The broad range of electronic commerce solutions offered include:

- EDI Solutions
- Gateway Solutions
- Electronic Commerce Outsourcing Services
- Professional Services
- Extranet Solutions
- Electronic Marketplace Solutions

Company and contact information:

Date Founded: 1965
Worldwide Headquarters: Rockville, Maryland
Europe: Paris
Asia/Pacific: Hong Kong
Number of employees: 2,300 worldwide, 40 percent based outside the United States
GE Information Services
301 North Washington Street
Rockville, MD 20850-1785
800-560-GEIS
301-340-4000
www.geis.com

IBM

IBM provides its own definition of e-business on its Web site:

1. Improving business processes using Internet technologies.
2. Leveraging the Web to bring together customers, vendors, suppliers, and employees in ways never before possible.
3. Web-enabling your business to sell products, improve customer service, and get maximum results from limited resources.

Big Blue believes that e-business is a customer relationship management (CRM) issue, and its e-business solutions reflect that thinking.

Breaking down e-business into three categories—e-commerce, supply chain management, and business intelligence—IBM tries to throw a blanket over the entire customer management enterprise. According to IBM, the e-commerce process includes:

- Electronic presentation of goods and services
- Online order-taking and bill presentment
- Automated customer account inquiries
- Online payment and transaction handling

How does e-commerce become e-business enabled, IBM asks its customers? By implementing these e-commerce strategies with e-business in mind:

- Develop a dynamic, database-driven online catalog
- Provide for online ordering by securely integrating your front-end presentation with an order entry system
- Move static billing statement data to an interactive Web-based presentment server
- Accept electronic payment methods (credit cards, EFT, etc.) for full-transaction shopping or bill payment

That, IBM says, allows companies to:

- Improve margins by using a lower-cost online channel
- Reduce costs associated with paper-based processes: postage, printing, and handling
- Reduce float through the use of electronic transfers/just-in-time payments
- Give customers faster, more responsive service

IBM's solutions to its customers e-business challenges are a combination of end-to-end e-commerce solutions that integrate customer service and supply chain management (SCM) systems that fit into any environment so users can easily build on existing hardware and software. These solutions include:

- Commerce software solutions (Web servers, applications servers)
- Services for consulting, systems integration

- Integration/IFS relationship
- Billing and payment server solutions
- Payments expertise through Banking ISU (wholesale/retail/payment instruments)

On the supply chain management side, IBM believes that solving the SCM issue depends largely on optimizing business processes and business value in every corner of the extended enterprise—from a client's supplier's supplier to a client's customer's customer. SCM uses e-business concepts and Web technologies to manage beyond the organization so manufacturers and vendors can share sales forecasts, manage inventories, schedule labor, optimize deliveries, and improve productivity. Some of the processes included within SCM are procurement, inventory management, forecasting, warehousing, and logistics. Its solutions for these areas include:

- Self-service Web sites—IBM e-business Start Now Program, Web Self-Service Solutions allows users' customers to use the Web to answer questions themselves instead of tying up limited resources like phone operators and sales clerks. Is it cost-efficient? Last year, IBM handled over 29 million technical support self-service inquiries over the Web, resulting in more than $620 million in cost avoidance and productivity savings.
- Front-office CRM applications—Empowers employees with instant access to real-time information at every customer touch point. Uses the Web to expand upon and upgrade sales force automation tools, call center applications, and marketing campaign initiatives. IBM recently partnered with Siebel Systems, the world's leading supplier of CRM application software, to make such high-performance solutions not only possible but also completely dependable and scalable.
- Systems integration—Ties various IT systems together, simplifying access to the information customers need across all of their business channels.
- Business intelligence—Analyze customer data to maximize effectiveness and profitability and adjust customers' marketing efforts accordingly.

Specific IBM customer relationship management products include:

1. ETS Business in a Box—a complete solution for companies that want to use the Internet or intranets to manage their business. It enables e-business by automating and improving key processes and increasing office productivity. It contains over 20 different business applications and allows management of an information distribution home page and communication via e-mail. Completely customizable, it allows integrated and comprehensive Lotus databases, facilitating instant access to critical information.
2. GWI Collaborative Front Office—A comprehensive suite of applications for customer service, sales force automation, marketing, help desks, and knowledge management. It allows for leveraging Lotus Notes infrastructure, facilitating communication and collaboration across the enterprise.
3. IBM E-business Start Now Program, Web Self-Service Solution— Helps small and medium businesses start building relationships with customers via the Web. Delivered and customized by IBM Business Partners, this solution uses the data gathered through customer contact to support Web-based CRM tools like customer service, customer management, and campaign management applications.

Contact information:
1-800-IBM-7080 xCR01

Sybase

Sybase believes that with e-businesses, the problem is that the volume of information on corporate Web sites has exploded. And instead of allowing easy business transactions, a poorly implemented corporate Web site can severely complicate a customer's interaction. Specifically, two problems are the most prevalent: black holes and lost information.

Web users fall into black holes when they waste time clicking through a seemingly endless maze of documents in search of the information, only to find nothing relevant. Equally frustrating is lost information, when the information exists and is relevant but is either inaccessible or impossible to recognize as relevant.

Sybase says that by improving business-to-business processes, companies can reduce black holes and lost information on their corporate Web sites. The goal is to provide the customer with the information and transactional capabilities they need with a minimal amount of effort.

Sybase's solution to these problems is to take the best of breed applications and use them as building blocks. Its Sybase Global Solutions Group has helped a variety of customers achieve their business goals using Web technology. The group has participated in a diverse set of e-commerce projects, including development of Internet yellow pages for US West, creation of a Web-based thoroughbred registration system for the Jockey Club, and assisting the State of New York with its Electronic Death Certificate project, which streamlines the state's death reporting process.

Company and contact information:

Sybase
6475 Christie Ave.
Emeryville, CA 94608-1050
800-8-SYBASE
www.sybase.com

Ericsson

For more than 100 years Ericsson has been making history as a leader in the telecommunications industry. Starting with its expertise in wire line telephony, Ericsson has created strong leadership positions in virtually all major telecom technologies, including wireless networks, mobile systems, and cellular phones.

Today Ericsson says it's committed to demonstrating its leadership in a new world—the Internet. Ericsson's e-business offerings begin with fault-tolerant and highly secure network infrastructure, including product lines that feature ATM and label switches, gigarouters, and access servers. Its recently introduced IP@Service platform acts as an important link between network infrastructure and value-added applications and services by providing for security, charging, service management, service brokering, and resource management. In addition to providing a secure infrastructure for e-commerce services this platform supports intranet/extranet services, multimedia, IP telephony, and third-party applications.

Another important element of Ericsson's e-business offering is its Internet Professional Services. Their mission is to design, develop, deploy, and support total customer value-based solutions. The company uses partnerships with other leading e-business vendors to offer a variety of e-commerce products, including Open Market's Transact, LiveCommerce and ShopSite products, Interworld's Commerce Exchange, iCat Commerce Suite, Intershop, Microsoft Commerce Server, and CyberCash. Ericsson also works with SET standards and products, including those from Trintech Group, IBM, and Verifone. Capabilities range from initial consulting to building high-end, customized commerce-enabled sites featuring all the necessary links into back-end transaction engines and hosting.

Company and contact information:

Founded: 1876
Headquarters: Stockholm, Sweden
Ericsson
740 E. Campbell Road
Richardson, TX 75081
972-583-0000
Fax: 650-463-6366
E-mail: EUSKADA@am1.ericsson.se
www.ericsson.com

Commerce One

Commerce One, Inc. is an underrated global leader in business-to-business Internet commerce solutions, delivering significant cost savings and operational efficiencies to enterprise-class organizations by linking buying and selling organizations into real-time trading communities. Based in Walnut Creek, California, Commerce One is a privately held company backed by a strong team of investors. Additionally, Commerce One has strategic relationships: SAP America, Microsoft Corporation, PriceWaterhouseCoopers, MCI Systemhouse, and MCI.

Commerce One delivers a full suite of products and services that automate an organization's procurement process including the management of supplier catalog content and the interactions between buyers and sellers over the Internet.

"emm@" Is for Money

How mature is your online business? The question is becoming increasingly relevant as many merchants and service companies are coming to realize that it takes more than a glitch-free Web site to come of age in a digital economy.

A lot more, say the e-business advisors at PriceWaterhouseCoopers. Certain that a healthy dot.com, like any young organism, can only grow as it is developmentally ready, the firm has introduced a new maturity model to test the fitness level and sea legs of its clients.

Called emm@ (pronounced "Emma"), PriceWaterhouseCoopers' global E-Business Maturity Model works in a broad context that relates online initiatives to a full menu of established business criteria including more than 700 "good practice" standards across nine general domains, from systems technology to security to strategy.

Through an emm@ analysis, companies should gain a realistic assessment of their current e-business development: Are they too dependent on suppliers? What are the risks of changing the business model? Are they ready to transfer certain functions to outsourcing? Have they matured to the point of being able to apply their original online identity into new areas of business?

PriceWaterhouseCoopers released emmm@ in early 2000, along with a "growth chart" of e-business evolution. Does your e-business have the following growth characteristics?

- Online Presence—A company has developed static information on a Web site with minimal ability for any interaction beyond e-mail or company background. This elementary step is the equivalent of posting "brochureware" on the Web as a placeholder.
- Online Business—Otherwise known as "e-enabled," when a company legitimately begins to conduct business electronically, customers can browse its Web site and place orders but there is not yet a true integration of customers, suppliers, and partners.
- Integrated Online Business—A company has effectively integrated the customer-facing, front-end of its Web site with back-end systems linked to key suppliers and third parties.
- Fully Integrated E-Business—Here is where the company really begins to gain competitive advantage for its e-business, having seamlessly integrated its partners, suppliers, and customers into its online operations. The smartest players know enough to stick to core competencies and begin to outsource all nonessential e-business functions, from manufacturing to logistics.
- Continuous Evolution—The most advanced e-businesses are those that are continually changing, not only their original model, but their respective industry models as well. At the highest level, successful e-businesses push toward a state of "proactive destruction" in order to stay open to evolving parameters of electronic commerce—even as they stay true to their previous e-business incarnations. At this ultimate stage, companies are also able to apply their e-business strategy across multiple industries.

The linchpin is the Commerce One Commerce Chain Suite, a fairly comprehensive software solution comprised of three components: Commerce One BuySite Electronic Procurement Application, Commerce One Multi-Supplier Catalog, and Commerce One Electronic Commerce Network (ECN). The company claims the Chain Suite is the first to fully automate the procurement of indirect goods and services. Through automation of interactions and transaction with external suppliers, the Commerce Chain Suite allows organizations to extend cost savings and increase the return on investment (ROI) of standard internal procurement systems. Commerce One also provides, through ECN, prepackaged supplier catalog content that relieves the buying organization's burden in maintaining supplier catalog content and makes the implementation and maintenance of the application faster and easier.

Company and contact information:

Founded: January 1994 as DistriVision Development Corporation, became Commerce One in April of 1997
Headquarters: Walnut Creek, California
Number of employees: 120 and growing
Commerce One
1600 Riviera Drive
Walnut Creek, CA 94596
925-941-6000
Fax: 925-941-6060
E-mail: info@commerceone.com
www.commerceone.com

chapter thirteen

Guarding/Protecting Your E-Valuables

The e-business revolution continues to gather momentum with thousands of companies being established online daily. E-business is making trade, communication, and information gathering between clients and customers and suppliers and partners easier, faster, and more cost-effective than ever before.

Companies implementing secure Web commerce are saving millions of dollars in customer acquisition, product configuration, price quotation, inventory analysis, order fulfillment, and post-sales support, even if they still sell through traditional channels. Eliminated in the new Web commerce model are the various functions formerly handled by third-party product brokers. The "everywhere-at-once" capabilities of the Internet allow corporations to search for the best prices on products and supplies themselves, without the assistance of brokers.

Naturally the benefits of e-business security apply to those buying online as well. Although some product listing and pricing information is available online for a company's purchasing department to view, often information regarding bulk pricing and other pricing policies may be for view by authorized customers only. Plus, a buyer needs a secure system installed to place orders, make payment, and track shipment. Having this confidential product information on a secure Web page protected by a secure e-system saves time and eliminates layers of labor and paperwork that raise costs for both buyers and sellers.

Distributed Barriers

Like many technological advancements, though, e-business comes with some unexpected baggage. The perceived security risk of the Internet is holding back many companies from investing wholeheartedly in the technology—and holding back customers from buying from you online.

Then there is the network infrastructure that e-business is built upon. Twenty-five years ago, we had mainframe computers. As in medieval times, the mainframe was one castle, with many users and many remote terminals. Today, modern computing has blessed us with the computer network, with islands of computers spread out across the enterprise. With the diminishment of centralized computing, and the advancement of distributed computing, corporate information technology managers find that their data is exposed on a wide variety of fronts, and their ability to control the security of that data compromised like never before.

Consider a global investment bank that specializes in handling foreign financial transactions, payments, and related services. With an average transaction of $13,000, compared to $29.95 on the average retail Web commerce site, security is paramount.

Recently the bank decided to use an extranet for managing and executing international payments for the burgeoning roster of its e-business clients. The company considered a range of security options, including biometrics such as fingerprint or voice identification, smart cards, and one approach that required users to enter their personal

---

Is E-Business Safe?

Although Internet security breaches have gotten a lot of press, most vendors and analysts argue that transactions are actually less dangerous in cyberspace than in the physical world. Consumers don't really believe it yet, but experts say e-commerce transactions are safer than ordinary credit card purchases. Every time you pay with a credit card at a store, in a restaurant, or over an 800 number—and every time you throw away a credit card receipt— you make yourself vulnerable to fraud. That's because a great deal of credit card fraud is caused by retail sales employees who handle card numbers.

E-commerce systems remove temptation by encrypting the numbers on a company's servers. For merchants, e-commerce is actually safer than opening a store that could be looted, burned, or flooded. The difficulty is in getting customers to believe that e-commerce is safe for them.

identification number into a desktop reader every five minutes. But the company rejected those as too cumbersome. After all, e-business isn't about barriers.

Instead, the bank decided on digital certificates, which serve as a legal signature and produce a binding confirmation of a business transaction. That makes it hard for users to repudiate an agreement later. They also serve as proof that people are who they say they are.

The bank went through an extensive planning process before implementing the system. Planners identified 10 key policy areas, hashed out details and a timetable, and then started building. Every two weeks bank IT staffers tested an internal release of the digital certificate software.

Now, security is seen as a shared responsibility with customers. The bank issues a valid certificate and makes sure its software does the authorization. Each customer has an IT administrator who handles passwords and certificates.

Even with the digital certificates, customers using the e-business site need to provide client identification, a personal identification string, as well as a password that the bank dictates. It also restricts access on a per-function basis for each company.

The result? The use of digital certificates strengthens the site in the eyes of clients because it gives clients peace of mind knowing their transactions are secure. Individually signed certificates are irrefutable.

The more complicated or sensitive the information, the more secure a company's business-to-business networks need to be. In addition to providing security for the initial applications, companies also need to plan for growth. Within 18 months of starting an e-business project, most large companies will use the e-business site to support at least 10 and in some cases dozens of secure intercompany applications, says Giga Information Group.

Securing Your E-Business

That's just one reason securing your e-business site is perhaps the most important strategic step you'll take in your e-business campaign. E-business solutions are as common as a basic password-based security software package that verifies whether the people dialing in are who they say they are or as complex as the digital certificate technology that the global bank cited earlier used.

According to a recent Forrester Research report, 80 percent of companies state that security is one of the biggest barriers to creating electronic links with customers and partners. At the same time, business over the Internet is increasing, suggesting that companies may be engaging in e-business at significant risk to their vital information assets. The best security strategies are designed to help companies minimize the trade-off between security and e-business.

E-security solutions allow companies to manage the risk to information assets and to facilitate e-business processes safely, implementing the right level of security needed to capture immediate e-business opportunities while developing a lifecycle security program that can easily adapt to new threats and changing business practices.

"The demand for e-commerce and e-business applications has moved security from a back-end technology for protecting data to a critical business enabler," says John Becker, CEO and chairman of Axent Technologies, Inc., one of the world's largest e-business security providers. "Companies understand that security is critical to enabling e-business communications with their customers, partners, suppliers, and employees."

Becker cites the four critical areas of e-security:

- Assess vulnerabilities and ensure policy compliance to proactively reduce the business risk.
- Protect critical information with perimeter security and detect attacks to information to maintain business integrity.
- Enable secure Internet communications between mobile employees, remote operations, suppliers, customers, and other businesses to facilitate new revenue opportunities.
- Manage and administer users and resources to manage more with less.

E-Business Security Checklist

- Conduct a network assessment and look at external and internal security risks.
- Identify the tools needed—both hardware and software—to keep the e-business site secure.
- Analyze what type of traffic is carried on the e-business site. How valuable is the information carried via that traffic to your company and your competitors?
- Develop security procedures and educate your employees and business partners on the importance of following them.
- Maintain constant vigilance; run simulated attacks and vulnerability scans.

Enterprise Resource Planning

What steps does an e-business take to address Becker's four critical e-business security points? One method many e-businesses are adopting is the use of Enterprise Resource Planning (ERP) systems.

ERP applications are increasingly used by organizations to capture valuable data and improve and expand business processes. These ERP applications enable electronic commerce between internal business units and external supply chain business partners. Effective e-business solutions need to secure then selectively unleash this data to employees, partners, and customers across private and public networks.

In many ways, ERP applications and the Internet are ideal partners. ERP applications take advantage of the Internet to expand electronic business boundaries. The need to secure mission-critical transactions over this untrusted network increases as the value of online transactions and the number of online supply chain participants increase.

Web Directories

With e-commerce will come a definitive broadening of wide-area connections and interconnections. User populations—some stable, many others transitional—will soar as business-to-business links grow dramatically. All of this could create a chaotic environment, with corporations struggling with the tasks of adding and deleting new users/sites and constantly revising access rights of new and existing users. The example of a terminated employee best describes the potential dilemma: Once terminated, but having had multiple access to online, automated purchasing capabilities, how long can an organization tolerate the latency between a termination and the cancellation of critical privileges? Only a directory can solve these issues instantaneously. E-commerce will exacerbate most of these issues, and sophisticated directory services need to be implemented to handle these.

Once an afterthought to security-minded IT managers, directories are becoming more critical to e-commerce because they are designed to house important security and certificate information, as well as policy access to applications—all of which would have significant e-business implications. It may be through the directory, for example, that individual users will receive permission to access a browser for ordering some supplies but not have the clearance to order capital equipment. The directory role for holding security authentication, or for pointers to certificate authorities, is also well documented and will have to eventually be linked to business-to-business activities.

Today's directory technology is moving in the following directions, most of which apply readily to automated procurement and other e-commerce developments. These developments include the ability to:

- Centralize information access through a single, secure repository and distribute data over multiple systems;
- Maintain and update directory contents from multiple sources;
- Provide access to external public or private directories;
- Synchronize multiple third-party information repositories;
- Secure sensitive information through system-level and multilevel user access sites; and
- Simplify administration through a centralized management tool that supports remote access.

The Borderless E-Business

The Internet's widespread use has drastically increased unwanted activity by computer hackers, those who use network pathways to invade private spaces and steal data or disrupt operations. Computer virus and worm attacks have cost corporations billions of dollars. Because hacking tools are easily found and downloaded from Web sites, this activity is not limited to sophisticated external hackers who use the Internet to attack corporate systems. It also includes internal employee attacks on corporate systems. Hacker activity is encouraged by the lack of effective security tools. Restraint is lacking because hackers generally believe that their activities will not be discovered.

To respond to these new threats, many corporations are looking for new ways to approach Internet security, both external and internal. Many corporations are changing security policies, employing new software products and procedures to protect their business so that they can safely exploit the attractive opportunities of Internet business.

In the past, large corporations built firewalls, acting like perimeter defenses to protect internal data, communications, and transactions. All communications between the corporate local intranet network (including corporate databases) and the Internet funneled through a single firewall point where traffic was strictly controlled. This did help protect operations and data from interference or theft. But the restrictive nature of the firewall, however useful in preventing harmful traffic from entering the corporate network, had the undesirable side effect of crippling the many useful open aspects of Internet communication.

Says Greg Gilliom, chief executive officer at Network ICE Corporation, a security software applications developer, "Even the need of a CEO to access information from home or on the road may be blocked by such a restrictive system. When a company wants to install a sales automation application to keep road warriors in contact with corporate headquarters, tunnels through the firewall inherently reduce security. For example, a firewall is normally configured to block all traffic to and from port 8000. If MIS later installs a sales information server communicating through port 8000, the CEO or a salesperson outside the firewall can't get information on that server."

Gilliom adds that firewall administrators are under constant pressure to increase firewall penetration in order to take advantage of the growing power of the Internet. The security administrator, too, is hit with an onslaught of applications for Web-based video conferencing, Web-to-host applications, and business-to-business commerce applications—all of which require new types of access that undermine the effectiveness of the firewall and increase vulnerability to hackers.

In addition to making new holes in the firewall, the growth of mobile computing opens new points of weakness in overall corporate network security. Before the advent of the telecommuting and mobile employee, important corporate computer systems confined sensitive information within the firewall. Now, many key systems with important corporate information are outside the firewall—the most obvious example being the CEO's home computer where confidential documents and data have been downloaded to reside on its local storage. While this is a tremendous boon to productivity, it is a critical hole in the firewall defense. This means that critical, confidential data such as merger plans, customer lists, or financial data may be attractive targets to an Internet pirate.

In addition to the information on the home system, that system can be highly available as a stepping stone to central stores of corporate data. Outside the protection of the firewall, a hacker may install a remote-control Trojan horse that the hacker can send over the CEO's personal connection to breach the firewall, giving the hacker access to all data on the corporate network. Firewall and virtual private network software will not block this access because the CEO's home system is a trusted system.

Unfortunately, it is now difficult to define the edges of an active corporate network. Aggressive adoption of e-business initiatives, intercompany sharing of data over extranets, and remote access by employees over high speed "always on" access have increased the complexity of network configurations and access points. It has created what we call the "borderless" network. Such a network obsoletes traditional security approaches.

A security manager must still protect communications and data, but with mobile warriors, company executives, telecommuters, extended business partners, and other interacting computer systems now an integral part of the security domain, the concept of perimeter defense becomes less viable. Increasing the dilemma is the fact that a perimeter defense was always open to internal attack. Many described the firewall defense as "soft and chewy on the inside, hard and crunchy on the outside." This was meant to point out an advantage of the firewall system, which provided open, loose internal communications. It was, however, never a completely satisfactory way to protect data. It was outmoded from the start.

Now that the borderless network is here to stay, corporate security managers need to find new ways to allow open Internet communications while protecting valuable corporate data. Several steps are necessary to provide this protection. Some are relatively simple policy and personnel changes. Others require the deployment of new software.

First and foremost, every corporation should have security policies firmly in place, including user name and password. All systems and shared resources must have good user names and passwords with a combination of eight or more letters, numbers, and symbols. Guest accounts must be disabled and passwords changed on a regular basis. This shared resource and password policy must apply to systems within the corporate buildings and to all notebook computers and home systems that employees use to access the corporate network. These security instructions must be an important part of new employee orientations and reminder sessions. Several very good utilities for policing corporate password policy are available to help maintain security standards.

Just as important is teaching employees about the rights and restrictions of accessing corporate systems. All employees know that it would be wrong to go around the building checking doors to see if they are unlocked. All employees know that it would be wrong to go searching through the CEO's desk or file cabinet. But, for some reason, some employees do not feel it is wrong to search the network neighborhood and attempt to connect to servers or other workstations that they are not authorized to use. They may even try a few guesses at passwords to access the accounting server or human resources database. At employee orientations, every employee should be told that it is corporate policy for employees to access only servers for which they have permission. If they believe they need information on a different server, they should contact the system administrator and get a proper password. This policy should include notice that attempts to gain unauthorized access to corporate servers are considered a severe breach of corporate policy and may require severe disciplinary action.

Detective Software

In addition to improving personnel and security policies and procedures, a corporation needs to install software to help enforce the new policies—either vulnerability scanners that check systems for open resources with null passwords or a new generation of intrusion detection systems (IDS).

Until recently, both internal and external hackers knew that there was little chance they would be caught. The first generation of IDS used log files, listing attempts to break into a system in a log file that would later be analyzed to uncover intrusion attempts. Unfortunately, the time delay between break-in and detection gave hackers time to cover their tracks by tampering with the log files—or encouraged them to take what they wanted quickly, before the log file analysis caught them.

The second generation of IDS monitored live network traffic and reported intrusions in realtime. This method solved the time delay but could only be deployed in places where all network traffic passed a single point, such as on a shared Ethernet segment. This second generation still could not protect the extended enterprise with its borderless networks where there is no single point of passage for network traffic.

Where to Turn for E-Security Help

Here is a representative sampling of vendors that provide e-business systems monitoring tools and services.

EWatcher and Trinity Suite—Avesta Technologies, Inc., *www.avesta.com/*
PATROL—BMC Software, Inc., *www.bmc.com/*
ETEWatch—Candle Corporation, *www.candle.com/*
MasterIT and Unicenter TNG— Computer Associates International, Inc., *www.cai.com/*

Empirical Suite—Empirical Software, *www.empirical.com/*
SiteScope and SiteSeer—Freshwater Software, Inc., *www.freshwater.com/*
OpenView—Hewlett-Packard Co., *www.openview.hp.com/*
VitalSuite—International Network Services (INS), *www.ins.com/*
Perspective—Keynote Systems, Inc., *www.keynote.com/*
Distributed Monitoring—Tivoli Systems, Inc., *www.tivoli.com/*

Today, a few companies offer innovative third-generation IDS, called intrusion countermeasure software. This new generation is designed for deployment on every system in a corporation, yet it is "lightweight," meaning that it takes very few system resources on each system. It detects an intrusion from outside the corporate network in the same way as an intrusion that originates inside the network. Hacker identity is revealed, so one can determine whether the attack was launched from inside or outside. These new products provide protection for all levels of network elements, from big corporate servers to the CEO's home portable, and provide detection and protection for the mobile computer user. With real-time network intrusion detection on every system, this provides the pervasive hacker protection required by today's Internet active corporation.

Digital Certificates

Good e-businesses see the Internet as more than a networked resource for product and sales information. They recognize the Web as a medium to use to save money, improve service, and expand product reach into formerly untapped markets. Digital certificates enable organizations to transfer their legacy systems to the Internet in order to cut expenses and generate revenue via secure electronic commerce transactions.

Legacy systems support sales, inventory, shipping, customer service, accounting, human resources, or any other system used to run a business. These systems consist of a company's current information infrastructure including desktops, networks, file servers, databases, mainframe and minicomputer hosts, and commercial and customized software programs. Companies worldwide are making these systems accessible from a Web browser because doing so can reduce paperwork, cut infrastructure costs, simplify customer interaction and spur online sales—each a result that boosts profitability.

However, once legacy systems go online, security concerns mandate that only authorized users access the information found in what are often confidential resources. Implementation of digital certificates ensures that users with predetermined authorization can enter only the online applications and databases they need to access to conduct business. These certificates are in effect the passports or ID cards of Web users who are surfing secure sites.

Digital certificates are online documents that authenticate user identities, provide the codes that encrypt and decrypt messages over the Web, and ensure that transmitted data has not been altered. A certificate authority (CA) is the Web-based mechanism that distributes and revokes certificates and guarantees data integrity by digitally "signing" a user's certificate. By implementing CA-based e-commerce, information sharing over the Web is immediate and secure, accelerating the rate of projects, commerce, and profitability.

Digital certificates are also a great way to ensure production from far-flung workers in the new distributed business environments. As companies compete for top talent, being able to work from home, or telecommuting, is a major incentive. If the systems that are accessible at the office are also securely available through the Internet to positively identify employees at their homes, a company can become a much more flexible workplace for its employees. Additionally, as employees travel on sales, support, and marketing trips, they can remain directly linked to their support systems back at the home office.

CAs positively identify users and provide the distributed encryption necessary to enter Web pages or network systems that are secured against anonymous public access. CA-enabled electronic commerce creates a distributed office environment that uses the Internet as a secure backbone so a worker certified on an Internet VPN (virtual private network) can securely access confidential company files from anywhere that has Web access.

Benefits of Digital Certificates

Digital certificates provide several benefits that allow e-businesses and their consumers to utilize the Internet with confidence, such as authenticating the identity of participants on both ends of an online commercial transaction and authorizing credit card payments. Digital certificates also improve security concerns in noncommercial transactions by authorizing access to key information sources without passwords, providing nonrepudiation or legally binding proof of messages sent over the Internet, and verifying the integrity of information exchanged online.

More and more Internet companies are requiring the use of digital certificates by their customers to protect the security of the consumers and their own transactions. For online merchants, digital certificates act as a passport or driver's license and are becoming a critical tool for boosting consumer confidence in the security of their Web site and in online commerce in general.

Technically, a certificate is a password-protected, encrypted data file that has been digitally signed by a CA. The data file consists of a public and private key pair, which is simply a pair of numbers that has no inherent association with any identity. The trusted third party, the CA, is needed to bind an identity to a public and private key pair, preventing any individual from generating a key pair and falsely claiming to be someone else. A digital certificate signed by a CA binds a particular identity to a key pair, assuring the parties involved in a transaction that everyone is who they say they are.

Certificate Authorities Defined

The reliability of any digital certificate is directly related to the reliability of the certificate authority (CA) that issues and provides services for that certificate. The CA is the missing link that makes trusted Web sessions a reality. Because each party in the session trusts the CA, and because the CA has vouched for each party's identification and trustworthiness by signing their certificates, each party recognizes that they have an implicit trust in the other and the secure session can proceed without the risk of masquerading. Furthermore, since the two authenticated parties exchange public key certificates, they can encrypt and digitally sign session data, removing the possibility that others may eavesdrop on the session or tamper with data.

As a trusted third party, the certificate authority reviews information submitted by a company requesting certification, ensuring that it has properly registered and filed the appropriate paperwork to be a legitimate company in the area where it operates. Some CAs have "graded" authentication requirements for varying degrees of certification assurance. A CA does not check or guarantee the financial soundness of a company.

A reliable certificate authority normally charges a fee to the companies it certifies. In exchange, the certificate authority issues a certificate, also called a digital certificate or an authentication certificate, to an applicant company, which can then put the certificate up on its site. Certificates convey the name of the subscriber and other identification information such as an e-mail address, the public key of the subscriber, the validity period for the certificate, the name of the certificate authority that issued the certificate, and the certificate serial number.

Deploying a certificate authority system encourages the use of the electronic commerce transactions that:

- Lower communications costs by taking advantage of the dramatic savings of using the public Internet instead of expensive leased lines
- Quicken access to markets by utilizing the ever growing reach of the Internet, exposing products and services electronically to countless new customers
- Reduce cost of sales by discouraging unnecessary investment in corporate network infrastructure
- Improve remote access capabilities for telecommuting and traveling employees because only browser-based local Internet access is needed for a remote employee to gain access to a Web-based application

- Make a company more Internet-savvy by turning the Internet into a revenue-generating tool instead of just an information-gathering resource

Public Key Infrastructure Management

Securing mission-critical transactions allows organizations to safely transition from paper-based businesses to true electronic businesses. A PKI (public key infrastructure) provides a flexible, robust, and scalable security architecture for securing ERP transactions over intranets, extranets, and the Internet. By securing the data and establishing trust in the identity between communicating parties, a PKI enables the increase in mission-critical transactions being transmitted across business boundaries creating effective e-business solutions.

E-business with PKI keys and certificates securing mission-critical transactions can be accomplished by integrating a PKI with supply chain applications such as Web servers, virtual private networks (VPN), SAP R/3, PeopleSoft, EDI, and more. Integration of a complete PKI, which manages the keys and certificates used to establish and maintain a trustworthy networking environment, provides confidentiality, authentication, integrity, and trust for ERP transactions.

A PKI is the comprehensive system required to provide public key encryption and digital signature services across a wide variety of applications. In the world of cryptography, the term "key" is a numerical value used by an algorithm to alter information, making that information secure and visible only to individuals who have the corresponding key to recover the information. For public key cryptography, keys come in pairs of matched "public" and "private" keys. The public portion of the key pair can be distributed in a public manner without compromising the private portion, which must be kept secret by its owner. A message encrypted with the public key can only be undone with the corresponding private key.

PKI Usage

All users of a PKI system must present their public key in a way the user community believes to be valid and trustworthy. To provide this assurance, these keys are stored in a digital format known as a public key certificate. In much the same manner as a passport authenticates a person's identity, a digital certificate guarantees the authenticity of a network user or device.

Digital certificates are issued to users and applications throughout the supply chain. PKI-enabled ERP applications use these digital certificates to perform digital signatures to prove who the users are without the risk and cost associated with sharing and managing shared passwords. When done properly, certificates with a robust PKI provide a nonreputable mechanism to bind a user to a transaction.

The result of integrating a PKI with your e-business infrastructure, such as ERP applications, is a fundamentally more secure supply chain transaction environment. This trustworthy networking environment is conducive to reduced transaction costs, more frequent and higher value electronic transactions, reduced time to market, and ultimately greater competitiveness for the supply chain participants.

Virtual Private Networks

A VPN (virtual private network) is a data transmission infrastructure that provides secure and reliable exchange of messages and information among company employees. VPN's are growing in popularity with cost-conscious network managers because VPNs are a means of relieving operational management snafus while saving a buck or two in the bargain.

The technology's potential success lies in the way that network managers view internetworking. In short, network managers like the idea of making company-wide data available to everyone in the company, but they're justifiably concerned about security protection when transmitting company data over public infrastructures. Therein lies the primary difference between VPNs and intranets—two otherwise compatible technologies.

VPNs do what intranets do but only more securely by adding features like user authentication and data integrity assurance to private interworking infrastructures. VPNs can also be configured to exchange e-mail between different divisions of the same organization at separate geographical locations. VPN capabilities establish secure links over IP networks, enabling remote users to dial into the corporate infrastructure via a local call to an Internet service provider. Some vendors are even rolling out add-on capabilities that enable managers to manage remote access more effectively. Adaptive switching tools, for example, provide network managers with a switch with one primary rate ISDN interface to support multiple services such as e-mail, encryption, error corrections, and Internet link-ups. And extranets can be created that link up information databases at different companies, say Ford Motor and its largest parts supplier, who frequently share information. The fact that managers may also save big bucks on 800 numbers, long distance calls, and remote hardware outlays using VPN only sweetens the pot.

Certificate authorities are the user authentication and content verification mechanism of VPNs. A typical CA-based VPN configuration consists of a sender and recipient Web server protected by firewalls, each with access to the agreed certificate authority file system.

The benefits of CA-enabled virtual networks versus the open Internet or leased networks include:

- Industrial-strength security;
- A flexible architecture that uses multiple browser and server applications across platforms;
- A finely tuned level of access control that can grant access to different levels of users down to the document level;
- The ability to support various online and e-mail applications; and
- The ability to scale to thousands or conceivably even millions of users.

Confidentiality

A digital certificate-based VPN is dependent upon algorithms of various lengths (keys) that encrypt and decrypt information. Encryption changes data into unreadable code, making interception by Web hackers or other unauthorized surfers useless. Certificate authorities utilize a public key infrastructure (PKI)–based encryption architecture, using both shared and private keys to encode and decode data. Public keys are shared by both the sender and recipient over the Internet while private keys are based on something users possess, such as smart cards. Both keys are mathematically linked so that the data scrambled by a public key can be read only by the corresponding private key and vice-versa.

Identification

The encryption keys used to encode data are filed in directories made up of digital certificates, each of which identifies a user who is permitted to access the keys. These certificates are used to verify identities, providing a higher level of security than what is offered by password systems. Digital certificates contain the key, the user's name, the issuance date and the expiration date of the key, the name of the certificate authority that issued the certificate, and the digital signature of the issuer. Digital certificates containing encryption keys are distributed to users only after users verify their identity based on data previously posted in the CA data bank by a Local Registration Agent (LRA).

Data Integrity

During an Internet message or transaction, parties need to not only offer guarantees of their identities but ensure the integrity of data and confirm that the transfer of information did occur. They do this by generating digital signatures. Creating a signature begins when a sender produces a mathematical summary or digest of a message called a hash. The hash is encoded via the sender's private encryption key and attached as a fingerprint to the message. The entire message is then encrypted via the recipient's public key and sent to the recipient. The contents of the transmitted message cannot be changed without also changing the hash code. When the message is received, the attached hash code is compared to the hash code possessed by the recipient. If the two codes match, the recipient knows the message could only come from the sender and that the contents of the message have not been altered.

The components of certificate authority–based public key infrastructure systems include the encryption, user identification, user authentication, and data integrity capabilities provided by digital certificates and the additional CA maintenance capabilities shown earlier.

A certificate authority service manages and distributes these certificates and the electronic keys. A CA can be operated either in-house by a customer or outsourced to a trusted third-party CA service. A CA is responsible for the complex process of registering new users, securing Web servers, distributing and updating private keys and certificates, recovering lost or forgotten keys, and maintaining audit trails that track any administrative changes made to the system.

Value-Added Networks

The migration to Internet e-commerce can be accelerated by corporations examining the weaknesses of their first-generation private network solutions that are still in use. Previously, security needs were addressed by value-added networks (VANs) that were based on private, closed, leased-line or dial-up access. The development of VAN capabilities through EDI offered the advantages of a fast, high-volume transfer of data over a secure network.

VANs, however, are very limiting in comparison to VPNs and the Internet. VANs are usually expensive proprietary solutions that restrict users to specific hardware and software platforms. The number of companies sharing these networks is minuscule compared to the near-entirety of the developed world that is linked to the Internet, which usually requires local hub access or the less expensive local dial-in.

In addition, both companies communicating over a VAN have to agree on standard EDI format for purchase orders, invoices, and other electronic forms. Standard formatting is a hassle for one or both of the companies if existing electronic documents have to be redesigned. When considering abandoning proprietary systems for the Web, corporate IT departments must realize that VANs offer a secure platform but limit the ability to link with potential clients and customers throughout the world.

Cyber Security Laws

Global governments are keeping a close eye on e-business and its commerce-related variations. Some countries have already enacted tough antitheft cyber laws, while some are adopting a wait and see attitude toward e-business. As of early 2000, the countries that have cyber laws already in place are the United States, Australia, Canada, Germany, France, the UK, Ghana, Singapore, Malaysia, and India.

Most of these countries' cyber laws are pro-business laws that are framed for the growth of e-commerce. The United Nations Commission on International Trade Law (UNCITRAL) has framed a model law to support commercial use of international contracts in e-commerce. This law provides for acceptability of digital signature for legal and commercial purpose and supports the computer evidence in the court of law.

In the United States, apart from federal statutes, all the individual states have cyber laws in place covering computer-related crime; crimes against property; credit card offenses; fraudulent access to computers, computer systems, and computer networks; crimes against commerce; unlawful use of computers; offenses against the right to privacy; criminal mischief; and related offenses.

In most instances, cyber laws in other countries are very similar and address similar issues. The primary point of difference is the severity of punishment that is meted out to cyber criminals.

A Secure World

Thanks to the Internet, business are finding new and wondrous ways to conduct businesses with parties thousands of miles away. Strategies can be as simple as issuing a digital certificate, e-mailing it to the recipient corporation, and telling them the name of the sender's home page. If the sender's internal systems are already Web-accessible, that's all that is necessary. Better yet, many applications, browsers, and Web servers are already "certificate ready," and for others simple plug-in software is currently available. Certificate authorities can allow an enterprise to set up and conduct business on the Web in a matter of hours instead of a matter of months.

In addition to the security of a certificate authority–based virtual private network, corporations are finding they can open their trusted internal systems to authorized partners over the Internet. Early commercial deployment of the Internet, other than e-mail gateways, were basically electronic brochures that provided standard company information and marketing material. To successfully implement Web-based commerce, a company must create the forms and supply Web addresses for information that was previously relegated to proprietary networks.

But all information that a company posts on the Web can't be accessible to everyone with a browser; confidential information on the Web must be secured. When part of a secure e-business network—like a certificate authority or a virtual private network—trusted information detailing customers, business plans, product development, inventory, and other business processes can be posted on the Internet but accessed only by those approved by the certificate authority and authorized by fine-grained access control applications. With the help of a good security package, all of the systems needed to transact with remote partners are available to the select few granted access.

chapter fourteen

If You Take a Walk
They'll Tax Your Feet

anuary 31, 2000 was a banner day for economists, politicians,
business owners, and all Americans for that matter. That was the
day the roaring U.S. economy had grown for a record 107th
straight month, a new record for the longest economic expansion in
U.S. history. In a lead story in that day's *USA Today*, the reasons cited
for the economy's remarkable growth weren't presidential policy,
Federal Reserve interest rate intervention, or the end of the Cold War.
No, the primary reason that *USA Today* gave for the booming
economy was the Internet—specifically e-business.

"The typical paper purchase order," *USA Today* reported, "when
factoring in personnel and other charges, costs, on average, $50 to
$70. The same process done electronically not only is faster, but costs
$1 to $5. Those sorts of innovations have been behind the 2 percent
annual average increase in productivity throughout this expansion.
Sales over B2B networks have grown from nearly zero several years
ago to $114 billion today. At that rate, corporations around the world
will save up to $1.3 trillion by 2002—the equivalent of France's gross
domestic product—by adopting e-business."

That's quite a testimonial to a technology that is barely old enough
to date Woody Allen. But the growth of e-business—and the accompa-
nying growth of the U.S. and global economy—may be jeopardized by
government intervention in the form of taxes on e-business transactions
on both the business-to-business and business-to-consumer sides.

So just how will e-business affect tax revenues? There is plenty of
speculation but few clear answers. However, one point in particular is

apparent: more people will be doing business over the Internet, and some, but not all, of it will be more difficult to tax.

For governments, it means a possible erosion of essential tax revenues; for businesses, it means a new competitive landscape where those who are able to offer tax-free, Internet-based products and services stand to gain a competitive edge over their competitors who don't—or can't.

The question of taxing e-business meshes a large number of different issues, including indirect taxes (such as Value Added Tax [VAT] in Britain and sales taxes in the United States) and direct taxes (such as corporation tax and income tax).

The E-Business Tax Dilemma

Electronic commerce has moved U.S. commerce from an industrial economy where machines dominated productivity to an information-based economy where intellectual content is the dominant source of added value and which knows no geographic boundaries. Yet most existing tax law and regulations were established decades ago and were designed for taxing tangible products. Some state and local governments have nonetheless attempted to capture emerging technologies in their tax structure by simply expanding old concepts to new types of businesses. The detailed tax regulations developed generations ago, however, are not easily applied to modern technological realities and present serious compliance problems for ISPs, vendors, and telecommunications service providers.

Critics claim that ordering a product or service via a computer is no different than placing an order over the telephone or by U.S. mail. "A company that uses the U.S. Postal Service or United Parcel Service (UPS) to receive its orders and deliver its products is not considered to have entered into an agency relationship with the Postal Service or UPS and thus does not establish nexus from its relationship with the conventional carrier," says Carol Cayo, senior analyst for the Information Technology Association of America.

"Why should products or services ordered or delivered via the Internet be any different?" Cayo says the Internet is only a different medium of delivery. Taxation should be based on the substance of a transaction and the surrounding facts, not the incidental form of conveyance. To date, no court has held that the mere use by a business of a commonly available means of transporting goods or services creates an agency relationship and therefore imparts tax nexus to such a business based on the relationship.

Order from the Court

The U.S. Supreme Court recently weighed in on the e-business tax issue with *Quill Corporation v. North Dakota*. The court held that North Dakota's enforcement of its tax-collection responsibilities against an out-of-state mail-order company with no physical presence in the state, which merely mails catalogs into the state and fills orders by U.S. mail or common carriers, was an unconstitutional burden on interstate commerce (i.e., violated the Commerce Clause of the U.S. Constitution). The fact that the seller had licensed software in the state for use by customers to electronically order its products was considered insufficient to meet the nexus requirement of the U.S. Constitution Commerce Clause.

Says the ITAA's Cayo, "There is no reason to believe that the Supreme Court would have decided *Quill* differently if the sales there had been made over the Internet, because a vendor selling via the Internet involves even less physical contact with the state than catalogs mailed to North Dakota, and indeed may involve no physical contact whatsoever."

Compliance Questions

While many government officials maintain that there should be fair and equitable tax treatment of goods and services purchased over the Internet and in the tangible world, the technological makeup of the Internet makes taxing e-business difficult to do. After all, an essential tenet of any tax system is the ability of taxpayers to comply. The inability to discern boundaries in the electronic marketplace makes it difficult, if not impossible, for Internet providers or other businesses selling or licensing products and services electronically to identify the location where they are being used.

A customer on the Internet may use nothing other than an e-mail address and utilize a service from virtually anywhere in the world. His or her location usually cannot be determined. Where is a product or service being delivered when it is sent to an Internet address? A billing address may be available but may merely be a post office box. Even then, a billing address may only be known to a credit card intermediary company, not the vendor or ISP.

When a product is physically delivered to a location, the taxing jurisdiction is known, which is often not the case when a product is delivered electronically to an Internet address. Such transactions should be subject to the same transactional tax requirements imposed on the mail-order industry. Based on the Supreme Court ruling in *Quill,* a vendor that has physical presence, or substantial nexus, in the jurisdiction where the goods are delivered can be required to collect and remit sales tax to that jurisdiction. A vendor that does not have substantial physical presence in the jurisdiction where the goods are delivered cannot be required to collect and remit the tax. The purchaser of the goods, however, remains obligated to pay sales tax (i.e., use tax) to the jurisdiction where the goods are being used, if such a tax is applicable.

Of concern to ISPs and vendors operating on the Internet is that every effort be made by taxing jurisdictions to avoid the risk of double taxation. The adoption of consistent taxing terms, definitions, and concepts would eliminate many of the problems that will otherwise occur when one jurisdiction seeks to impose income tax based on one criterion while another jurisdiction embraces a conflicting taxing criterion.

Critics also ask why states should not expect to benefit from e-business. Many say they already are. Many people don't realize it, but Internet-related activity is already being taxed. Both Internet access providers and their customers already pay taxes on the telecommunications facilities used to provide access to the Internet. As more and more people access the Internet, states are benefiting from increased tax revenue they are receiving from increased use of telecommunications facilities. They are also benefiting from increased purchases of tangible property such as personal computers, printers, servers, and peripheral equipment.

It is also logical to assume that as industry grows and hires more people to meet the increased demand for goods and services, states will reap the benefits of economic growth through the increase in income taxes, sales taxes, property taxes, and payroll taxes being paid, as well as expanded availability of disposable income. Other benefits include expansion of educational opportunities, better health care, increased quality and reduced cost of government services, and a new way to reach rural areas and inner cities to provide services.

There's also little doubt that unreasonable tax burdens will hinder the growth of the Internet, a medium with great potential for contributions to the economic health of the states and the welfare of their citizens. If the Internet is going to be a benefit, it will also be a benefit to the states. Any new public policy should remove obstacles to achieving the maximum economic growth possible, enable more Americans to use the Internet to take advantage of the rich resources in information, communications, and computing technologies, and create the largest possible marketplace for U.S. providers of high-technology products and services.

U.S. Government's Internet Tax Strategy

Some Internet observers say that Uncle Sam has no business taxing e-business transactions, that state and local governments have a responsibility to create an environment that will facilitate economic growth and make available to its citizens the many benefits new technology has to offer. Still, the U.S. government moved quickly to address the tax as well as other regulatory and legal questions raised by the global e-business revolution. In late 1996 and mid-1997, the government issued two major policy discussion papers, one covering general legal and regulatory issues and the other authored by the Treasury Department covering in detail the tax policy implications of global e-business.

The Treasury Department's paper, "Selected Tax Policy Implications of Global E-Commerce," the first national paper of its kind, was intended to stimulate a discussion on the federal, international, and compliance issues that emerge from advances in communications technology and use of the Internet. The Treasury paper raised questions about permanent establishment (PE) and the character and source of income without making specific recommendations other than to indicate that:

- The United States would seek to apply existing international tax principles, appropriately modified, to e-commerce;
- The United States would not take an aggressive stance on taxable presence;
- The new software regulations might be expanded to cover other digitized material;

- The principle of neutrality is favored to ensure that income from electronic transactions is treated the same as income from similar physical transactions; and
- In sourcing income from e-commerce, a residence-based approach appeared to be the most workable.

Also in late 1996, the IRS issued proposed regulations (which were finalized in 1998) on the characterization for international tax purposes of transfers of computer programs. The software regulations deal with an issue that had been under debate for a long time: under what circumstances will a transfer of software constitute a sale, a license, or a service? Resolution of this issue will advance the resolution of other tax characterization questions relevant to e-commerce.

The Internet Tax Freedom Act

In response to concerns regarding state and local taxation of the Internet, Congress enacted the Internet Tax Freedom Act (ITFA) in October 1998. The IFTA places a three-year moratorium (until October 2001) on new taxes on Internet access fees and prohibits "multiple and discriminatory taxes" on e-commerce. It does not, however, prevent tax authorities from imposing a previously existing tax on e-commerce transactions, if the tax is equally applicable to e-commerce companies and traditional companies. In addition, the ITFA contains a grandfather provision that allows states that had previously imposed and enforced taxes on Internet access fees to continue to apply these taxes.

The ITFA created a congressionally appointed 19-member Advisory Commission on Electronic Commerce, comprised of representatives from government and industry, to study Internet taxation issues and draft a report to Congress by April 2000, outlining recommendations regarding the moratorium and application of current tax laws to e-business transactions. The Advisory Commission's recommendations may result in dramatic changes to the existing sales and use tax system, which would affect almost every company's existing sales tax collection and information reporting systems. For example, the commission could propose an arrangement whereby companies making "remote sales"—such as Internet, mail-order, and telemarketing companies—agree to collect and remit sales and use taxes on all sales. In return, the companies would enjoy a significantly reduced administrative burden associated with collecting and remitting taxes. Such measures might include establishing a uniform statewide tax rate, as well as consolidated statewide tax returns, limitations on tax rate changes, and uniform definitions of which products and services are subject to tax. Commission members also may consider "technology solutions" when reviewing potential

Glossary of E-Business Tax Terms

apportionment formula. Most states use this formula to calculate which revenues should be apportioned to their state. It's based on a taxpayer's relative percentage of gross receipts, payroll, and property compared to other states.

digitized product. Items that can be reduced to bits and bytes, generally in a physical form such as music, books, newspapers, or software. Questions exist whether digitized products are tangible or intangible.

intangible property. Valuable business assets without any physical manifestation such as trademarks, copyrights, and customer goodwill.

level playing field. Similar economic transactions are treated the same for tax purposes to prevent distortion (i.e., taxing a computer program purchased on a diskette versus the same program downloaded).

neutrality. Similar to level playing field, tax laws should not be applied differently on the channels of commerce (i.e., retail store versus mail order versus e-commerce purchases).

nexus. The degree of business activity/presence required before a state or local tax jurisdiction can impose tax or require a company to collect sales and use tax. (The U.S.

Supreme Court has ruled that nexus requires a physical presence.)

permanent establishment (PE). The degree of presence that would result in taxes being imposed in another country.

tax pyramiding. Pyramiding occurs when a business pays sales tax on supplies and equipment that are later factored into prices charged to customers, who also pay sales tax when they purchase the same product.

uniformity. Each of the states has its laws, rate structures, definitions of what is taxable, and exemptions of tax in applying sales and use tax. Lack of uniformity makes compliance with all the varying tax rules a complex and costly undertaking that imposes a significant administrative burden on multistate tax issues.

use tax. The complement to sales tax, it usually accrues when the item is used in a state other than the state in which it was purchased. For example, if a California resident purchases a computer from an out-of-state vendor, that resident is responsible for filing a use tax return as a part of the self-reporting use tax collection process.

Source: Deloitte & Touche

changes to the existing sales and use tax system. At this time, no one can predict the recommendations the commission will make.

Foreign Trade Compliance

In addition to the federal tax issues, foreign businesses selling services and digitized information to customers in the United States may need to comply with state income and sales and use taxes. The ITFA was an important development in this area, which limits the states' ability to implement new state sales or use taxes that discriminate against e-commerce.

The Treasury paper suggestions on U.S. domestic law include the following:

1. Soliciting through a Web site will not constitute a U.S. trade or business. Mere accessibility of a foreign person's Web site on computers in the United States will not be sufficient presence to constitute a U.S. trade or business.
2. The mere presence of a computer server in the United States will not be a U.S. trade or business (part of the reasoning seems to be that the server easily could be moved to another jurisdiction, thus making such a jurisdictional basis of taxation illusory).
3. The use of service provider, such as an Internet service provider (ISP), will not create an imputed trade or business to a nonresident. On the issue of PE, the Treasury paper suggests that:

   - The presence of a computer server belonging to a foreign vendor should not be deemed to constitute a PE (analogizing a server to a facility used solely for the purpose of storage, display, or delivery of goods or merchandise). However, a different result may ensue for telecommunications service providers or ISPs because, unlike the case where a foreign person sells data that is stored on a server in the United States, operation of a U.S.–based server for the sale of Internet access to United States and foreign customers is integral to the "actual realization of profits" of these companies.
   - Mere accessibility of a foreign person's Web site on computers in the United States will not be sufficient presence to give rise to a PE.

The IRS Office of Electronic Commerce

The IRS has also set up a group that will consider the technical and audit issues involved in e-business, including:

- The treatment of advance payments for on-line services
- Whether Web site development costs should be expensed or capitalized
- Whether Web site development costs should be eligible for the R&E credit
- Whether income is created if two companies have linking banners on their Web sites

The IRS also has started measuring tax compliance from Internet activities and will develop audit techniques for e-commerce.

U.S. Sales Tax View

E-commerce raises complex issues for both domestic and foreign businesses in the sales and use tax arena because of the possibility to deliver digitized products traditionally sold in tangible form, like software on disk or CD-ROM. The ability to avoid fixed points of distribution (for example, by using mirror Web sites) and the difficulty of determining the location of the consumer, particularly if electronic money is used to effect the transaction, make it nearly impossible to determine the appropriate tax jurisdiction's rates and rules for certain transactions. As these transactions become more prevalent, the tax stakes and risks will increase significantly.

Online sellers are faced with the task of resolving controversial tax issues such as what products and services are taxable, the base on which tax is imposed, who is responsible for collecting the tax, and what jurisdiction is entitled to the tax, simply to be in compliance. On the tax administration side, because of co-branding and unclear relationships between the retailer, the Web host, and the fulfillment company, it is often difficult to determine who the true seller is, and where the seller is located.

Companies that sell throughout the United States face the prospect of multiple sales tax rates and multiple tax exemptions that can be imposed by a staggering 30,000 state, city, county, and special purpose taxing authorities. Such companies may be required to submit more than 6,500 different sales tax forms each year. Most startup e-businesses lack the resources to understand and comply with the rules of a myriad of taxing jurisdictions. The rapid evolution of e-commerce, as well as its culture, is simply not conducive to thoughtful compliance with complex and often unclear state sales tax laws.

States' Rights?

While Uncle Sam has adopted the stance of no additional Internet taxes for now, state governments are grappling with the issue individually. Texas taxes not only Internet access charges, but also all the money collected when content providers sell online subscriptions as well as the fees charged by Web developers for building sites. On the other hand, New York decreed that Internet access charges are not subject to state sales or telecommunications taxes. Currently nine states tax Internet services, and six states, including California, have moratoriums on Internet taxes.

Most states still don't know what to do, according to the accounting and consulting firm Deloitte & Touche, which published a comprehensive guide called *Taxation in Cyberspace*. Some states, like Texas, claim the location of a computer server creates tax liabilities for either the Internet service provider or the vendor that hosts its Web site. Even though ISPs and vendors typically don't own the server and are unaware of a Web site's location, some states persist in asserting nexus. Multiple servers in different cities are commonly used to avoid problems in the event that one server has crashed. And ISPs and vendors can easily move the location of a Web site—a Web site in Texas today may transfer to California tomorrow. Under the ITFA, the definition of discriminatory tax includes a state asserting that "the sole ability to access a site on a remote seller's out-of-state computer server is considered a factor in determining that remote seller's tax collection obligation."

Variances in state sales tax rules also create a huge administrative cost burden. The big players in e-business—either Fortune 500 companies or well capitalized start-ups—are spending anywhere from $25,000 to $75,000 per year for high-end sales tax software. These companies are also spending anywhere from $100,000 to $200,000 and up for research materials to understand the laws and to hire people who can interpret these laws.

The key to Internet taxation is uniformity, which produces a level playing field, rather than dealing with 50 sets of rules. The lack of uniformity is driven by the actual economic situation in each state (i.e., market state versus a manufacturing state, or provider versus consumer state). Most variations in state and local tax rules have been developed intentionally, either to benefit particular industries or to raise revenue based on captive industries that can't easily relocate, such as oil and gas industries or wineries.

The ITFA specifically prohibits multiple taxation. However, this provision isn't intended to block different apportionment formula schemes among states. Under existing law, the differences can create the potential for multiple taxation. In a worst-case scenario, the lack of a uniform apportionment approach among all states can result in taxation of more than 100 percent of a business's income. At the opposite end of the scale, this lack of uniformity could create "nowhere" income, untaxed by any state.

Tax News from Abroad

Tax administrations around the world and the Organization for Economic Co-operation and Development (OECD) have embarked upon a review of their fiscal policies and collection procedures in contemplation of the likely effect of Internet taxation. In 1999, the OECD held a conference in Ottawa on developing a framework for e-commerce. It ended with an agreement on two key principles that could well guide global governments' responses as they grapple with the question of taxing e-business. The first principle is that e-business taxes, where they are applicable, should be applied at the point of consumption (the browser) rather than at the point of supply (the server) in an attempt to stop countries generating lower tax rates in the hope of attracting e-businesses.

But the OECD ran into the same roadblock that everyone else has run into after examining the Internet tax landscape: Nobody can figure out how you can actually police or tax intangible goods. One of the main reasons for this is that if you're looking at the flow of information over a wire, there is no real way you can work out which pieces of data represent the delivery of packets of intellectual property.

At one point, according to a European Commission study, it looked as though there might be some support among governments for a "bit tax." This tax would effectively levy a charge on each bit (eight bits make a byte) of information transmitted.

But momentum for such an initiative is slow, if not nonexistent. In fact, the probability is that, on a global basis, e-businesses are not going to be subject to a whole new constellation of international income tax rules or taxes. The U.S. Treasury and OECD pronouncements both recently stated that there will be no "bit tax," no "tollbooth on the information superhighway," or any other kind of new Web tax. Some might disagree (note the recent U.N. suggestion for a one-cent [U.S.] tax on every 100 e-mail messages sent over the Internet).

One area that the OECD is encroaching upon is the area of e-business "softgoods" (i.e., commodities' legal or accounting services, digitized text, music, and other information services). A vendor selling these products electronically would not be subject to royalty treatment and withholding tax unless the customer is granted the right to copy for distribution to the public. On the other hand, sellers of software and digitized content to non-OECD (and some OECD) countries may not be relieved of the withholding tax burden anytime soon. In addition, the European Union (EU) is working on changes to the VAT rules that would eliminate the existing opportunity for non-EU sellers of softgoods to sell VAT-free to individuals in the EU.

Merely having a Web site that is accessible to customers in foreign countries is not likely to create a taxable presence in those countries. However, if the server is loaded with a digitized product and is programmed to process and deliver orders, some countries might view it as a permanent establishment (PE). Accordingly, server locations will have to be selected with care.

Indirect taxes—such as VAT, GST, and U.S. state and local sales and use taxes—will continue to present challenges to both taxpayers and tax authorities because of the multiplicity and variety of taxing jurisdictions and disparities in rules and compliance burdens.

The Offshore Threat

The wild card for e-businesses worldwide in the Internet tax wars is the threat by such companies to move their businesses to tax-friendly offshore locales like Bermuda or the Cayman Islands. While it's true tax havens can be considered for offshore Internet operations, a counterbalancing primary concern will be the telecommunications infrastructure (e.g., T1 lines) and the absence of tax treaties with such countries. Aside from Bermuda and the Cayman Islands, among the low-tax jurisdictions with treaties that have set out to be Internet friendly are Ireland and Singapore. The latter, for example, has upgraded its infrastructure and passed the Electronic Transactions Act and the Approved Cyber-Trader tax incentive regime to promote e-business within its borders.

A principal concern of tax authorities is that the highly mobile nature of the new Internet technologies will lead to the proliferation of tax haven operations that will further erode their tax base. For the country where the business is owned, the question is the effectiveness of any tax (or antitax) legislation, which may or may not capture all types of income derived in e-commerce. For the countries where the customers are located, the feared tax base erosion will be offset by the collection of import VAT and customs duties on goods and withholding tax on payments that are characterized as royalties. Few countries have tax treaties with tax havens, so the typical treaty reduction or elimination of withholding taxes on royalties would not be available.

Industry Impact

The expansion of e-business undoubtedly will impact companies and industries of all stripes. As we've seen throughout this book, most businesses operating in the physical world have or are in the process of taking their business onto the Web. Well known established names have added Internet resources to their existing distribution structure, including Charles Schwab, Ford, General Motors, Barnes & Noble, and the Gap. The Web has spawned a variety of Web-only businesses, such as Amazon.com, E*Trade, and eBay—companies that have no stores or other traditional facilities but sell entirely over the Internet. The Web also has opened up worldwide markets for small players as well, as small and medium-size businesses now will benefit from access to a global consumer base.

Uncertainty is one of the biggest issues facing businesses and consumers engaging in e-commerce. In the tax arena, uncertainty stems from two key issues: geography is meaningless on the Internet, making sales and use tax collection problematic; and no one knows if the current tax system can be adapted to serve the mercurial nature of e-commerce.

While the Internet Tax Freedom Act (ITFA) has imposed a three-year moratorium on implementing new taxes, taxation remains a concern for companies and consumers conducting business via the Internet. Under a grandfather provision for states that began taxing Internet access prior to October 1998, some states can continue to collect sales and use taxes on Internet access fees. The ITFA moratorium applies only to Internet access fees and "multiple and discriminatory taxes" on e-commerce. If a company has to collect sales taxes on mail orders, it must also collect tax on its Web-based sales.

Another pressing issue for e-businesses involves designing computer systems that capture and process transaction information. If you launch a complex Web site to interactively serve customers and take orders, consider inputting fields requesting zip codes and calculating sales tax on each bill of sale. These fields won't have to be active until Congress or state and local governments mandate certain taxes. However, the functionality ensures that billing information will be captured for future compliance. Two years from now, upgrading your IT infrastructure to support new tax functions could be a very expensive undertaking, so design and act now.

For now, e-commerce providers such as AT&T are treating Web purchases much like mail-order sales. The providers collect taxes if the merchant has a significant presence in the state where the buyer resides.

The Current Tax Outlook

So where do e-businesses stand today regarding Internet taxation? Let's face it, increased economic activity fostered by e-commerce has the potential to generate significant additional tax revenues. In addition, this will allow the government to provide better services at a lower cost.

Everyone agrees that there's a lot of money at stake in the domestic and global quest to address Internet taxation issues. A recent report by Forrester Research estimated that global Internet commerce sales will reach $3.2 trillion in 2003 if business and governments effectively collaborate to solve issues raised by the Internet—such as taxation. But sales will reach only $1.8 trillion if business and governments fail to work in unison.

Reports differ on just how much revenue states stand to lose from the growth of e-commerce. Frank Shafroth, director of state and federal relations for the National Governors Association in Washington, says states lost $4 billion in revenue in 1998 from untaxed remote sales. However, another study by Ernst & Young says states lost only $170 million, less than 1 percent of collected taxes. Either way, they will lose more and more as e-commerce continues its blistering growth.

To eliminate the loss of taxes from remote sales, states and other local governmental groups are pushing for tax assessment based on where the purchaser lives rather than the seller's location. This way, consumers lose all tax incentive to favor one type of retailer or another.

But e-businesses fear such an approach—and for good reason. There are roughly 6,500 taxing jurisdictions in the United States created by separate state, county, and city laws. Complying with all of these statutes could bury a company in a mountain of tax forms.

For the time being, nobody is paying sales taxes when they buy books, clothing, or anything else on the Net. Given that the average sales tax rate in the United States is about 6.3 percent, that means state and local governments are giving e-business a huge subsidy. University of Chicago economist Austan Goolsbee estimates the value of this gift was $430 million in 1998.

The big hope of many Net merchants is that the tax holiday will last forever. It probably won't. Sales taxes account for about 49 percent of all state tax revenues—more than individual and corporate taxes combined. And in cities and counties, sales levies account for about 16 percent of all taxes collected.

This means that the nation's governors and mayors need sales taxes to balance their budgets—not to mention to pay for schools, law enforcement, highway repair, and the other important work they do. As e-business accounts for a bigger chunk of the economy, there's no way they're going to let sales tax revenues dwindle away.

This will have a huge impact on e-biz. Net shoppers are nothing if not price sensitive. In a recent study of 25,000 consumers by the University of Chicago, online spending would drop by 30 percent or more if taxes were suddenly imposed. This short-term blow wouldn't kill healthy e-businesses, but it would certainly threaten many marginal ones.

Steps to Take

What can e-businesses do specifically to get involved directly in the Net tax discussion? The commissions appointed to study the Internet's tax implications, like the ITFA and the OECD, provide important forums for business and government to discuss and resolve tax issues. The public's input could prove valuable in guiding the commissions' work. Companies should contact commission members, follow current developments impacting the taxation of electronic commerce, and make their concerns known.

Above all, if you're entering the brave new world of e-business, make sure these considerations are part of your business plan:

1. Follow the current government and industry developments affecting online business.
2. Understand that while taxes should not drive e-commerce business decisions, tax involvement in upfront planning is absolutely critical.
3. Maintain flexibility of your IS systems to accommodate tax law changes. This will save the prohibitive costs of upgrading your system at a later date.

The good news is that with strategic tax planning, you can minimize, and in some cases, avoid tax problems. Business owners venturing into

---

Internet Taxation: Points to Ponder

- Despite the passage of the Internet Tax Freedom Act, which imposes a three-year moratorium on new taxes, a grandfather provision allows states that implemented Internet access taxes before October 1998 to continue to collect sales and use taxes on Internet access fees.
- Leaping into e-commerce without considering taxes could be a recipe for disaster. But that doesn't mean tax issues should drive your e-commerce decisions. Tax implications will become clear once a solid e-commerce business plan is in place, taking into account such key areas as customer service, process re-engineering, security, privacy, and other legal issues.
- By 2002, Deloitte & Touche predicts that e-commerce and marketing will be a necessity for staying in business for 70 percent of companies. Increased economic activity fostered by e-commerce has the potential to generate significant additional tax revenues. Subsequently, this will allow the government to provide better services at lower costs.

e-businesses should proceed with caution by first developing a savvy business strategy for the Internet. While tax issues are important, they shouldn't drive your e-commerce business decisions. CEOs and CFOs should plan how to provide exemplary customer service and consider what their competitors are doing. And they shouldn't forget process re-engineering, security, privacy, and other important legal issues.

Should e-commerce activities fall under the same legal corporate entity as an existing retail business, or should a new entity be created, such as a corporation, a limited liability company, or a limited partnership? Once a business strategy for e-commerce has been devised, then tax implications can be evaluated.

chapter fifteen

The Future of E-Business

While experts have different views on how e-business will grow over the next decade or so, everyone's on the same page when it comes to the monumental impact technology will have on global commerce in the years ahead. In a recent study released by Nortel Networks, the company predicts that the value of the global Internet economy will rise to $2,800 billion in 2003—about 7 percent of the global domestic product. More than half this sum represents the investment that will be necessary to build up the Internet infrastructure to cope with the growth in demand. The study says that upgrading the Internet will cost $1,500 billion a year in 2003, while e-business will have grown to reach $1,300 billion a year. Most of the growth is expected to be in business-to-business commerce, which will be six times as big as business-to-consumer revenues.

This growth is causing companies—and investors—to throw cash around like drunken sailors. When China.dot.com launched an initial public offering (IPO) for just under $100 million on the NASDAQ, it received more than $4 billion in offers. Months later, the company went back for more, raising $422 million in a second offer that was 10 times oversubscribed.

What Have You Done for Me Lately?

As the intense interest by investors in online commerce demonstrates, the future of e-business is about much more than an online, alternative means of payment. Over the next two to three years, the emergence of pervasive electronic commerce applications will transform the manner in which e-companies conduct their most basic business functions. This transformation will be signaled by ubiquitous and uniform access to networked computers, collaborative initiatives among institutions and business solution providers, and legislative reform of key regulatory law. The results will include reduced operating expense, enhanced service quality delivery, the outsourcing (or co-sourcing) of non-core-business operations, and a return to a focus on education and research.

By linking people through a pervasive tapestry of interactivity, and keeping track of their transactions, e-business-based systems will enable enterprises to respond to customers' needs, facilitating a range of customized transactional experiences, support applications, and administrative services.

Culturally, future e-business trends signal the diminishment of the term "e-commerce" in our lexicon. While retail e-commerce—the Amazon.coms and Gap.coms of the world—stole most of the Internet commerce headlines in the late 1990s, the 2000s are a different story. Now e-business, which encompasses e-commerce's click-to-buy mantra but also includes supply chain inventory flow, virtual bids, and other short-term online business needs, will grab most of the world's attention.

"Millions of e-businesses will emerge in the early 2000s," says e-business guru and author John Patrick. "The winners and losers won't be determined by who is on the Internet (since everyone will be), but by who handles all their normal, day-to-day business needs via the Web." Patrick cites as prime examples of new e-businesses IntraLinks, which handles document flow for loan syndication ($250 billion worth of loans closed in two years), and SciQuest, the "Internet Source for Scientific Products," with 300,000 items to search through. Internet2, addressing the major challenges facing the next generation of university networks, has 40 companies involved, including AT&T, IBM, 3Com, Cisco, MCI, Ameritech, Lucent, Microsoft, and over 150 universities.

Patrick is one of an army of Web observers who believe that the ability to conduct business on open electronic networks is vital as it helps companies coordinate their activities faster and more cheaply on a global basis. They say that efficiencies will arise as technology replaces manual processes and as e-business technologies create structures that operate across firms and supply chains.

Across all industry sectors, 37.1 percent of organizations already have e-business operations in place, and more are on the way, according to Computer Economics.

E-Business Implementation

Industry	Percentage
Manufacturing	34.9
Discrete Manufacturing	33.3
Retail Distribution	35.5
Wholesale Distribution	33.3
Banking and Finance	52.9
Insurance	48.1
Health Care	21.8
Trade Services	36.8
Professional Services	21.7
Utilities	26.9
Transportation	57.2
Federal Government	25.0
Local Government	37.5

Source: Computer Economics

The annual "Information Systems and E-Business Spending" report by Computer Economics predicts that another 46.8 percent of firms are planning to engage in e-business in the future.

Future Shock

As e-business is a dynamic, fluid new commerce model, it's hard to keep track of all the changes. But the research shows that there are some things company managers can count on when it comes to e-business in the years ahead.

Applications

E-business applications should continue to grow user friendlier, as buyers and suppliers alike are getting hooked up to the World Wide Web and Internet technology is moving forward rapidly. Analysts say that in the not-so-distant future, many buyers will use e-procurement systems to communicate changing market demand in realtime and adjust future supply needs automatically. Indeed, this already is being done in high-tech manufacturing markets. And the e-marketplace will mature, allowing communities of buyers and suppliers to interact in a manner that opens and speeds communication and creates a more competitive—and efficient—business environment.

E-commerce also offers great potential to improve materials management. Thanks to technology that makes it possible for better communication between all links of the supply chain, analysts see a business world with less inventory and more customized products.

Some experts believe that 2000 will mark the "second wave" of Internet procurement. The first wave focused primarily on automation of the internal workflow—things like the implementation of ERP systems and placing catalogs online—but the second wave will offer applications that provide decision support as well as reporting and analysis tools.

Thus far, purchasing applications have been used primarily to buy nonproduction goods and services, such as MRO supplies, and they are often linked up with fewer than ten suppliers. (Electronics manufacturing, which is already seeing e-commerce for production purposes, is an exception.) E-business applications of the future will continue to support the traditional purchases of nonproduction goods and services but will extend to the production realm as well.

This second wave of Internet commerce will also consist of companies sharing analysis with the supply base. These new applications will enable many procurement organizations to interact with a multitude of suppliers, creating a more competitive bidding process. But they will also extend the forecasts of internal commerce applications, such as MRP and ERP, out to that supplier base.

Technology will allow buyers to provide suppliers with their material resource planning forecasts and, utilizing this information, suppliers can make more value-added bids that better meet a company's specific needs. The new phase is going to enable users to manage supplier collaboration planning, basically extending the enterprise out to the supply base.

The third aspect of e-commerce that buyers can look forward to will be the rise of open Internet marketplaces or exchanges. These online marketplaces will benefit both supplier and purchaser, as suppliers will be able to acquire new business and purchasers will be able to accept bids in a more competitive environment.

These e-marketplaces, reads a white paper authored by Charles Shih, a business-to-business e-commerce expert and a former research director with the Gartner Group, provide two fundamental services that will enable and scale e-commerce. The Gartner Group paper says the first fundamental service is that e-marketplaces aggregate buyers, sellers, content, and business services, making the traditionally fragmented markets more efficient. The second service is that e-marketplaces provide a single point of integration for buyers and sellers to interact, eliminating the friction that is inherent in connecting to trading partners directly. The paper says that this friction is and will continue to be the biggest obstacle to widescale deployment of EDI and most software-only integration solutions.

Also according to Shih's paper, e-marketplaces come in two forms: vertical marketplaces that specialize along a specific industry or market, and horizontal marketplaces that specialize along a specific business process or a set of related business processes. The paper goes on to say that there is both overlap and synergy to be found between the offerings of the horizontal and vertical e-marketplaces. Together, Shih wrote, they form a quilt of trading communities that number close to 500 today, and will, according to the Gartner Group, grow to 7,500 by the year 2002.

The paper says that the vast majority of these e-marketplaces, 95 percent, will be of the vertical variety and the transaction value that will flow through them, estimated by the Precursor Group, will be between $50 and $100 billion by 2002. And, according to the Gartner Group, almost 80 percent of the Global 1000 companies will participate in these business-to-business e-marketplaces to some extent by the end of 2002. Meanwhile, the major e-business application vendors will redouble their efforts to grab a bigger slice of the burgeoning online market.

For vendors like IBM, Microsoft, Oracle, and Sun Microsystems that want to extend their existing franchises through new products, acquisitions, and partnerships, that means getting closer to offering a complete "stack" of the base-level technologies. Over the past couple of years, all but Microsoft have focused significant energy on application servers as distinct components—environments for multiple operating systems that manage programming objects, database transactions, and Web programming. Microsoft has instead defined these capabilities as integral to its server operating system—thereby hindering it somewhat because many promised improvements were dependent on the release of Windows 2000. But the linkage is only more pronounced in Microsoft's case. Each of the others also aims to sell a stack of other technologies with the application server—Java, Solaris, and server hardware for Sun, the database and packaged applications for Oracle, and a range of enterprise integration technologies for IBM.

At the Gartner Group, analysts have begun talking about an "e-business platform" that exists above the level of hardware, operating systems, and databases. The vendors that own one or more of those traditional platform assets may have an advantage, but upstarts like Allaire Inc. and Bluestone Software are also showing leadership. Both expanded their product lines beyond application servers to support multiple styles of programming, multiple modes of interaction, XML-based application integration, and personalization.

Key to staying in the e-commerce race is choosing the right technology to build on. Gartner says that in Europe mobile and wireless technologies will be the main driver for e-commerce. One of the main technologies is Wireless Application Protocol (WAP), which allows applications to be accessed via a mobile handset. It's expected that over 95 percent of new mobile phones shipped in 2004 will be WAP-enabled.

Auctions

One business model native to the Internet is the auction site. In the past, auctions were limited to high-value goods such as antiques or very active markets such as commodities. On the Net, the improved economics of coordination and communication allow the model to apply to more products.

As more people access the Web, negotiated pricing mechanisms will increase in use. Most sites today use auction systems developed in-house. Now application vendors are beginning to offer products that include this technology.

"Auction-based market makers open new channels for small and medium-sized enterprises to reach customers that would have been too widely dispersed to reach before," says a report by PriceWaterhouseCoopers.

PriceWaterhouseCoopers also forecasts that in the next two years consolidation will reduce the number of payment mechanisms. "In 1999 more solutions are proposed than are necessary," they say.

They expect no single payment method to emerge as dominant. In the United States, payment card transactions will remain dominant with some growth in the use of electronic checks. In a pilot scheme, the U.S. Department of Defense issued more than 1,000 electronic checks per day to suppliers.

For most countries, where direct debit is already in use, businesses will couple this method with electronic billing to distribute invoices over the Internet.

Security

Some companies do remarkably well with e-business. Look at the success of General Motors and Navistar, for example. For General Motors, the cost of setting up a purchase order went from $57 to 14 cents when the process was moved online. The manufacturing giant Navistar saved $167 million in its first year of use. These are the kinds of concrete customer examples—not just talk or hype—that will keep e-business moving forward.

One barrier standing in the technology's way is security. Cutthroat global competition is causing companies to protect their proprietary information tighter than ever. Studies show that concerns over security is the biggest reason more companies don't go online.

But help is on the way. Further technologies beyond security and payment will become integrated to connect businesses. PriceWaterhouseCoopers forecasts that suppliers of enterprise resource planning (ERP) systems will add secure e-business functions to their products for suppliers, distributors, and customers. The software will become easier to use with configuration technologies available at manufacturer and retailer sites.

Future E-Business Trends

- Security—public key infrastructure led by certification authorities
- Payment—various methods that users choose depending on cost, efficiency, convenience, and trust
- Applications—enterprise resource planning suppliers will integrate e-business functions into their products
- Integration—enterprise application integration will mature to connect different business areas. Standards will replace proprietary interfaces and consolidation will occur

Corporate buyers will integrate their procurement applications with ERP systems and will use purchase systems to handle catalog and availability, then run the order through secure ERP software. Secure electronic data interchange using proprietary value-added networks will continue to grow, although at a lower rate as new users access EDI through the Web.

The Supply Chain

How will the value and power in the supply chain change and what are the opportunities that e-business can support? Understanding the information flows and the structure of the supply chain in the near future will be important for determining how to position your company and the best strategy for migrating toward e-business. Certainly there will be major changes in the supply chain with a shift in the boundaries between the delivery of goods and services and a simultaneous shift in the value chain. Similarly many goods and services currently delivered in a physical format will be delivered electronically creating structural changes that existing players will need to adapt to or die.

Currently, e-business is moving along two parallel lines on the supply chain. E-business is causing supply chains to shrink as buying corporations seek to streamline their purchasing and save large amounts of money by channeling more business to a core group of preferred providers with whom they can share a highly automated process, rich amounts of information, and low prices. It is creating compact, intimate supply chains with more teamwork as familiar players work together to make the whole supply chain hum.

Simultaneously, e-business is causing supply chains to expand as the power of the Internet knocks down old walls. Selling organizations with well crafted Web sites and marketing strategies are now reaching customers they never knew existed. Buying organizations are finding a host of new suppliers out there bidding for their business and offering products, services, terms, or prices that are better than they could get before. Relationships proliferate as cyberlinks are forged quickly and opportunistically to bring in unfamiliar players with value to add.

One trend that Web analysts say will drive supply chain e-business models in the 2000s is collaborative, or "c-commerce." The term, first coined by the Gartner Group in 1999, describes the collaborative and fluid interaction of a community of personnel, business partners, and customers that is joined together by the Internet, component, and integration technologies, resulting in agile but highly integrated "virtual" multicompany enterprises.

By enabling multiple trading partners to work interactively online, Gartner says that c-commerce strategies will produce lower costs, improve the quality of products and services, increase innovation, and optimize trading opportunities. "C-commerce is the next issue that business applications such as enterprise resource planning will have to address," explains Gartner Group analyst Bruce Bond. "Current ERP and supply chain applications are focused on supporting transactions and optimization within the single enterprise or, at best, within and among the enterprise and its more traditional, strategic trading partners. C-commerce applications will move beyond that level of support to enable multiple enterprises to work together online within a dynamic trading community, or 'cybermarket,' in which relationships are far more fluid and opportunistic." Current leaders in applications and infrastructure, including IBM, i2 Technologies, Microsoft, Oracle, and SAP, are developing c-commerce strategies and software applications.

Some business segments in the manufacturing and distribution industries—such as high-tech electronics and automotive—are already using more proactive, collaborative technologies including:

- Digital mockup technology, which enables a real-time 3-D design session to be invoked across a project Web site between a manufacturer and the manufacturer's suppliers, is used to collaboratively design a product, thus reducing cost and product time-to-market.
- "Processware," which enables inter-enterprise business processes and workflow, can substantially reduce inventory and manufacturing/distribution cycle times.

While these examples deal with immediate trading partners, c-commerce applications will ultimately expand capabilities across the supply chain. For example, supply chain "available-to-promise" functionality will enable enterprises to offer customers a more accurate reflection of when and how much of an order may be distributed based on looking beyond the next upstream supplier all the way to the supply chain source.

C-commerce will also bring about an increase in application hosting as enterprises look to c-commerce vendors to manage the c-commerce "traffic" and tackle the integration challenges that will require specific and scarce skills.

What is driving the creation of c-commerce? The emergence of global shop floors and virtual enterprises, as well as the proliferation of marketing and delivery channels, is creating the need for c-commerce communities. Moreover, the speed at which business is transacted and the increased emphasis on time-based competition enables the substitution of technology for human contact in high-velocity information and knowledge exchange applications.

The technologies that are enabling c-commerce evolution include the growth of the Web, component architectures, acceptance of emerging standards such as XML (Extensible Markup Language), and collaborative technologies including agents. In addition, integration technologies from more established IT vendors such as IBM, Microsoft, and SAP are gaining wider acceptance as de facto standards, according to Bond.

The next evolution of business applications, including ERP, enterprise asset management, engineering, supply chain planning, and front-office systems, will have to incorporate c-commerce strategies. Application vendors that do not build c-commerce infrastructures (and

E-Commerce Revenue by Industry (in billions)

	1998	2003
Computing and electronics	$19.7	$395.3
Motor vehicles	$3.7	$212.9
Petrochemicals	$4.7	$178.3
Utilities	$7.1	$169.5
Paper and office products	$1.3	$65.2
Shipping and warehousing	$1.2	$61.6
Food and agriculture	$0.3	$53.6
Consumer goods	$1.4	$51.9
Pharmaceutical and medical	$0.6	$44.1
Aerospace and defense	$2.5	$38.2
Construction	$0.4	$28.6
Heavy industries	$0.1	$15.8
Industrial equipment	$0.1	$15.8
TOTAL	$43.1	$1,330.8

Source: Forrester Research, Inc.

most will not) will have to enable their products to connect to them. IT managers will have to develop strategies so that they align with the vendors that demonstrate a strategic focus on the enterprise's industry—for example, demonstrating an understanding of consumer packaged goods, automotive, financial services, health care, and others.

E-Business Market Makers

E-commerce today is dominated by a large number of seller-centric Web sites and a small but growing number of buyer-centric internal networks. But a third alternative is starting to appear as new ventures spring up, usually focused on a single industry, that attempt to create portals or online marketplaces where multiple sellers meet multiple buyers. The rules and formats are dictated by neither buyers nor sellers but by the new market makers, in whose systems the transactions occur.

They represent the return of a new breed of middleman. The formula for a successful online, multiseller, multibuyer marketplace is far from clear at this point, but the would-be market makers generally tilt toward buyers and push sellers toward standardization and commoditization, sometimes under an auction-like bidding process where the lowest bid gets the business.

Arthur Andersen, the Chicago-based Big Five public accounting firm, has been studying the emergence of these vertical market makers. "Previously, a business buyer might have to go to dozens of different suppliers to get what he needed," reports Robert D. Randolph, AA's marketing manager for knowledge enterprises. "Some industries have more than 2,200 product lines, where even the biggest suppliers or distributors carry no more than 300 of them at any given time," he notes. "An Internet vertical market-maker adds value by letting a buyer use one site to source products from multiple suppliers."

The vertical suppliers are building what some call "transactional hub sites," describing their role as intermediaries in a many-buyer, many-seller marketplace—one site where a buyer can find many sellers and a seller can find many buyers. Hub sites typically take a middleman's cut, but if it's not too much, it can be a good deal for both buyers and sellers. If the hub sites become greedy, buyers and sellers will find a way to deal directly and eliminate the middleman.

Administrative Support

As institutions begin to develop their e-business capabilities, they will start to transform administrative operations. Traditional services that today are characterized by data-intense, paper-based, clerical-mediated delivery will become self-service, no-stop-shop applications. Business trading partners will emerge to provide powerful co-sourcing enterprise delivery mechanisms to further reduce complexity and cost and make applications more user friendly. Enhanced services in back-office transaction processing will leverage the scale economies of the networked technologies and enable institutions to focus on front-office personal counseling, instruction, and value-added services.

Administrative and support utilities will emerge in the next decade. E-business will enable the surgical outsourcing, or co-sourcing, of many administrative operations. Some of these co-sourced functions will work like utilities, with institutions charged for the number of transactions or amount of services consumed. Powerful new applications will create virtual front and back offices, dramatically changing the way enterprises handle administrative and academic support functions. A new generation of co-sourcing relationships will emerge.

Partnerships

When it comes to building e-business enterprises, so far companies have had to choose between building their own proprietary systems or farming out the job to a Web specialist. That should change as e-businesses take a closer look at a third option: partnerships. Already, more and more e-business-bound companies—including Office Depot , Paccar, and Delta Air Lines—are making equity investments in their e-commerce partners.

While hard numbers on the trend are elusive, financial consultants say it's clear that such investments are on the upswing. Experts cite deals such as Delta Air Lines's $125 million stake in Priceline.com, announced in November, and Ford Motor's September investment in Microsoft's CarPoint venture.

The deals, experts say, can cement long-term working relationships between e-business providers and their customers, and that can benefit both sides. Customer/investors get increased access to the experts, developing technologies that support their e-business plans, and may also get a cash payoff if they invest in a startup that later launches a successful IPO (initial public offering). E-business technology vendors receiving the investments gain cash to pour into R&D while waiting for profits to appear. They also get a visibility and credibility boost if they attract a big-name customer/investor.

There is a catch, however. You should choose your investments wisely, experts say, because taking an equity stake in the wrong partner might prove costly in more ways than one: Your company's investment could so south and, perhaps worse, you might stick with an inferior product longer than you should if you've invested in the vendor.

Management

While it's no longer surprising to hear a CEO or CIO cite e-business as a top priority, executives are struggling with how best to manage their e-business operations. Recent research by KPMG and the research and consulting firm Benchmarking Partners suggests the e-leadership role remains up for grabs.

The study interviewed executives at 48 companies—most of which had more than $1 billion in revenue—and found that only 26 percent had one person charged with leading e-business efforts company-wide. Fewer than half of the companies surveyed had an executive with an e-business or e-commerce title, and only 40 percent of those executives managed a budget for e-business. Typically, the initiative and budget is coming from a group such as marketing or supply management that sees an opportunity and starts implementing an Internet strategy.

Decentralized IT initiatives let business-unit managers push projects far into development before they face scrutiny from outside their departments. In a study looking at the role of centralized IT leadership, the Working Council for Chief Information Officers, an arm of the Corporate Executive Board, says some companies reported that in-depth audits found more than $100 million in unbudgeted IT spending.

E-business further complicates the delicate task a CIO has of balancing centralized IT projects and responsibilities to business units. It has become common for some IT personnel to report to both an IT department and a business-unit manager. But the emergence of e-commerce officers and specialized e-business units could result in the future CIO sharing turf—or fighting for it—more often. Since the CIO's responsibility is to ensure that the organization has an appropriate alignment of IT with business requirements, the sharing of turf is natural and beneficial. Those CIOs who insist that they control the business process and infrastructure for e-business are focusing on the wrong targets. "Their job is to help ensure that the infrastructure is in place to permit the multiple new business initiatives which the Web allows, not to control the businesses themselves," says Bud Mathaisel, CIO of electronics manufacturing services company Solectron Corp. in Milpitas, California, and former CIO at Ford Motor Co. "That's because many of those projects are being led by marketing. This may be a major phenomenon—the IT people within marketing groups moving onto the fast track to CIO."

With the growth of e-business, the career path for the techno-savvy manager is becoming broader yet more complex. At the top, e-business is tying IT more directly to the bottom line and expanding technology's role in every corner of the business. This makes it more likely that successful CIOs—e-leaders—will be seen as having the breadth of experience needed for higher executive jobs.

For the aspiring professional a few steps down from CIO, there have never been so many career tracks: leading the technical side of an Internet startup, joining the e-business team at a large company, changing the culture within a large traditional IT department. IT people should find it easier to move into nontechnology management positions as companies increasingly fill senior management jobs with IT executives. "It's conceivable that a warehouse system management developer might become the site logistics manager," says one human resources manager.

So what experience makes sense for tomorrow's e-leader? Two skill sets are clear: people skills, to explain an idea and inspire support for it; and business knowledge, to know a company's place in the market and how it needs to change. A more pressing issue concerns what technical skills an e-leader needs.

Stressing management knowhow over technical prowess, the person has to have led complex projects, especially assessing the risks for the business and allocating resources, and also must have managed senior staff, not just fresh-from-school IT grads. But profit-and-loss financial understanding also is very important, something IT managers can sometimes be insulated from at larger companies.

So far, there's no standard educational pedigree for tomorrow's e-leaders. But business schools are rapidly adding e-business to their curriculum. Carnegie-Mellon and Columbia Universities last year launched programs specifically designed to teach technology–business management, using business school and computer sciences faculty. Students learn the finer points of marketing, along with the relative strengths of different programming languages.

To bring all this together, the biggest test of e-leaders will come in their ability to inspire people. E-business by its nature must become dispersed through an enterprise. Leading that effort requires motivating and managing people with widely different interests to rally behind common goals—from business-unit executives with their eyes on next quarter's results to IT employees looking for a cutting-edge project.

What the Future Will Bring

Here are some more predictions from around the world on where e-business is headed in the next few years:

- Gartner Group analysts have warned that in the run up to 2003, almost 75 percent of European companies will underbudget e-business transformation costs. Despite this, the company said there is absolutely no reason Europe cannot catch up with the e-business leaders in the United States.

- According to Forrester Research, one-third of all Europeans will use the Net via mobile phones in 2004. Operators will try to control content and commerce services in the early years, but by the end of 2002 new mobile Internet providers will deliver open access to the Internet. "European Internet leaders think that deploying sites for mobile phones will generate new revenues and increase customer loyalty. Nine out of 10 plan to launch mobile Internet sites, and more than half have already started development," said the company in a report.

- Sixty-seven percent of Asian CEOs surveyed by PriceWaterhouseCoopers in 1999 stated they believe that e-business will have a significant impact on competition in their industries, while 47 percent stated they believe financial services will be the sector most significantly impacted by the Internet in the next two years.

- The same survey respondents associate the Internet primarily with sales and marketing: 42 percent cite "building awareness of the company" as the primary function of their corporate Web site, followed by "customer interaction" (29 percent) and "advertising products or services" (17 percent). Paradoxically, in light of this view of the Internet as a "front-end" channel, 62 percent of respondents believe that e-business will have "only some" or "no" impact on their brand strategy. For the 30 percent of companies that conduct business on their Web sites, business-to-business transactions outpace business-to-consumer transactions (35 to 28 percent).

Great Quotes from Industry Leaders

What do the great technological minds of our time have to say about the future of e-business? Here are some quotes from the best:

The ultimate horizon in great interface is taking the computer from being such a dumb device, and teaching it to see, listen, and learn.

—BILL GATES, CHAIRMAN, MICROSOFT CORPORATION

The future is about the Internet. It's about having access to all of your data, anywhere you happen to be. It's going to be a phenomenal, new economy.

The next thing is that products are going to evolve into services. In the future, you won't buy electronic mail (e-mail) systems for business use, as e-mail systems for businesses will be available on the Internet; and your whole company will rely on an Internet service provider for it. The same will apply to file storage. You'll just be storing your data in data centers that will be hosted by somebody who knows how to manage them professionally.

—WILLIAM HOUNG-LEE, MANAGING DIRECTOR, ORACLE SYSTEMS

The enterprise resource planning (ERP) market will continue to grow at current rates given the move to Web-enabled inter-enterprise applications. While the promise of the Internet is that any corporation can move its business online and perform transactions and interactions at zero incremental cost, the reality is that doing so takes far more than a Web browser and an Internet connection. So ERP growth will be driven by business requirements for the integration of front-end functionality with robust, scalable and open back-office systems.

The Internet will continue to grow exponentially and become the overwhelming method of doing business. But beyond the mere sales of goods and services, electronic business (e-business) will see new business relationships formed around the Web and the emergence of global villages of industry collaboration.

Organizations may choose to no longer own their IT hardware and software with the emergence of "apps-on-tap," a one-step solution for hardware, software, and services delivery via the Internet with payment options including rental or transaction fees."

—KHATIJAH SHAH, MANAGING DIRECTOR, SAP MALAYSIA

We see the PC becoming a personal server, connecting and managing complementary, handheld informational devices such as pagers and personal organizers.

The next major change will occur with greater penetration of broadband technologies, which is a way to provide superfast Internet connections. Broadband is a massive catalyst for people to get online, as rich audio, video, and graphic content becomes widely accessible.

—RON GOH, VICE PRESIDENT, ASIA, DELL COMPUTER CORP.

It is predicted that PCs will lose out to Internet-enabled devices such as mobile telephones, personal digital assistants, and thin clients, as the device of choice for users to access information on the Web.

Currently, mobile phone sales and worldwide penetration are already greater than PCs. As Internet access standards are adopted, more powerful mobiles capable of performing a wide variety of tasks will outstrip the unwieldy PC.

—GOVINATHAN PILLAI, MANAGING DIRECTOR,
SUN MICROSYSTEMS MALAYSIA

E-commerce will no longer be a buzzword but instead, be part of normal sales and marketing operations.

—YOHANI YUSOF, COUNTRY MANAGER, INTEL ELECTRONICS

We will hear more about the Web economy with buzzwords such as iUtility, Web appliances, wireless broadband Internet, Web enterprises or e-companies, portals, and cyber marketing. Three key trends which will dominate the news are technology innovations, liberalization or globalization through virtualization, and e-companies with new business models and work processes.

The Internet will be a key platform for globalization through virtualization. Eventually, computing will be affordable to all, connectivity will be pervasive, businesses and governments will have transformed to coexist with the virtual world, and we will improve our quality of life.

RAFEE YUSOFF, VICE PRESIDENT FOR
APPLICATION DEVELOPMENT, MIMOS BERHAD.

appendix

E-Business Resources on the Web

W e've covered a lot of ground inside these pages, but we didn't cover everything. For more information on business and technology resources, read on.

Resources for Small Businesses

Are you trying to raise new capital or improve your marketing strategy? Perhaps you just want to consult with other small business owners. Whatever assistance you seek in running your company, you'll find it at these Web sites:

- The Business Resource Center (*www.morebusiness.com*)—The Business Resource Center is for those who already know the basics of business and are ready to strike out on their own. If you're looking to get involved in a new business, check out what the center considers the top 500 franchise opportunities. If you already have a business up and running, get advice on building a Web site. You'll also find tips on financing, management, taxes, legal issues, and a list of upcoming trade shows.
- CommerceNet (*www.commerce.net*)—Connect with CommerceNet to get your small business's e-commerce plans off the ground. The mission of this nonprofit market- and business-development organization is "to make electronic commerce easy, trusted, and ubiquitous." Once you join, CommerceNet can introduce your company to other members to help you network, improve your

site, and get more exposure on the Web. The site also provides public-policy information and daily news, training materials, research, and conferences for its members.

- The International Small Business Consortium (*www.isbc.com*)— The International Small Business Consortium tries to match small businesses offering specific products and services with other companies in need of the same. For example, a small business looking for an advertising agency or construction assistance could check the site to see if there were any other businesses in its area that provided such services.

  It costs nothing to register your business on the site or to perform a search of a small business that could provide a needed service.You'll also find other information and services aimed at small business users, including discussion forums and a list of funding services. And when you think that your business will never get off the ground, go to the consortium's list of quotes, such as the one from a Western Union memo from 1876 stating that the telephone has "too many shortcomings to be seriously considered as a means of communication."

- National Federation of Independent Business (*www.nfibonline.com*)— Small businesses can find a wealth of resources at the Web site of the National Federation of Independent Business (NFIB). Stop in for daily workshops, where you'll learn simplified marketing tactics, how to keep in touch outside of the office, or how to spend wisely when investing in technology. If you haven't got the time to check it out online, NFIB can deliver the workshops and its daily news column directly to your mailbox.

  NFIB offers the latest information on taxes and laws that affect small businesses and ways to contact your state representatives. In addition, if you're looking for advice from other small business employees, check out the online forums.

  You'll also want to turn to NFIB for links to sites and articles with valuable information on how to write a business plan, publicize your organization, and keep up with current market trends and abreast of your competition.

- Small Business Administration (*www.sba.com*)—No matter what type of business you're in, the site of the Small Business Administration (SBA) is worth frequent visits to get the latest on financial assistance and other resources available to your company. A section on financing lists available loan programs and explains how company size affects the loan process. Another area reviews legislation and regulatory issues affecting small businesses. If you are searching for a bargain on equipment or property, check out the Assets for Sale section, where you'll find a list of assets that the SBA has acquired while administering its loan programs and information on how you can acquire them. Most sections also include a list of outside resources to which you can turn for additional information.

Here are some additional small business sites with an e-business flavor that are worth checking out:

Bplans.com (*www.bplans.com*)
Business Know-How (*www.businessknowhow.com*)
Business2Business (*members.tripod.com/~mysec/flag/ b2b.html*)
The Emerging Companies Network
      (*www.capital-network.com/entp.htm*)
The Idea Cafe (*www.ideacafe.com*)
Internal Revenue Service
      (*www.irs.ustreas.gov/prod/bus_info/index.html*)
The Marketing Resource Center (*www.marketingsource.com*)
Small Business Administration (*www.sba.gov*)
The Small Business Advisor (*www.isquare.com*)
The Small Business Journal (*www.tsbj.com*)
Young Entrepreneurs' Organization (*www.yeo.org*)

E-Business Reports, White Papers, and Speeches

A great Web site for all things e-business is Creative Networks Inc.'s Research and Analysis Web site (*www.cnilive.com/publications/html/ all_publications.html*). Some research is free and some is not, but it's all good stuff. Here's a sample of what you'll find there:

The Business Case for Outsourcing E-Business (Subscribers Only)
The Business Case for Outsourcing E-Business—Executive Summary (Free)

Enterprise Directory Applications, Costs, Staffing and Service Levels:
A Survey of Customer Experiences (Subscribers Only)

Enterprise Directory Applications, Costs, Staffing and Service Levels:
A Survey of Customer Experiences—Overview (Free)

Email: A Strategic Corporate Asset (Free)

Messaging Costs: The Highs and Lows in Mid-Sized Companies
(Free)

Messaging Costs: The Highs and Lows in Mid-Sized Companies
(Subscribers Only)

Alignment: The Key to Success for Transforming Your Organization
to E-Business (Subscribers Only)

Lower TCO and Higher ROI for Microsoft Exchange: The Impact of
Using External Services (Free)

Email Archive and Retrieval: A Hidden Enigma, A Hidden Cost
(Free)

Webmail Management: Marrying Email to the Call Center
(Subscribers Only)

Thin-Client Architectures (Subscribers Only)

Electronic Procurement and the Heterogeneity Hazard (Subscribers Only)

Cowboy UP: Time to Ante Up for E-Commerce (Subscribers Only)

E-Commerce Is Fine, But What About Infrastructure? (Subscribers Only)

Exchange and Notes/Domino: TCO vs. Value (Subscribers Only)

Hewlett-Packard OpenMail: Customers Speak Out (Free)

The Directory Dilemma (Subscribers Only)

Why Deploy an Enterprise Directory? (Subscribers Only)

The Status of Enterprise Directories (Subscribers Only)

Shifting Sands in Retail Economics? (Subscribers Only)

Benchmark TCO: Microsoft Exchange and Lotus Notes/Domino in
the Enterprise (Free)

The IT Value Proposition: Why TCO Isn't Enough (Subscribers Only)

The BusinessNet: Delivering Competitive Advantage (Subscribers Only)

Workflow and Process Automation (Free)

Electronic Commerce and the Web (Subscribers Only)

Groupware (Free)

Internet and the World Wide Web (Free)

Electronic Forms (Free)

Intranet Messaging: Usage Patterns and User Experiences—
Executive Summary (Free)

Electronic Commerce and the Web—Executive Summary (Free)

Group Calendaring and Scheduling (Free)

Intranet Messaging: Usage Patterns and User Experiences (Subscribers Only)

Electronic Messaging (Free)

Electronic Commerce (Free)

Document Management (Free)

Directory Services (Free)

The World Wide Web: Costs and Applications (Subscribers Only)

The World Wide Web: Costs and Applications—Executive Summary (Free)

Groupware, the Web, and Lotus Notes (Subscribers Only)

Electronic Commerce: A CNI Overview (Free)

Securing Your Email (Free)

Is Web Collaborative Computing Ready for Prime Time? (Subscribers Only)

Great E-Business Web Sites

There's no shortage of great e-business Web sites. In the course of researching this book, these are at the top of the list:

EpayNews.com (*www.epaynews.com*)—Links explaining the new businesses practices and approaches within e-commerce and in the physical world are contained on this page.

Business-to-Business Links (*www.epaynews.com/links/biz2biz.html*)

B2Business Net (*www.b2business.net/*)—Great e-business discussion boards.

Business in Cyberspace (*www.deloitte.co.nz/ebusiness/*)

Impact of Cashless B2B (*www.arraydev.com/commerce/jibc/9811-18.htm*)—from the *Journal of Internet Banking and Commerce.*

CyberAtlas's e-business statistics page (*cyberatlas.internet.com/big_picture/stats_toolbox/article/0,1323,00.html*)

Andersen Case Studies in eCommerce (*www.ac.com/overview*)

E-Commerce Times (*www.ecommercetimes.com/*)

Electronic Payment Systems (*ntrg.cs.tcd.ie/epay.html*)—Details of a book explaining e-payment mechanisms.

Will Web Banking Replace the ATM? (*www.zdnet.com/yil/content/ mag/9811/banking.html*)—ZDNet feature on online banking.

Basics of Online Banking (*www.bankrate.com*)

CIO Magazine's E-Business Center (*www.cio.com/forums/ec/*)

MicroPayments Explained
(*www.idg.net/idg_frames/english/content.cgi?allowFeedback=false &referer=&outside_source=cnn&url=http%3a%2f%2fwww% 2ecomputerworld%2ecom%2fhome%2ffeatures%2ensf%2fall% 2f980223micropaylinks&doc_id=39084*)— From *ComputerWorld*.

Online Auctions Explained
(*news.cnet.com/news/0-1007-201-338739-0.html?st.ne.180.head*)
—Source: News.com.

Internet Wallet Choices and Answers (*www.bankinfo.com*)

IBM Multi-Payment Framework (*www.bankinfo.com*)

Special Report on Online Financial Services
(*www.industrystandard.com*)

Dispelling myths of using a credit card on the Web
(*www.ecompupublishing.com*)

A Practical Guide to Internet Payment Processing
(*www.owlstrategy.com/whitepaper.html*)—Source: Optimal
Web Leverage.

The eSupply Chain Is Coming...and Fast (*ebiz.ittoolbox.com/ browse.asp?c=EBIZPeerPublishing&r=http%3A%2F%2Fwww% 2Emfg%2Derp%2Ecom%2F11perform%2Epdf*)—Source: RM
Donovan Managing Consultants.

11 1100000101001000   01110100010 001111010001101   11101010
    0   1 0101   0000   1 100 1   1 00   0111   1   1
   1 0   0   1   0 0   1   01   0   1
  0 1 111 0   00   001010 10   00   1 0001   010100 010

Glossary of E-Business Terms

Here's a list of key e-business terms compiled by Trintech.com:

AADS. For account authority digital signature. A payment mechanism where smart cards and PIN codes interact to generate a unique digital signature for each transaction. Removes the need for third-party authorization of payments, thereby reducing the risk of payment details being intercepted in transit.

acquirer or **acquiring bank.** The institution or organization where a merchant has an account to process transactions and credit payments.

AMESA (Asia Mobile Electronic Services Alliance). A Visa-backed initiative representing the first Asia-Pacific partnership to integrate the power of the smart card, mobile phone, public key infrastructure, and open standards.

ASP (Application service provider). A body that licenses, maintains, and rents third-party software systems to business clients.

audit trail. Messages created as a byproduct of data processing runs or mechanized operations for recording purposes.

authentication. The process of identification of individuals and businesses through the use of digital certificates.

authorization. This is the process where permission is granted by the card issuer (the financial institution) allowing the payment transaction to proceed. It is during this process that the issuing bank checks that the available credit on the card is not exceeded.

batch. A composite of captures and credits accumulated over a period of time, generally no more than one day, that are waiting to be settled with the merchant's acquiring financial institution.

batch close. The process of sending a batch to the financial institution for settlement.

biometrics. The measurement of a living trait (retina scan, fingerprint) used to control access. Refers to the interpretation of personal traits for access control purposes in place of password or ID verification systems.

browser plug-in. Additional software that is installed on your computer, which extends the functionality of your Web browser.

BSP (business service provider). An emerging breed of software developer that rents its services to vertical industries such as banking or airlines.

capture. A procedure performed on a previously authorized transaction after a merchant has shipped goods or services to the customer. This transaction triggers the movement of funds from the issuer to the acquirer and then to the merchant's account.

cardholder. An individual or business that has established an account with a credit or debit card issuer. A cardholder is eligible to initiate a payment card transaction.

CDMA (code-division multiple access). A type of circuit-switched mobile network with a global user base of 30 million subscribers. Likely to upgrade to CDMA-2000 before reaching UMTS level.

CDPD (cellular digital packet data). A standard capable of transmitting Web data to personal digital assistants (PDAs) such as Palm Pilots. Whenever a lag occurs in data transmission, CDPD squeezes data into reserved spaces between analog cell channels. Although this data is low priority, carriers charge per packet.

CEPS (Common Electronic Purse Specification). Initially developed by Visa before being handed over to the European Committee for Banking Standards (ECBS), this is a unique standard for the global interoperability of smart cards.

certificate authority (CA). This is the service a bank provides that digitally signs public keys sent to it by a Web browser or by the merchant's server software. It issues and validates digital certificates associated with SET transactions.

challenge-response. A common authentication technique for smart cards whereby an individual is prompted (the challenge) to provide some private information (the response). The built-in security system presents a code (the challenge) to the user, which he or she enters into the smart card. This generates a new code (the response) that the user can present to log in.

credit. A transaction resulting in a credit to a cardholder's account.

cryptography. The practice of digitally scrambling a message using a secret key or keys.

CSP (computer service provider). Enterprises resembling utilities firms in functioning as server farms to host ASPs, CSPs, and e-commerce ventures.

digital cash. Consists of two main mechanisms: "digital coins" that can be downloaded to the user's PC from a participating bank, or the set up of a digital money account with a bank. Both (encrypted) forms of cash can be sent to merchants for payment.

digital certificate. Online identification that authenticates a consumer, merchant, or a financial institution. Digital certificates are used to encrypt information exchanged in SET transactions. A certificate is a public key that has been digitally signed by a trusted authority (the financial institution) to identify the user of the public key.

digital money. The same as digital cash, but it can also involve the use of software-based secure credit card transactions.

digital receipt infrastructure (DRI). Utilizing this infrastructure enables consumers and organizations to prove that electronic transactions and events actually took place. In legal terms, these serve as a digital trail, as opposed to a paper trail.

digital signatures. An electronic signature that cannot be forged. It is generated from a computed digest of the text that is encrypted and sent with the text message. The recipient decrypts the signature and retrieves the digest from the received text. If the digests match, the message is authenticated and proved to be from the sender.

digital wallet. Software that provides the equivalent of a wallet for electronic commerce. A digital wallet, or e-wallet, holds digital money that you purchase, similar to travelers' checks. A digital wallet may also hold your credit card information along with a digital certificate that identifies you as the authorized cardholder.

disintermediation. The practice of cutting out the middleman to achieve convenience, savings, and fast turnaround time for consumers. Refers to the bypassing of traditional retail channels for direct selling by Web-based companies.

ECC (elliptic curve cryptography). Cryptographic solution requiring less bandwidth to offer increased security for online transactions. Twice as much power is needed to crack a 97-bit ECC key than a 512-bit RSA key.

ECML (Electronic Commerce Modeling Language). A new standard developed by a consortium of industry players including American Express, Compaq, Dell, IBM, Microsoft, SETCo, Transactor Networks, Trintech, and Visa USA. Consequently, one-click purchasing at all compatible Web sites is facilitated.

electronic bill presentment and payment (EBPP). Comprises two components of Internet billing, bill presentment involves the online delivery of bills to customers with electronic payment instead of through paper check.

electronic checks. Currently being tested by several companies, electronic checking systems such as PayNow take money from users' checking accounts to pay utility and phone bills.

electronic commerce or **e-commerce.** All types of transactions that are conducted using digitally transmitted data methods.

electronic document interchange (EDI). The electronic communication of business transactions such as orders, confirmations, and invoices.

electronic wallet. Software, residing as a plug-in in the Web browser, that enables a cardholder to conduct online transactions, manage payment receipts, and store digital certificates. Like your real wallet, your digital wallet stores your credit card number and shipping details. This wallet initiates the data encryption in a SET transaction.

EMV (Europay, MasterCard, Visa). Usually refers to EMV 96, which is a set of three specifications covering debit/credit cards, terminals, and applications. EMV supports applications enabling issuers, retailers, and consumers to use chip cards and terminals with added security. The term "EMV compatible" is used when referring to terminals that meet level 1 of the EMV 96 specifications.

ETSI (European Telecommunications Standards Institute). A nonprofit organization whose mission is to determine and produce the telecommunications standards that will be used for decades to come.

extranet. An extension of a company's intranet, extranets connect the internal network of one company with the intranets of its customers and suppliers. A combination of intranets, extranets, and the

Internet makes it possible to create applications covering all aspects of a business relationship, from ordering to payment.

FIX (Financial Information eXchange Protocol). The messaging standard for the real-time electronic exchange of securities information.

gateway. An electronic application that accepts transactions from online merchant storefronts and routes them to a financial institution's processing system.

GPRS (General Packet Radio Services). An extension of the GSM standard allowing the transmission of packet data to wireless devices at speeds of up to 150 kbps.

HDML (Handheld Device Markup Language). A markup language adapting Web content for display on mobile handheld devices such as cell phones, pagers, or PDAs.

HSCSD (High Speed Circuit Switched Data). A software upgrade for the GSM standard that provides enhanced, cost-effective, high speed data services across existing networks.

Identrus. A global banking consortium established to "trust-enable" every stage of a transaction through to actual payment. Promotes the use of public key infrastructure (PKI) systems within the financial industry.

IMT-2000 (International Mobile Telecommunications-2000). An ITU-approved standard, employing three wideband-CDMA (W-CDMA) specifications. The single carrier portion is intended as a 3G bridge for current GSM networks.

Internet keyed payment (IKP). Created by IBM, a group of secure payment protocols that enables customers to purchase goods and services securely over the Web.

intranet. An internal company network based on Internet protocol. Intended for speedy and convenient distribution of corporate information.

issuer. A financial institution that issues payment cards, such as credit or debit cards.

Joint Electronic Payment Initiative (JEPI). Proposed by CommerceNet and the W3 Consortium, an Internet payment standard focusing on data security and interoperability between payment schemes.

MAOSCO. The open industry consortium behind the MULTOS smart card operating system. A full member of the European Telecommunications Standards Institute (ETSI).

MEPS (Malaysian Electronic Payment System). A joint venture established by 18 banks in Malaysia. Operator of the country's only payment gateway, which does not itself secure online transactions, so the consortium is promoting the SET protocol.

merchant. Collective term applied to Web-based retailers that may have online storefronts.

message digest. The basis for digital signatures in providing a digest of the random message being transmitted. As a result, they are difficult to reverse.

MExE (Mobile station application Execution Environment). As defined by the European Telecommunications Standards Institute; relates to PDA (personal digital assistant) devices such as Palm Pilots.

micropayments. Low-cost transactions of between 25 cents and $10. Payments are typically made prior to downloading graphics, games, and information.

MTP (Micropayment Transfer Protocol). A W3-defined software-based system for micropayments, this protocol is optimized for use in low-value transfers between parties who have a relationship over a period of time.

MULTOS. Abbreviation for Multiple Operating System, comprises a platform for smart card development. Favored by MasterCard, Mondex, Europay, and Discover credit card brands.

nonrepudiation. Process by which a customer cannot deny having paid for an order after it is conducted.

online storefront. A Web site containing e-commerce software, available on a public network such as the Internet, which offers goods and services for sale. An online storefront is the equivalent of a store or place of business that a customer would visit to purchase goods and services.

Open Financial Exchange (OFX). A financial data markup language to facilitate online data exchanges between businesses, consumers, and financial institutions. Holds implications for online banking in its support of real-time online transactions on Web sites and in financial software.

Open Trading Protocol (OTP). Protocol to align various electronic payment mechanisms and render them interoperable. Mainly used for transactions in the financial services sector.

point of sale. In the physical world, this is the point at which a product is paid for and delivered. On the Internet, this is the software that enables merchants to accept transactions on their online storefronts and conduct follow-on transactions with their financial institution.

public key encryption. An encryption system using two keys, a public key for encrypting messages and a private key for decrypting messages, to enable users to verify each other's messages without exchanging secret keys.

public key infrastructure (PKI). An interoperable security solution incorporating the use of digital signatures to ensure the integrity of transmitted information. Also supports user authentication and non-repudiation.

SCSUG (Smart Card Security Users Group). Established by the major card organizations to establish recommendations for chips and operating systems within smart cards. Is defining a protection profile for both credit and debit applications based on recommendations for chip card security.

Secure HyperText Transfer Protocol (S-HTTP). A secure version of HTTP, providing general transaction security services over the Web.

Secure Sockets Layer (SSL). A public security protocol developed by Netscape, creating a secure link between a Web server and its communicating browser. In an SSL session, all data sent is encrypted. SSL does not authenticate either the sender or the receiver.

SET (Secure Electronic Transactions). A secure payment protocol developed by MasterCard and Visa designed to ensure security for bank card transactions over the Internet. In denying merchants access to credit card information, details are secured between the shopper and the bank.

SET mark. The mark or logo that assures that the transaction software being used is SET compliant.

SET protocol. An open industry standard developed for the secure transmission of payment information over the Internet and other electronic networks.

settlement. The step in the clearing process when the acquirer credits the merchant account with the amount of a credit card purchase and the bankcard association (such as Visa and MasterCard) credits the acquirer and debits the card issuer for the transaction.

shopping basket or **shopping cart.** As you shop online, you add items to a "virtual" shopping basket. The basket is simply a list of the items you have selected to buy, together with the necessary details (number selected, price of each item). You can review what's in your basket at any time as you shop.

smart card. Similar in size to a credit card but containing electronic memory and possibly an embedded integrated circuit (IC). If this is the case, the cards are termed integrated circuit cards (ICCs).

SSLeay. Free shareware developed by RSA Data Securities, which enhances SSL capabilities to offer RSA, DSA, and DH algorithms. Also offers Transaction Layer Security (TLS).

TCPA (Trusted Computing Platform Alliance). Initiative by several PC vendors to collectively establish a security standard for B2B transactions. Participants are to develop hardware and software security specifications for release by the second half of 2000 prior to licensing to the PC industry.

time division multiple access (TDMA). Circuit-switching mobile data network transferring data between a mobile device and a base station. Involves GSM capabilities, hence likely to upgrade to GPRS. Has 210 million subscribers worldwide.

transaction. Any action between a cardholder and a merchant that results in activity on the account, such as an authorization and settlement. Merchants and financial institutions also conduct follow-on transactions that affect the cardholders' account, such as a capture and credit.

Transaction Layer Security (TLS). A revision of SSL offering increased security mechanisms within the protocol. Currently in draft with the Internet Engineering Task Force (IETF).

UMTS. Stands for Universal Mobile Telecommunications System, part of the International Telecommunications Union's vision of a global family of "third-generation" (3G) mobile communications systems. A key role is expected in the future mass market for high quality wireless multimedia communications that will approach 2 billion users worldwide by the year 2010.

virtual sales slip. Detailed information on a financial transaction, which is generated by the merchant's online store and downloaded to your digital wallet. Typical items contained in the virtual sales slip are confirmation of your order, shipping details, and total amount of sale.

WAP (Wireless Application Protocol). An emerging protocol whereby Web-coded information is adapted for use in mobile access devices such as cell phones, pagers, or alternative means.

W-CDMA (Wideband Code Division Multiple Access). A standard facilitating the delivery of high speed data to compatible mobile phone handsets.

WML (Wireless Markup Language). A markup language providing a "light" version of a Web site for viewing on handheld devices.

Web browser. A client program that runs on an end-user's computer, linking it to the World Wide Web.

Index

About the Author

Brian O'Connell has 10 years experience covering business news and trends, particularly in the financial, healthcare, and high technology sectors. He's authored three books; most recently *The 401(k) Millionaire*, a "Book of the Month Club" selection, and *Generation E*.

A former bond trader and seasoned business writer, he left Wall Street in 1989 to embark on a writing career. Since then he became senior editor at *DEC Professional* magazine and contributing writer at *LAN Computing* magazine. From 1989 through 1994, he covered the high technology sector in-depth, writing numerous articles and attending many seminars, trade shows and product demonstrations devoted to the industry. He also wrote frequently and effectively on the standards, tools and platforms that laid the foundation for the growth of technology and the Internet in the 1990's.

O'Connell's work has appeared in many top-tier publications, including *CBS News Market Watch*, *TheStreet.com*, *Worth Magazine*, *Dow Jones Investment Advisor*, *The Robb Report*, *The Boston Herald*, *E*Trade Magazine*, *Better Homes and Gardens Family Money*, *Massachusetts Psychologist*, *Continental* (the in-flight magazine for Continental Airlines), and *CBS Sportsline*. He has also appeared as an expert commentator on business and finance issues on CNN and Fox News.

He lives in Doylestown, Pennsylvania with his wife and three children. He can be reached via e-mail at Bwrite111@aol.com.

FIND MORE ON THIS TOPIC BY VISITING

BusinessTown.com
The Web's big site for growing businesses!

☑ **Separate channels on all aspects of starting and running a business**

☑ **Lots of info on how to do business online**

☑ **1,000+ pages of savvy business advice**

☑ **Complete web guide to thousands of useful business sites**

☑ **Free e-mail newsletter**

☑ **Question and answer forums, and more!**

Accounting
Basic, Credit & Collections, Projections, Purchasing/Cost Control

Advertising
Magazine, Newspaper, Radio, Television, Yellow Pages

Business Opportunities
Ideas for New Businesses, Business for Sale, Franchises

Business Plans
Creating Plans & Business Strategies

Finance
Getting Money, Money Problem Solutions

Letters & Forms
Looking Professional, Sample Letters & Forms

Getting Started
Incorporating, Choosing a Legal Structure

Hiring & Firing
Finding the Right People, Legal Issues

Home Business
Home Business Ideas, Getting Started

Internet
Getting Online, Put Your Catalog on the Web

Legal Issues
Contracts, Copyrights, Patents, Trademark

Managing a Small Business
Growth, Boosting Profits, Mistakes to Avoid, Competing with the Giants

Managing People
Communications, Compensation, Motivation, Reviews, Problem Employees

Marketing
Direct Mail, Marketing Plans, Strategies, Publicity, Trade Shows

Office Setup
Leasing, Equipment, Supplies

Presentations
Know Your Audience, Good Impression

Sales
Face to Face, Independent Reps, Telemarketing

Selling a Business
Finding Buyers, Setting a Price, Legal Issues

Taxes
Employee, Income, Sales, Property, Use

Time Management
Can You Really Manage Time?

Travel & Maps
Making Business Travel Fun

Valuing a Business
Simple Valuation Guidelines

businesstown.com